CONTENTS

Contributors   *vi*

Introduction. The City and its Worlds   *vii*
    Terry Brotherstone & Donald J. Withrington

PART I: UNION STREET AND BEYOND
  1. Aberdeen since 1794: as Place and as Community   2
     Donald J. Withrington

  2. Union Street and the 'Great Street' in Scottish Town Planning   25
     Ranald MacInnes

  3. Advertising Made a 'Fine Art' in Victorian Aberdeen   40
     Edward Ranson

  4. Aberdonians Abroad: Two Centuries of Human Exports
     from North-eastern Scotland   62
     Marjory Harper

  5. The Added Values of Learning   82
     John Hargreaves

PART II: ISSUES IN SOCIAL, POLITICAL AND CULTURAL HISTORY
  6. 'All New Works of Interest Received on Publication':
     Aberdeen and its Access to the Printed Word, 1800–1850   94
     Iain Beavan

  7. 'A Woman's Greatest Adventure': the Development of
     Maternity Care in Aberdeen since the Eighteenth Century   115
     Lesley Diack

  8. Healing for the Body as Well as for the Soul: Treatment
     in the Aberdeen Royal Lunatic Asylum during the
     Nineteenth Century   130
     Seamus Lobban

  9. 'No Mean City'? The Growth of Civic Consciousness in
     Aberdeen with Particular Reference to the Work of the
     Police Commissioners   150
     Rosemary Tyzack

10. Aberdeen into Parliament: Elections and Representatives,
    1832–1865   168
    Michael Dyer

11. Aberdeen and Holland: John Forbes White and the Scottish
    Fascination with Dutch Art, 1860–1880   194
    John Morrison

PART III: CAPITAL AND LABOUR
12. Aberdeen 1800–2000 AD: the Evolution of the
    Urban Economy   211
    Clive Lee

13. Neither Parochial nor Soothing: Aberdeen and the Future
    of Labour History   224
    Terry Brotherstone

Index   239

CONTRIBUTORS

The authors of this book all work at, or have strong connections with, the University of Aberdeen.

Iain Beavan is a sub-librarian in the Department of Special Collections and Archives.

Terry Brotherstone, Lesley Diack, Marjory Harper, Edward Ranson and *Rosemary Tyzack* teach in the Department of History and Economic History.

Michael Dyer is a lecturer in Politics.

John D. Hargreaves is emeritus professor of History.

Clive Lee is a professor in the Department of Economics.

Seumas Lobban, a recent post-graduate student in History, is now editing technical journals in London.

Ranald MacInnes, who is Principal Inspector of Historic Buildings with Historic Scotland, is an honorary research fellow in History.

John Morrison is a lecturer in the History of Art.

Donald J. Withrington is reader in Scottish History.

Ken and Angela
for the
Saxon, June 1996.

The City and its Worlds
Aspects of Aberdeen's History since 1794

The City *and its* Worlds

Aspects of Aberdeen's History since 1794

edited by

Terry Brotherstone & Donald J. Withrington

C R U I T H N E   P R E S S

1996

GLASGOW

The cover photograph, by George Washington Wilson, is reproduced by permission of the Aberdeen University Library.

1996

© The authors

Cruithne Press
197 Great Western Road
George's Cross
Glasgow G4 9EB

British Library Cataloguing in Publication Data

A catalogue record for this book is available from the British Library.

ISBN 1-873448-12-0

Set in Palatino by JAZZ CORNETS
and printed and bound in Great Britain by Redwood

The City and its Worlds

Terry Brotherstone & Donald J. Withrington

Alike in its economic variety, its types of social responsibility, and its range of educational opportunity, Aberdeen deserves close study. This isolated and independent centre gives the best example of the continued vitality of an eighteenth-century inheritance of individual responsibility, optimism and benevolence. New conditions might produce varied social tensions but they developed rather than overthrew the accepted tradition.[1]

Laurence J. Saunders, *Scottish Democracy, 1815–1840.*

The City and its Worlds derives from a conference held in the Town and County Hall in the Aberdeen Town House on 19 and 20 November 1994. It was an academic but also a public occasion. Our first thanks must go to all who attended and participated, whether from Aberdeen and its environs, or from other parts of Scotland. To them this book is dedicated.

The conference was part of the celebrations held throughout the year to celebrate the 200th anniversary of the planning of Union Street, which, as Ranald MacInnes details in chapter two, was – and is – Aberdeen's 'great street', the *sine qua non* of the modern and contemporary city. Called 'Union Street and Beyond', the event was organised by the editors of this volume on the initiative of Alan Fulton, the City Librarian, and Allan Macinnes, professor of History at the Univer-

sity of Aberdeen; and it also had the support of Lord Provost James
Wyness. To all three, and to the many Council staff who assisted in
making a success of the conference, thanks are due. To that should
be added our gratitude to the Librarian for making this consequent
volume financially viable, and to Gillian Brown of the Department of
History and Economic History at the University of Aberdeen for all
that she did in helping to prepare it for publication. Our publisher,
Ross Samson, has also been very tolerant and helpful.

The intention of the conference was, at the same time, to add to the
sum of knowledge about Aberdeen's past, to contribute more generally
to the study of British urban history, and to launch a discussion
amongst the citizens of Aberdeen about their history. Conscious that
the City Council, in a last throw of the dice before the Scottish local
government reorganisation of 1995–96, had commissioned a two-
volume history to appear towards the end of the decade, we felt merci-
fully relieved of any obligation to be comprehensive. The conference
highlighted various aspects of the city's history since approximately the
time at which Union Street became a gleam in the planners' eyes; and
this book attempts to do no more.

While the book argues no general thesis, the editors, in the course of
its production, have become increasingly clear that Aberdeen's history
deserves much greater scholarly attention than it has until now received. And that *The City and its Worlds* should, accordingly, be seen as
an important step towards attracting such interest. The quotation from
Laurence J. Saunders' 1950 study *Scottish Democracy, 1815–1840*, which
leads off this short introduction, draws attention to the way in which
particular features of 'isolated and independent' Aberdeen in the
nineteenth century may make the city's history not only fascinating in
itself, but also an instructive comparator for more industrial urban
centres which are often taken as typical. As John Butt has written more
recently:

> If there is a lesson arising from [the urban Scottish] twentieth-
> century experience, it is perhaps best found in Aberdeen: it is
> best to have little in the way of an integrated industrial base, as
> the negative experience of Dundee and Glasgow had de-
> monstrated . . . A combination of diversity in economic activity
> linked with constant industrial innovation is perhaps the safest
> policy.[2]

The authors of the chapters which follow have not engaged in any

systematic, collective investigation, but there is much here which contributes, sometimes explicitly and often by implication, to the further examination of such arguments. Nor did we set out to put any particular theory of, or approach to, urban history to the test. Yet the method exemplified here, which draws together apparently diverse pieces of empirical research about one very particular place, may nonetheless be seen as illustrating at least one possible way forward for the subject as a whole.

R. J. Morris and Richard Rodger recently suggested that urban history has usually consisted mainly of *either* an attempt to explain how land was built on in the way that it was; *or* an examination of social, political and cultural battles for control and domination.[3] *The City and its Worlds* is a practical example of how collective work can unite the two approaches. Aberdeen, furthermore, is a place which, by its distinctive nature, insists of its historians that they pay attention to the nuances of how the battles for control were fought out: it does not respond to attempts to impose the cruder sociological models of class or status conflict, which sometimes yield up apparently plausible results for students of more industrially dominated cities.

A study of Aberdeen uninformed by consciousness of work done on other urban centres, and indifferent to the contribution it can make to social history more generally, would be of limited interest. But it also needs to be stressed that, if such a study is to play its part in further developments in British social history, it must show sensitivity to the way in which the distinctiveness of the regional capital of north-eastern Scotland has frequently reasserted itself. Knowledge of what happened in Aberdeen can contribute to urban history as much by highlighting contrasts as by simple comparison. This point may perhaps relate to one also made by Morris and Rodger, who argue that 'the institutional structures and histories of specific towns' have to be given their full place in constructing general judgements. In speaking in broad terms of British (or Scottish) 'urbanisation and its problems' that is to say, we must pay attention to the remarkable local variations in the ways in which municipalities have evolved, and their commitment to social and community services has developed.[4]

We have preserved the memory of the November 1994 conference in the sub-title of our first section 'Union Street and Beyond'. Here Don Withrington provides an overview of the evolution of city, and its ethos, since the late eighteenth century, and examines particular aspects of Aberdeen's distinctiveness; Ranald MacInnes shows that

Union Street's construction owed as much to practical need as to aesthetic vision, but also sets his story within the context of street-construction more generally, in Scotland and elsewhere; Ted Ranson entertains and instructs with the tale of Samuel Martin, whom, in deference to Lewis Carroll, he has elsewhere dubbed 'the Mad Hatter' of Union Street;[5] Marjory Harper voyages far beyond Union Street to explain why and how 'human exports' played such a big part in Aberdeen's contribution to the wider world; and John Hargreaves explores, with an eye jaundiced by the higher education policies of recent British governments, whether the success of the United Kingdom's fifth oldest university can be assessed by the extent to which it produced 'added value' – as opposed to merely performing the old-fashioned function of educating its students.

Section two – 'Issues in Social, Political and Cultural History' – begins with Iain Beavan's exploration of bookselling and librarianship and their contribution to the creation of an informed citizenry in Aberdeen in the nineteenth century. There follow chapters by Lesley Diack, tracing the history of the science and practice of childbirth in the city from the mid-eighteenth century to the present; by Seamus Lobban, dealing, from an Aberdeen standpoint, with important issues raised by the historical study of the treatment of those classified as insane; by Rosemary Tyzack, showing, by detailed examination of the history of the Police Commission from 1795 to 1871, that the first steps towards the creation of the infrastructure of water supply, sanitation, and public health provision, regarded as indispensable in cities today, were taken with the greatest difficulty – yet with a growing civic-mindedness; by Michael Dyer on electoral politics between the two parliamentary Reform Acts of 1832 and 1867; and by John Morrison, who elevates us above the practicalities of the sewers and the manoeuvrings of the politicians to show the leading part played by Aberdonian patrons in fostering 'the Scottish fascination with Dutch art'.

The book ends with two chapters under the collective title 'Capital and Labour'. Clive Lee outlines the evolution of the modern city's economic base, which he sees as determined by the success of the 'market system', and writes optimistically about the prospects ahead. Terry Brotherstone, in conclusion, calls for an approach to 'labour history' which might engage the attention of scholars, concerned citizens and political activists alike; and sees Aberdeen as an excellent base for such an initiative.

As a new millennium approaches, Union Street is entering on the

third century of its history; the University of Aberdeen embarks on its sixth; and a new Aberdeen City Council is beginning its work. We hope this book will be seen not only as a report on the past, but also as a stimulus for the future – that it may help to open up a period of more systematic study of the history of Aberdeen. We are sure that the city's history has important lessons to teach – both to its own inhabitants, and to others far beyond its unique location.

NOTES

1. Laurence J. Saunders, *Scottish Democracy, 1815–1840* (Edinburgh, 1950), p. 135.
2. John Butt, 'The changing character of urban employment, 1901–1981', in George Gordon (ed.), *Perspectives of the Scottish City* (Aberdeen, 1985), p. 232.
3. R. J. Morris and Richard Rodger (eds), *The Victorian City: a Reader in British Urban History, 1820–1914* (London, 1993), pp. 14–17.
4. Morris and Rodger, *The Victorian City*, p. 31.
5. Edward Ranson, *The Mad Hatter of Aberdeen: the Life and Times of Samuel Martin* (Aberdeen, 1996).

Part I:

Union Street and Beyond

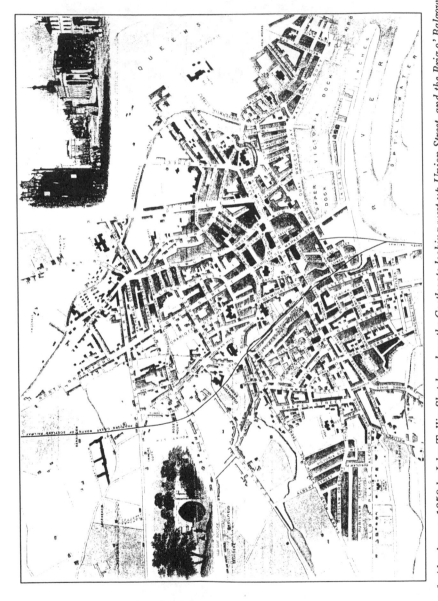

Map 1. Aberdeen c. 1850 by John Tallis. Sketches show the Castlegate looking west up Union Street, and the Brig o' Balgownie.

Aberdeen since 1794: as Place and as Community

Donald J. Withrington

In 1796 the ministers of Aberdeen, in their return for Sir John Sinclair's *Statistical Account of Scotland*, carefully described the town not only as 'the capital of the county of Aberdeen', but also as 'the metropolis of the northern division of Scotland'.[1] A century and a half later its predominance remained unchallenged – 'in truth it is still the capital city of the north of Scotland . . . the centre of trade and professional services.'[2] Throughout, Aberdonians maintained a self-conscious pride in this 'metropolitan' status and, in the 1790s, when Edinburgh was being graciously extended and rebuilt to much public admiration, the town council and citizens of Aberdeen determined also to give their city a new, 'modern', and improved physical setting – particularly with the scheme to begin the construction of Union Street, and to carry it westwards.

By the time that Francis Groome, preparing his valuable *Gazetteer of Scotland*, came north in the early 1880s, he could not contain either his surprise or his admiration at what had been achieved: 'the land approach from the south is singularly repulsive . . . till it bursts at once on a new view of the Dee and the city . . . Both the city and its surroundings, as first beheld, are very beautiful.' Once arrived in the town centre, he announced that it was 'enchanting' and approvingly quoted the comment of another traveller about Union Street, which

possesses all the stability, cleanliness, and architectural beauties of the London west-end streets, with the gaiety and brilliancy of the Parisian atmosphere.[3]

Groome was all the more impressed when he heard from local observers about the unimproved Aberdeen, at a time when it had still been contained within the bounds of the old royalty:

an assemblage of narrow, ill-built and badly-arranged thoroughfares without any good openings into the country . . . crowded with buildings and abominably filthy; . . . the thoroughfares leading out to the Dee and also to the north were steep, rough, narrow and malodorous.[4]

In 1911 Professor David Masson, native of the town and an alumnus of Marischal College, recalled the old royalty as it had been in the 1820s, before 'the noble length of Union Street' had been completed. The ancient jumble of streets, he said,

all remained, still useful thoroughfares, with good shops in them, but others [were] hideous in the squalor into which they had degenerated as the old parts of towns do; and one or two of them [were] doubly hideous from the effects of moral putridity at the mouths of their ugliest and narrowest courts. To go through Justice Port, even in the daytime, was to hear, within one or two minutes, full excerpts from the foulest wealth of anatomical and physiological words known to the British vocabulary; and even the Justice Port was as nothing compared with one narrow lane called the Vennel, in whose double row of ghastly houses, the windows stuffed with rags and old hats, brutality was more quiet only because more murderous.[5]

The contrast of these scenes with the graciousness of the new, extended town was keen in Masson's memory, as he applauded the developments which were in time to remove such eyesores. But even the Aberdeen of the 1820s had itself changed, something which is revealed in another sharply observed recollection of 'improvements', not only physical this time, and made by a rather soured old man and long-time resident of the city. In a private diary which spanned the previous half-century,[6] Sir Alexander Bannerman of Elsick wrote of the 'constant revolution' he had seen in local society. For instance, social graces and manners were being refined, and there was much new assumed gentil-

ity among the upper and middle orders – with far greater regulation in the giving and receiving of hospitality, so that genteel dinners were *de rigueur*, in contrast to the homely and more friendly suppers of previous times. There had come to the fore many men with new fortunes, striving for a status earlier enjoyed only by the families of long-standing landed gentry. These social upstarts had usually been helped to success by their own or their relatives' commercial or administrative activities in the Far East. By the 1820s, the main streets of the town, old and new, which had once seen only the occasional carriage of some local nobleman, were thronged by 'chariots, imperials, dickies, all with their valets and ladies' maids' – a signal of a new and much grander style of living, reflected also in the splendours of the new housing. 'Now look at Union Street,' wrote Bannerman, 'here we have palaces without number, some costing [£]5 or [£]6 or £8,000, mostly built for lawyers who spring from nothing or nobody.'

This straining after sophistication was not, apparently, relaxed in the remainder of the nineteenth century for, in the 1890s, William Keddie of Glasgow was writing of Aberdeen that 'the middle and upper classes of its community exhibit a metropolitan polish and tone of feeling and intelligence, entitling them to take a high rank amongst the people of Scotland.'[7] Leading Aberdonians could and did revel in such affirmations of their own, usually quietly observed, and purring self-assessment.

In the mid-nineteenth century, however, the general welcome for the physical improvements in the town was qualified by something like a wave of nostalgia which swept over Aberdeen. In the 1860s the local newspapers carried a series of articles on local history, dealing mainly with the recent rather than the more distant past, and also published reminiscences (as well as fictional stories about earlier days), often written in local dialect. These sometimes included regretful comments about older identities and communal activities which had been lost.[8] Local historians, such as James Rettie, produced pamphlets and books which were directly intended to preserve, in drawings and in word-pictures, at least the vestiges of a fast-disappearing past, for the benefit of younger as well as the older inhabitants.[9] And yet, by this time, although the town had certainly increased greatly in population, its geographical boundaries had not matched that increase. Aberdeen trebled in population between 1811 and 1871 (from some 35,000 people to about 100,000), but the area occupied increased only from 1,200 acres to 1,780. Some of the social consequences were noted by

Groome in 1883: the Aberdeen improvements

> have produced the evils of placing grandeur and meanness side
> by side, and of greatly augmenting the density of the poorer
> population. No fewer than some 60 narrow lanes and about
> 168 courts or closes, of an average breadth of at most 7 feet,
> still exist; are mostly situated in the immediate or near-vicinity
> of fine new streets; and occasion the average distribution of the
> inhabitants of St Nicholas to stand at so high a ratio as 16.8 to
> each house; and of the royal burgh at 14.8. Some closes such as
> Smith's and Peacock's, adjacent to the east end of Union
> Street, exhibit the lower grades of civilisation only a few steps
> apart from the higher; and other places, such as the courts
> branching from the Gallowgate, are about the dingiest and
> most unwholesome to be found anywhere in a British town.
> Nevertheless, the death-rate per 1,000 diminished from 22.5
> during 1867-72 to 21.7 during 1873-78, being thus below the
> average of other large Scottish towns; and in 1879 it further
> sank to 20.9.[10]

Even those who could, easily enough, have left the old royalty
seemed to want to remain, to be part of the old huddling community
of earlier decades. James Rettie provides perhaps an extreme example.
He carried on a thriving family business – as japanner, jeweller and
lamp manufacturer – which moved from Broad Street to the Union
Buildings when they were erected, and then westwards up Union
Street. But throughout his long life, he resided where he had been
born, in Rettie's Court off Broad Street. He died there in 1896 just
before it, and a number of other old crowded lands and courts, were
pulled down and cleared. Even those who did leave the courts and
lanes of the old royalty seem not to have gone far away: in the 1880s it
was being said that it was a very strange thing to find a townsman living
more than a mile from the Castlegate or from the Links. By the mid-
1880s, indeed, the march westwards had progressed only to Fountainhall Road and, while Rosemount was filling up, and Victoria Park had
been established, there was little or nothing beyond, north or west of
Argyll Place (see maps 1 and 2 at pages 2 and 7).[11] In fact, the period
between the early 1860s and early 1880s had seen something of a slow-
down in the town's expansion, although population still rose significantly. In the mid-1880s and after, however, another perhaps even more
dramatic phase of the 'constant revolution' began.

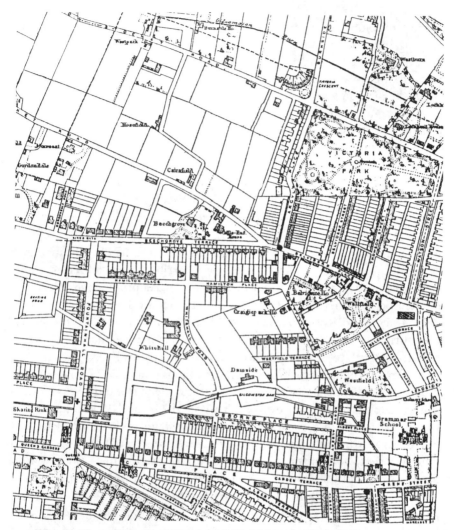

Map 2. Plan of Aberdeen, 1886, by Gibb & Hay: section showing area west of Esslemont Avenue.

A NEW PHASE OF IMPROVEMENT

There was then a discernible change of the tone in which the news-papers and other commentaries reflected on what was almost a century of improvements. An earlier, often grudging acceptance of the changes, social as well as physical, and a nagging nostalgia for the past, gave way to a very positive and resounding welcome for the new developments. And the town's leaders, elected on a much extended franchise, re-

turned to more expansive and visionary policies. To the still strong existing industries, Aberdeen added the benefits of steam trawling and an even greater reliance on fishing and on fish-marketing.[12] There was a new buoyancy, a sense of having 'made it', the rightful enjoyment of worked-for success – and a renewed pride in living in what visitors referred to as a 'show city', throwing 'its brightest lustra' over its region and over Scotland as a whole.[13]

As early as 1881 a sharply satirical local magazine, the *Northern Figaro*, was already warning the citizens of what was to come: a new, Liberal-dominated town council, it remarked, was threatening 'to become the most extravagant of modern times' and would be forever seeking 'new ways of spending the citizen's money'.[14] The council did not disappoint the *Figaro*'s editor. In 1881, amid other road-building and road-making, the Victoria Bridge was opened, leading southwards across the Dee to Torry, and 460 acres of territory were added to Aberdeen. Yet more private bills put through parliament gave the town council powers in 1883 to build a viaduct over the Denburn, providing decent access to Rosemount; to widen Schoolhill; to bridge the Ferryhill Burn and open up a route from Bon Accord Terrace to Fonthill; and to extend to the Links both Castle Street and Urquhart Road, where much building of 'workmen's dwellings' was to take place in the next few years. A scheme was also begun to clear the old Shorelands – thus sweeping away such eyesores as Pork Lane and Water Lane – as well as parts of Shiprow and Exchequer Row. And the council turned its attention to a still grander development, westwards and parallel to Union Street, concentrating much effort on Schoolhill and Belmont Street. A new public library was planned, which would incorporate the old Mechanics' Institute Library from Marischal Street. A new art gallery was erected and then, close by, a new school of art – with, between them, a grand new gateway to Gordon's College. A statue of William Wallace was at first intended for the Duthie Park, recently gifted to the town as a recreational area on the north bank of the Dee; instead it was to be placed in Schoolhill to embellish the new development – and the enhanced public standing of the area was soon re-emphasised by the plans to erect a new girls' school for the town across Schoolhill from the art gallery, in Belmont Street.[15]

To the town's annoyance – but to the expectation of those in the know – just as it was preparing to host the annual meeting of the prestigious British Association for the Advancement of Science in 1885, and then meetings of the British Pharmaceutical Society and the

[8]

Sanitary Association of Scotland, an enquiry into the town's hospital at Woolmanhill was completed. The *Northern Figaro* called it 'a crusher'; worse was to come, for it was quickly followed by a highly critical report on the town's health, with much pointed comment on the inadequacies of the existing sewerage arrangements.[16] (Rosemary Tyzack discusses the earlier background to this in chapter nine.) The councillors were shamed into immediate action. And the result – apart from another wave of slum clearance – was a most remarkable and foresighted scheme for an improved water supply, including new reservoirs at Mannofield and much new tunnelling. The long-used sewerage farms on the King's Links were abandoned, as were the older sewage outfalls into the Dee at Abercrombie's Jetty and at the suspension bridge. With the introduction of new pumping stations, it became possible to site the main outfall far to the south and well out to sea, at Girdleness Point.[17]

Contemporaries seem to have been aware that something like a new era had opened for Aberdeen. The new water supply, available in all areas of the existing town by a remarkably well-designed system, undoubtedly in the longer run improved living conditions: it also stimulated further building to the west and north. Indeed the council had acted so positively in improving the supply of water that at the turn of the century the municipal system could provide forty-five gallons a day per head of population – but for an estimated population of 227,000 inhabitants, nearly twice as many as there were in 1900.[18] Aberdonians judged their's as more than a fair match for Glasgow's renowned Loch Katrine scheme. Moreover industries which were water-dependent were secured and could expand. Hence the odours to be met with around the harbour and the railway station were at least changed, and generally much for the better.

The impact of these and other developments in the 1880s and 1890s is made plain in a useful and informative publication of 1907. Twenty-one years earlier the *Figaro* had been joined by another satirical magazine, the *Bon-Accord*, which was to have a long career. If its tone was less sharp, it was closer to the local political scene (it was full of in-jokes about the councillors), and it may have been intentionally less aggressive than the *Figaro*; but it was still able to deliver its own style of cutting commentary. That Aberdeen should spawn two substantial journals of this kind is itself notable, and an index perhaps of a new and assured civic consciousness. When *Bon-Accord* reached its majority year in 1907, the owners and editor marked the occasion with a special publication

intended to review, commemorate – and generally extol – the changes which their city had seen since the mid-1880s. [19]

Perhaps one feature stands out above all others: the sheer extent of the expansion of municipal services. Not only was water municipalised, but also gas and electricity. The transport system, tramways and buses, had been taken over and developed. Leisure facilities across a wide spectrum of activities had been provided – from public halls and galleries for all kinds of music and the fine arts, to public libraries, to better arrangements for sea-bathing and for horse-racing on the Links. The council also provided pitches galore for cricket (which in the summer of 1885 the *Figaro* could describe as 'the national game') and for soccer; and Aberdeen was widely praised, by visitors and by its inhabitants alike, for the numbers, spread and management of its public parks.[20]

The development of the road system, the bridging of the Dee to Torry, the swift expansion of tramways and then bus routes, all aided an extraordinary spreading outwards of residential areas. This, however, happened in ways which further emphasised what had already been growing more evident – the sharpening of the social class divisions between different districts of the expanding city. As the distances increased between newer residential areas occupied by different social classes, so too were the opportunities reduced for their 'natural' mixing, whether in leisure or cultural pursuits, in church-going or community gatherings – leaving only those formal and socially regulated contacts such as took place at work. As we shall see, there was after 1872 far less opportunity for any social mixing in schools than had been the case as late as the middle of the century. Yet the physical expansion of the city was still remarkably constrained, and remained so until after World War II: only then was there that enormous expansion in the provision of council-housing and the wholesale emptying of the remaining old residential areas of the town centre, which took so much of the population to Mastrick, Northfield, Summerhill and Kincorth. Map 3 shows how in 1950 there was still no large-scale building west of Anderson Drive, just as there was no expansion yet into Airyhall and other areas which today are dominated by housing built for the middling and professional classes. On the whole, for all its expansion, nineteenth-century Aberdeen retained to a surprising degree its old sense of 'community' – something which earlier writers recognised as having been so strongly maintained despite the first stages of the town's improvement. The early tramways, for instance, along their consider-

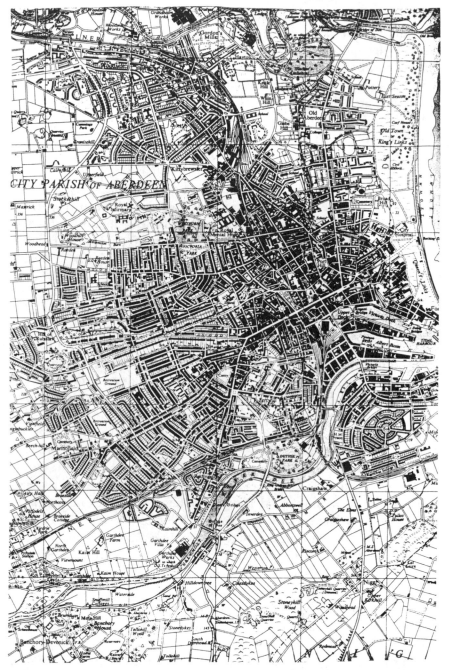

Map 3. Aberdeen in 1950: Kincorth being laid out for housing, but Northfield and Mastrick still untouched.

able lengths, had generally served a wide cross-section of the town's population. But new patterns of schooling and church-going were often to be more socially divisive than the earlier spreading of the different classes into distinctive residential areas. Not until the present century, and even then later rather than earlier, did housing developments in particular act so directly in breaking up what remained of that cohesiveness which had for so long marked Aberdeen society.

The history of Aberdeen in the nineteenth century, and even in the twentieth, readily provides instances of the distinctive course it has so often taken in comparison with the other major Scottish cities. Here we must here restrict ourselves to three examples which serve to highlight the individual and particular ways in which Aberdeen responded to general social developments: Chartism, the Disruption of 1843 in the Established Church and its aftermath, and the changing provision of schooling.

Aberdeen Chartism

In the past quarter of a century historians have grappled with the often problematic course of 'the Chartist movement in Scotland' or the 'Scottish context of Chartism' – thus implying a rather different perspective from older studies of 'Scottish Chartism' as something firmly denoted by its own specific character, and having its own particular motivations.[21] The more recent writings have, it should be noted, tended to concentrate their attention on the central belt of Scotland, especially Glasgow, and to seek out evidence which, so far as possible, provides parallels with the Chartist movement south of the border. Thus we are told that Chartism in Britain 'was political first and foremost'; that it was in Scotland, as in England, a mainly political response to those particular economic and social stresses of the 1830s and 1840s which closely affected the lower orders; and that it should be accounted for in terms of its immediate causes.[22] But then we are also told that the Scottish movement was 'too incoherent' properly to parallel that in England (and was, we are evidently meant to infer, the worse for that). Nonetheless, much effort is expended on interpreting the Scottish experience in English terms: as a manifestation of an emergent or sharpening class conflict; of a battle between labour and employers; of a new popular riotousness, strongly politicised and often overlaid with sectarian animosities, which in turn, of course, would demand a survey of Chartist attitudes to the immigrant, Catholic Irish of the south-west. [23]

Chartism in Aberdeen is usually given a side-glance or two, but little more, because it does not seem to 'fit'. What is known of it, indeed, goes to underline in a marked way the lack of 'cohesiveness' in Scottish Chartism as a whole. In fact we know a great deal about Aberdeen Chartism, for it has been thoroughly researched by Robert Duncan since the 1970s, and his conclusions sit uncomfortably with the now usual line of interpretation.[24] Thus, Duncan emphasises the long-term roots of the movement as it developed in Aberdeen, and also the relative lack of upset it brought in social class relations. Scottish Chartism – at least in the form and character it took in Aberdeen – was not some spontaneous reflex to social distress arising from trade depression, was not an episode in what is often called 'hunger politics' and should not be interpreted from a narrow, institutionalist, 'labour history' approach.[25] In Aberdeen, Duncan maintains, Chartism should be placed in that continuum of 'plebeian radicalism' which existed at least from the 1790s, and which had been constantly stimulated in the local community by vibrant popular traditions – in a political ideology consistently opposed to 'old corruption', but also in community activism and in cultural and social ambition.

This popular attack was directed throughout at the social, as well as political, results of the objectionable ways in which patronage, privilege and power were confined in the hands of the landed aristocracy. It was a plebeian radicalism which disputed, whenever it could, the privileges of establishment in Church and state alike, not least in the ways these were sustained by the alliance of parish ministers and the heritors.[26] For Duncan, the struggle as it was to be found in Aberdeen was one of 'people versus aristocracy and Establishment' rather than of 'labour versus capital'.[27] Moreover, in professional, commercial and mercantile Aberdeen – less dominated than some other cities by manufacturing – there was a vociferous middle class. Many of its members shared the distaste for patronage as it was managed; opposed uncontrolled aristocratic powers and also the Church Establishment or at least its worst features; favoured reform of the electoral system; were highly sympathetic to demands for better education, and better and more fairly-directed welfare systems; and warmly supported such schemes of collective self-help as friendly societies. They could find common ground with local Chartists, more or less, in attacking the Moderates in the Church of Scotland; in their disgust at Westminster's resistance to reform of the Corn Laws; and in demands for free trade and anti-landlord legislation – which were fiercely fuelled by the editorials of James

[13]

Adam of the *Aberdeen Herald*.[28]

Duncan notes that only once in the Chartist era was the military called out in Aberdeen to suppress a riot, and that was not until 1848 and was against an old-fashioned meal mob rather than a Chartist demonstration.[29] Indeed, as he remarks, when Aberdeen Chartists held their meetings – and one of them in August 1838 attracted 10,000 people – these took place not in the streets of the town but at the traditional place for all public demonstrations, on the Broadhill. Duncan rightly stresses the socio-cultural strengths of Aberdeen Chartism – in pressing for educational reform; in moves to self-preparation for full 'citizenship'; in demanding a strengthening of the moral and religious character of its supporters. He notes too that, when political reform was at the forefront in Aberdeen, it tended to take the form of an alliance between the Chartists and middle-class supporters of the further extension of the franchise – to the point at which middle-class social reformism would envelop the constitutional radicalism of the Chartists.[30] There was coherence here, but apparently not of the kind that readily led to cohesion with the Chartists of the south, whether of southern Scotland or of England.

ABERDEEN AND THE DISRUPTION

If some historians have found Aberdeen awkwardly 'different' in its Chartism, it has been otherwise with accounts of the Disruption. Here the Aberdeen experience – as meticulously described by Allan MacLaren[31] – has been taken as a model. MacLaren was, by a long way, first in the field with his study of the social as well as the ecclesiastical impact of the Disruption in a Scottish town. He set a framework which others expect to replicate elsewhere in urban Scotland. What historians expect to find, therefore, is a very substantial secession of ministers in city parishes to the Free Church – in Aberdeen all fifteen went out in the summer of 1843, two or three, it must be said, with some hesitation. They look also, in the post-Disruption presbyterian churches, especially the new Free Churches, for the Aberdeen example of domination by middle-class memberships and managements to be reproduced. Some researchers have recently been rather perplexed, for instance in studying selected districts of Glasgow, because their findings do not sufficiently match MacLaren's account of Aberdeen.[32] But why be surprised? Was not Aberdeen again demonstrating its distinctiveness? It is only possible here to look at one aspect, in making our

Table 1. The Disruption in Scottish cities, 1843.

| | Church Affiliations after the Disruption (nos) | | | | | | Attachment after 1843: within cities (%) | | |
| | Parish ministers | | | Chapel ministers | | | All ministers | | |
	C of S (Mod)	C of S (Evgl)	FC	C of S (Mod)	C of S (Evgl)	FC	C of S (Mod)	C of S (Evgl)	FC
Aberdeen	–	–	6	–	–	9	–	–	100
Dundee	3	1	3	1	–	7	27	7	67
Edinburgh	7	4	14	1	1	17	18	11	71
Glasgow*	1	4	5	2	9	17	8	34	58
TOTAL	11	9	28	4	10	50	13	17	70

* Glasgow here includes the parishes of Gorbals, Govan and Barony

comparisons between Aberdeen and other major cities in Scotland. Table 1 indicates the decisions made in 1843 by the sitting Church of Scotland ministers (Moderates and Evangelicals) in Dundee, Edinburgh and Glasgow, on the question of whether to join the Free Church.

The question in reality is not why other Scottish cities did not match the Aberdeen pattern of secession, but rather why in Aberdeen the Disruption took such a unique course. And the answer to that is not too difficult to uncover.[33] Aberdeen was very late indeed in dividing the original town's parish, St Nicholas – which, in the 1820s, had three ministers to serve the population – into new legal parochial units to match the rise in numbers, and the new geographical spread, of the citizenry. Not until 1828 were six independent *quoad civilia* parishes set up, two of these on the basis of existing chapels (Greyfriars' and St Clement's – the latter serving mainly the fishertown of Footdee) and the other four, North, South, East and West, replacing the old St Nicholas. Apart from St Clement's, all these churches existed cheek-by-jowl in the city centre and were, from the beginning, 'gathered' churches, adhering but little in the formation of their congregations to their new parish boundaries.

With patronage so crucial an issue in the ecclesiastical politics of the 1830s, how were appointments made under arrangements with the town council? As it happened, the council seems to have acted with great sensitivity towards the known desires of the congregations. There is evidence that any successful candidate for St Clement's had to have strong congregational support. The Greyfriars' ministry had long been combined with the principalship of Marischal College, the actual serving of the cure being left to preacher-catechists who, the town council

ensured, were acceptable to the congregation. Existing ministers of St Nicholas were allotted their new charges with marked deference to congregational opinion. Thus, in 1828, James Foote was given the East Church because he was 'the people's choice', and James Murray was transferred to the North Church in recognition of his 'popularity' with his new hearers. The patronage of the South Church, newly built by subscription, was in effect made over to the subscribers, and we read of 'elections' being held in 1832 and 1836.[34] Only in the case of the West Church, the old first charge of the original parish, is there a lack of evidence that the town council took formal soundings in the congregation; but that new charge, attended by a socially very important section of the community, no doubt made its congregational wishes known in the right quarters. In short, long before the final crisis in the Church arrived in the years 1839 to 1843, only the merest vestiges of old-style patronage remained: it was hardly exercised at all, or was exercised only with the greatest sensitivity.

The remaining nine charges within the Establishment in Aberdeen in 1843 were chapels of ease, some of them long standing. In 1834 four – Gilcomston, Trinity, Bon Accord and Union – were made *quoad sacra* parishes by the General Assembly, newly dominated by the Evangelicals. In 1835 these four were joined by Holburn, and, in 1839, by the former secession church of Melville. All these churches had their own constitutions. The ministers at Gilcomston were appointed by its managers, in Trinity by the communicant seat-holders. The Mariners' Chapel, formed only in 1839–40, certainly elected its own minister, as did the older Gaelic Chapel and John Knox; elsewhere the congregations, through elected managers, seat-holders, or the male heads of families, held the right of appointment.[35] Hence, exceptionally, patronage was in Aberdeen hardly a live issue, either in *quoad civilia* or in *quoad sacra* parishes, and, in the late 1830s, all the ministers were known and mostly voluble adherents of the Evangelicals' cause. That they seceded in 1843, and were accompanied by very substantial portions of their congregations, was no surprise to contemporary observers.

The time has surely come to look beyond MacLaren's findings for the 1840s and 1850s – for the distinctive religious history of Aberdeen does not stop there. There are, for instance, some surprises if we look at tables 2 and 3 below which allow us to compare the enumerations of church memberships in Aberdeen in 1851 and 1891 with the recorded attendances by congregations of the various sects in these same years. [36]

What is immediately apparent, especially in the attendance figures in

Table 2. Aberdeen church affiliations, 1851 and 1891.

Sect	1851 sittings	attendance	1891 attendance	members
Church of Scotland	22.4	18.7	36.9	49.9
Free Church	40.3	41.6	33.0	29.5
United Presbyterian	11.5	6.9	6.8	5.7
Congregationalist	12.2	11.2	5.0	4.1
Episcopalian	5.6	13.4	6.1	5.0
Roman Catholic	2.3	3.0	3.6	3.4
Others	5.8	5.2	8.6	4.3

Figures represent percentages of totals in each column.

Table 3. Aberdeen church attendance as percentage of population, 1851 and 1891.

Year	CofS	FC	UP	Cong	Episc	RC	Others
1851	7.26	16.14	2.67	4.35	5.18	1.16	2.04
1891	8.53	7.63	1.57	1.16	1.40	0.84	1.99

table 2, is the striking recovery by the Established Church, significantly overtaking the Free Church in the numbers of all churchgoers and then alone (see table 3) increasing its proportion of attenders in the population at large in the forty years from 1851 to 1891. Moreover, the dominance of the two largest presbyterian churches in Aberdeen was maintained in the period, at some 70 per cent of all attenders: in that respect, we can find revealing comparisons with the other large towns in Scotland (table 4, next page). The statistics there relate to presbyteries (Church and Free Church) in which the towns are sited, and thus contain figures for some nearby rural or part-rural parishes. To make comparisons easier, church membership is given as a proportion of the total population in the appropriate presbytery. [37]

The domination of the two major presbyterian churches in Aberdeen is thus, by and large, not shared by the other major towns in Scotland – even by Edinburgh, which likewise had no large influx of Irish Catholics in mid-century. But Edinburgh alone parallels Aberdeen in one notable respect, that it shows a marked recovery in the later part of the century by the Church of Scotland (and at the same time a decline in Free Church attachment). These tables serve mainly to throw up questions which have still to be answered, not least by those

Table 4. Membership of Established and Free Churches in Scotland in proportion (%) to population, 1871–1891. Returns by presbytery.

Year		1871	1874	1879	1883	1884	1887	1891
Aberdeen	CofS		19.0	17.8		19.5	20.1	20.9
	FC	12.6		12.0	11.1		10.7	10.2
Dundee	CofS		11.8	12.8		12.5	12.9	13.4
	FC	6.7		6.9	6.8		6.8	6.8
Edinburgh	CofS		10.9	12.1		11.7	13.2	13.8
	FC	8.3		8.1	8.0		8.0	7.7
Glasgow	CofS		7.5	8.2		8.0	8.1	7.9
	FC	4.5		5.2	5.3		5.4	5.4
Paisley	CofS		10.0	10.8		10.6	10.5	11.5
	FC	4.8		5.2	5.0		5.1	5.0
Greenock	CofS		8.0	8.8		9.3	9.9	9.8
	FC	6.4		6.6	7.2		7.2	6.5

Totals (CofS + FC)	1871–74	1879	1883–84	1887	1891
Aberdeen	31.6	29.8	30.6	30.8	31.1
Dundee	18.5	19.7	19.3	19.7	20.2
Edinburgh	19.2	20.2	19.7	21.2	21.5
Glasgow	12.0	13.4	13.3	13.5	13.3
Paisley	14.8	16.0	15.6	15.6	16.5
Greenock	14.4	15.4	16.5	17.1	16.3

who may wish to continue MacLaren's work. There are highly distinctive developments in later nineteenth-century Aberdeen – not only as here in religion, but in so much else – which cry out for investigation of their background and their causes.

SCHOOLING IN ABERDEEN

Aberdeen shared with other Scottish cities a long-held concern to make adequate provision for the education of its citizenry. In 1834, responding to a government enquiry, the parish ministers of all Scottish cities were very positive about the sheer quantity of available schooling, claiming that no parent, however poor, was without access to education for

Table 5. Schooling in 1838–39: percentages.

Type of school	Aberdeen			Dundee			Edinburgh		
	Burgh/ Sessional	Private	Total	Burgh/ Sessional	Private	Total	Burgh/ Sessional	Private	Total
elementary	34.8	27.7	62.5	17.1	53.6	70.7	15.6	67.5	83.1
commercial/ modern	–	11.5	11.5	–	–	–	1.2	4.7	5.9
classical/ modern	0.5	15.3	15.8	–	13.8	13.8	2.2	4.5	6.7
classical	5.2	4.9	10.1	–	15.5	15.5	0.9	3.4	4.3
Total	40.5	59.4	99.9	17.1	82.9	100.0	19.9	80.1	100.0

his or her children – at least to instruction in the rudiments: and this schooling was provided in a range of institutions which in many instances offered their services gratis, or at very low fees. True, a few ministers – especially in Glasgow – were aware that some parents were not using these opportunities to the full and a few were withdrawing their children too early, or were not sending them to school at all, in order to capitalise on their wage-earning potential: but the provision for them was there. Such schooling in the great towns, as elsewhere, was supported in many different ways; much of it by public bodies, such as town councils, endowment trusts, churches, national and local charities, all of whom could (and usually did) make efforts to offer instruction cheaply, or free if required; in addition, there were many schools, large and small, supported by private individuals or by subscription, charging a wide range of fees for wide-ranging and often more adventurous curricula.[38]

Another government enquiry, in 1838–39, allows us to compare the character of the schooling which was available in Edinburgh, Dundee and Aberdeen (the Glasgow data are much less full).[39] In the table above, the schools in each town have been categorised by the curricula they taught and by their providers (whether 'public' or private); and the results converted into percentages for easy comparison. 'Modern' subjects here include book-keeping, practical mathematics, geography, modern languages, navigation and so on.

Again Aberdeen appears to be distinctive. There was markedly greater school provision made by public bodies there – another index of its commitment in community-based enterprise? – and also wider public

Table 6. Types of school in Scottish cities, 1896.

	Aberdeen	Dundee	Edinburgh	Glasgow/Govan
Elementary:				
board	75.3	70.0	65.4	75.6
non-board	12.8	21.9	12.4	16.8
hospital etc.	2.2	2.5	1.2	2.1
other endowed schools	–	1.4	3.0	–
private/adventure	2.2	–	0.1	0.9
subtotal	92.5	95.8	82.1	95.4
Higher-class (Secondary):				
board	3.8	–	1.1	0.8
non-public	3.6	4.2	16.8	3.8
subtotal	7.4	4.2	17.9	4.6

provision for classical training; nonetheless, over a quarter of all Aberdeen schools also offered instruction in non-classical or modern subjects – a substantially greater proportion than in Dundee or Edinburgh.

Half a century and more later, in 1896, and twenty years and more after the government intervened more directly in schooling through the 1872 Education (Scotland) Act, we have data from which we can again compare the character of educational provision in the Scottish cities, including Glasgow this time.[40] The categories of schools are those used by the government inspectors in their returns to the Scotch Education Department. Once again, for each city the figures represent the percentage of schools in each category.

The 1872 act had brought Scottish schooling much more extensively into the public domain, through the institution of local school boards with powers to raise rates, together with an extensive system of highly regulated government – that is Scotch Education Department (SED) – grants awarded to 'efficient' schools. A new uniformity, more or less, was introduced as a result: only Edinburgh had a substantial proportion of secondary schools in the private or non-public sector; only Aberdeen retained a strong public element in its secondary schooling. Aberdeen's commitment to public schooling (elementary and secondary), at almost 80 per cent, was the highest in all the cities. Despite the 1872 act, however, some of the earlier traits and emphases remained, and still differentiated the responses in schooling, city by city. Aberdeen, indeed, was renowned in the fifty years after 1872 for the positive

way it responded, time after time, to pressures from the SED in the name of efficiency. It galloped ahead in building very large elementary or primary schools ('grey barracks' some opponents called them) which at the same time as changing significantly the school experience of Aberdeen children also solidified the growing class divisions in the town by their geographic positioning, which determined the particular residential catchment areas they served. It deliberately limited the curriculum in these elementary schools, separated 'elementary' from 'secondary' education, then later added supplementary (vocational) classes in elementary schools. It also marched ahead with the government's scheme for post-school 'continuation education' (developing the town's Central School and then totally changing the character of the training offered in vocationally-oriented Robert Gordon's College). It did all this in the effort to maximise the level of government grants and contain the inevitably increasing level of school-rates. [41]

ABERDEEN AND ITS HINTERLAND

When in 1903 a local worthy, William Watt, addressed the Aberdeen Philosophical Society on the changes which Aberdeen society had undergone in the previous fifty years, he keenly looked for those developments which distinguished it from other major Scottish towns.[42] Typical of an age all but obsessed with questions of national health, and the presumed eugenic decline resulting from the worst features of expanding urban life, Watt remarked on two aspects which he believed set Aberdeen apart. Although the 'best specimens' of robust and capable youth were being lost to the locality through high levels of emigration – which involved especially the loss of many highly educated professionals to the empire – yet the physical calibre of the town's population seemed to have been maintained (in contrast to Glasgow, for instance). He offered two reasons to account for this apparent anomaly. Firstly, Aberdeen in the 1880s and 1890s had experienced an extraordinary advance in its prosperity and thus in the general standards of living of its citizens (something which, incidentally, made him and others rather bewildered at the assertive radicalism and increasing readiness of the city's labouring population to strike in the 1890s and after). Watt proudly pointed to the 1901 census which showed that only 39 per cent of Aberdonians lived in one- or two-roomed houses (compared to 62 per cent in Glasgow and 63 per cent in Dundee); and that 41 per cent lived in three- or four-roomed houses (the percentages

in Glasgow and Dundee were 26 and 27 respectively). Some of the worst effects of urbanisation had thus been avoided. Secondly, genetically and intellectually, the city of Aberdeen had been constantly refreshed by the numbers and quality of young people who came to live and work there from the rural north and north-east. Aberdeen was 'much more than compensated numerically by the attraction of recruits to the city to aid in its work and participation in its lot'. [43]

The close interrelationship of the city of Aberdeen and its rural hinterland has long remained a mark of its distinctiveness. In 1979 Dr Ian Carter still commented on the intense cultural cohesiveness of north-eastern Scotland, something which (surprisingly to him as an 'outsider') so clearly cut across social class lines. And it was a cohesiveness, having its own vital impact on Aberdeen as place and as community, which was underpinned by the continuing phenomenon of that rural immigration observed and welcomed by William Watt a century before. After World War II, this cohesion had perhaps its greatest vitality among the city's professional and managerial groups, for these so often had and were at pains to retain their rural links. Indeed, Carter amusingly recounted that

> If you should find yourself pinioned in social conversation with an Aberdeen lawyer or surgeon, searching with increasing desperation for something to talk about, then I strongly recommend that you turn the conversation to the local history of agriculture. All of these urbane, sophisticated men seem to have had an auntie in Echt or a cousin in New Pitsligo. [44]

'Metropolitan' Aberdeen – for all the recent impact on it of the oil industry – still retains the marks of its roots in its own highly distinctive past. And that past, not least in the two centuries since the town broke out of the confines of the old royalty, and began its majestic march westwards up Union Street and beyond, deserves much more scholarly attention that it has received so far.

NOTES

1. D. J. Withrington and I. R. Grant (eds), *Statistical Account of Scotland 1791–1799*, vol. 14 (Wakefield, 1982), p. 255.
2. Henry Hamilton, 'Introduction', in Hugh Mackenzie, *The City of Aberdeen* [Third Statistical Account of Scotland] (Edinburgh, 1953) p. xv.
3. Francis H. Groome (ed.), *Ordnance Gazetteer of Scotland* (Edinburgh, 1882), vol. 1, p. 6.

4. Groome, *Gazetteer*, p. 7.

5. David Masson, *Memories of Two Cities: Edinburgh and Aberdeen* (Edinburgh, 1911), p. 193.

6. National Library of Scotland (NLS) ms. 1685, Bannerman of Elrick, vol. 1.

7. NLS, ms. 1685, ff. 72–73.

8. The importance of 'didactic fiction' of this kind in Scottish newspapers is well described and analysed in William Donaldson, *Popular Literature in Victorian Scotland: Language, Fiction and the Press* (Aberdeen, 1986), esp. chapter 3.

9. E.g. James Rettie, *Aberdeen Fifty Years Ago* (Aberdeen, 1868).

10. Groome, *Gazetteer*, p. 7.

11. D. J. Withrington, 'Aberdeen in the mid-1880s', in *Aberdeen Grammar School Magazine*, no. 89 (100th anniversary number, June 1985), p. 13.

12. Withrington, 'Aberdeen in the mid-1880s', p. 15.

13. *Aberdeen Today: a record of the life, thought and industry of the city* [majority number of *Bon Accord*, 1886–1907] (Aberdeen, 1907), pp. 11–12.

14. Withrington, 'Aberdeen in the mid-1880s', p. 15.

15. *Aberdeen Today*, 'City Improvements', pp. 19 et seq. Aberdeen University Library's Department of Special Collections also contains the cuttings of a 48–part *Short History of Aberdeen*, contributed by John Malcolm Bulloch to local newspapers in 1900; volumes of other cuttings by Bulloch provide much worthwhile commentary on 19th-century developments in Aberdeen.

16. Withrington, 'Aberdeen in mid-1880s', p. 15.

17. *Aberdeen Today*, pp. 31–35.

18. *Aberdeen Today*, p. 35.

19. *Aberdeen Today*, pp. 12–14. Given the subtitle 'Encyclopaedia Bon-Accordia', *Aberdeen Today* was intended to measure her achievements in 'the years of Aberdeen's greatest commercial activity and her brightest artistic renaissance' and to show how 'radical and far-reaching have been the changes, in almost every field of thought' and also to mirror 'the peculiar pride in our city which is not the least dominant note in the character of the Aberdonian'.

20. Withrington, 'Aberdeen in the mid-1880s', p. 16. The *Figaro* in 1885 claimed that cricket was Aberdeen's 'most popular summer pastime'; in September 1885, two of its soccer teams dismayed the town by their performances in the first round of the Scottish Cup – Aberdeen Bon Accord lost 36–0 to Arbroath (still the record score in cup matches) and Aberdeen Rovers went down to Dundee Harp 35–0.

21. Alexander Wilson, *The Chartist Movement in Scotland* (Manchester, 1970); W. Hamish Fraser, 'The Scottish context of Chartism', in Terry Brotherstone (ed.), *Covenant, Charter and Party: Traditions of Revolt and Protest in Modern Scottish History* (Aberdeen, 1989); Leslie B. Wright, *Scottish Chartism* (Edinburgh, 1953).

22. Fraser, 'Scottish context', esp. pp. 66–78.

23. Fraser, 'Scottish context', pp. 73–74.

24. Robert Duncan, 'Chartism in Aberdeen: radical politics and culture, 1838–48', in Brotherstone, *Covenant, Charter and Party*, pp. 78–91; and his 'Artisans and proletarians: Chartism and working-class allegiance in Aberdeen, 1838–42' in *Northern Scotland*, vol. 4 (1981), pp. 51–67.

25. Duncan, 'Chartism in Aberdeen', pp. 78–79.

26. Duncan, 'Chartism in Aberdeen', pp. 82–84.

27. Duncan, 'Chartism in Aberdeen', p. 83.

28. Duncan, 'Chartism in Aberdeen', pp. 86–88.

29. Duncan, 'Chartism in Aberdeen', p. 79.

30. Duncan, 'Chartism in Aberdeen', pp. 88–89.

31. A. Allan MacLaren, *Religion and Social Class: the Disruption years in Aberdeen* (London, 1974).

32. Peter Hillis, 'Presbyterianism and social class in mid-19th century Glasgow: a study of nine churches', in *Journal of Ecclesiastical History*, vol. 32 (1981); and 'The sociology of the Disruption', in S. J. Brown and M. Fry (eds), *Scotland in the Age of the Disruption* (Edinburgh, 1993), esp. pp. 52, 55–56. The statistics in the table which follows are derived from James McCosh, *The Wheat and the Chaff* (Perth, 1843), which allows us to divide those ministers who remained in the Establishment into old-style Moderates and known Evangelicals who might have been expected to go out in 1843.

33. See MacLaren, *Religion and Society*, pp. 51–58; Alexander Gammie, *The Churches of Aberdeen: historical and descriptive* (Aberdeen, 1909), passim; Hew Scott (ed.), *Fasti Ecclesiae Scoticanae* (new edition, Edinburgh, 1915), vol. 6, pp. 1–42.

34. Gammie, *Churches of Aberdeen*, p. 39; *Fasti*, vol. 6, p. 15. 'Election' may here refer to the final and formal process before the town council, but, if so, this was most likely a formality, after there had been a well-supported congregational call and the known and firm support of the subscribers.

35. MacLaren, *Religion and Social Class*, pp. 52–54; Gammie, *Churches of Aberdeen*, pp. 19, 23, 32, 73, 81, 92, 150–51, 179–80, 222.

36. The data in these tables are calculated from *Commission on Religious Worship and Education, Scotland: report and tables* (London, 1854); and see also MacLaren, *Religion and Society*, pp. 213, 215; and James Howie, *The Churches and the Churchless in Scotland* (Edinburgh, 1893).

37. This table is based on the membership figures which were presented intermittently or regularly to the General Assemblies of both the Established and Free Churches, and printed in their annual reports and proceedings; and also on data in Howie, *Churches and the Churchless*.

38. Education Enquiry. *Abstract of the Answers and Returns made pursuant to an Address of the House of Commons dated 9th July 1834: Scotland* (London, 1837).

39. *Answers Made by Schoolmasters in Scotland to Queries Circulated in 1838, by Order of the Select Committee on Education in Scotland* (London, 1841).

40. *Returns for School Districts in Scotland of Rateable Value, School Rate, Population, Accommodation and Number in Average Attendance in Public, State-aided and Elementary Schools Recognised as Efficient, 1896*, Parliamentary Papers (PP), 1897, vol. 71, p. 223.

41. *Aberdeen Today*, pp. 67–79.

42. William Watt, 'Fifty years of progress in Aberdeen', *Transactions of the Aberdeen Philosophical Society*, vol. 4 (1910), pp. 99–124.

43. Watt, 'Fifty years of progress', p. 116.

44. Ian Carter, *Farm Life in Northeast Scotland 1840–1914: the Poor Man's Country* (Edinburgh, 1979), p. 5.

2

U*nion Street and the 'Great Street' in Scottish Town Planning*

Ranald MacInnes

Could there be such a thing as a great city with tramcars, electric lights, hotels, and cathedrals so far away among empty fields so near the North Pole as we were going? [1]

S*ir John Betjeman* was a famous admirer of the 'glories' of Aberdeen. The English poet's delight at encountering a city of such consequence after travelling through miles of 'wilderness' echoes Groome's[2] remarks on Aberdeen's 'repulsive' hinterland quoted in chapter one. But Betjeman's attitude perhaps sprang from a Home Counties' world-view: in his time, the south-east of England was well on its way to becoming more or less one massive suburban conurbation, with only token strips of green belt separating the various centres of population. And as Betjeman noticed, with all its mountains and moorland, Scotland is nevertheless one of the most urbanised countries in the world. This chapter is concerned with the most dramatic episode in the making of the modern city of Aberdeen – the creation of Union Street. It deals with Union Street's place in the history of Scottish town planning; with the 'bridge street' concept, which was central to it; and its relationship to Edinburgh's 'bridge street' – South Bridge.

The facts concerning the building of Union Street are well docu-

mented. The idea originated in a proposal designed to open up communications by road with inland Aberdeenshire and beyond. The scheme involved compulsory purchase, demolition, and construction on a large scale – with massive under-building and vaulting in addition to the Union Bridge itself. The area was cleared, the street laid out and the bridge built between 1802 and 1805 by the surveyor Thomas Fletcher, with advice from Thomas Telford (plate 1). David Hamilton's winning three-arch design (plate 2) was shelved after it was discovered that the Glaswegian architect had miscalculated the levels. John Rennie was consulted and submitted three designs, including one for a single cast iron arch. Thomas Fletcher then proposed a single-arch design but in stone. The 'architectural' part – the parapet and piers – was designed by James Burns. The bridge was later widened in line with the street. But how did Aberdeen arrive at such an ambitious and expensive solution, a great commercial adventure that began life as a mere road improvement?

Scotland has specialised in new towns and indeed has occasionally taken the concept overseas to Europe and North America. Eighteenth-century Russian experiments in town planning were taken forward by Scottish architects such as Charles Cameron and Adam Menelaws. Robert Mylne's prize-winning design for a great square is another early example of a Scottish export in town planning. Mylne was the first architect from the UK to win the Concorso Clementino, at that time the most prestigious architectural prize in the world. Another example is Robert Adam's remarkable scheme for Lisbon. Often dismissed as a student exercise, it in fact involved a serious attempt by an experienced architect to plan on a large scale. After the earthquake of 1756 Adam proposed to do nothing less than to re-build the Portugese capital. [3]

There is certainly an accomplished tradition, a cultural confidence in new towns and town planning in Scotland, but there is also the closely related fascination with the monumental in architecture. The two come together in the very firmly rooted idea of the city as *itself* a monument – the idea that each building or square is only part of a greater architectural composition to be shaped and added to, over time and as circumstances permit. The foremost example of this commitment to the city over time is of course Edinburgh, where the initial idea was institutionalised into a city planning framework which long outlived its original mid-eighteenth-century proponents, continuing even into the twentieth century. Broadly speaking, Scotland could be said to have a culture of renewal. This is one of the reasons why it has specialised in

Plate 1. Union Bridge as built, c. 1810: from the guide book Scotia Depicta (reproduced by permission of University of Glasgow Library, Special Collections).

New Towns, new solutions: the twelfth-century burghs of David I; Edinburgh New Town (or *Towns*); Inveraray, New Lanark and countless eighteenth- and nineteenth-century planned towns and villages; the redevelopment of Glasgow and Dundee by the respective City Improvement Trusts[4] with grand streets and tall buildings after the fashion of Baron Haussmann's Paris.

Although perhaps reluctantly at first, Aberdeen made an astonishing contribution to this long and varied tradition with a bold but simple idea which overcame the disadvantages of geography. That idea became Union Street. The medieval street pattern and natural obstacles such as the Denburn did not allow for the simple cutting through of a straight, level street on the model of, for example, Glasgow's Trongate/Argyle Street. Union Street became therefore one of only two major 'bridge streets' developed in late-eighteenth-century Scotland. But where are the roots of the concept?

An attitude had developed throughout Scotland – within the eighteenth-century drive for 'improvement' – which reached its peak in the capital during the boom years of the 1820s. Between 1750 and 1830, the idea that towns could be organised according to architectural principles had become almost commonplace. In the nineteenth century, the word 'improvement' acquired added and urgent meaning: it was

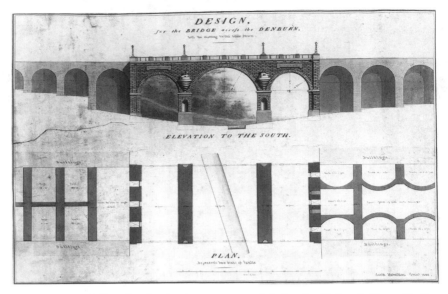

Plate 2. David Hamilton's winning, unexecuted design for Union Bridge with its associated vaulting, 1801 (reproduced by permission of Aberdeen Art Gallery).

seen as the alternative to revolution. In the eighteenth century, on the other hand, the main questions had not concerned how to ameliorate the condition of the poor, but rather how to house the burgeoning middle classes and urban gentry, how to relate them structurally to one another, and how to avoid the ever-present dangers and nuisances represented by the urban 'mob'. Rioting and small-scale 'riotous assembly' were growing problems in Scottish towns, terrifying town dwellers. Architecturally, this fear, especially after the Gordon Riots and the French Revolution, might be expressed through an exaggerated stratification of urban life, coupled with more effective policing to replace the ad hoc arrangement of night watchmen and volunteer militia. The notion of planning of urban space was suddenly broadened to include whole districts, whole cities. Union Street, like Robert Adam's South Bridge scheme (plate 3), addressed the problem of rational planning, but found the solution through a *vertical* hierarchy, with bridges treated as buildings in themselves. Throughout Scotland, geometric 'rational' settlement planning, framed within a monumental form, was at the heart of eighteenth-century experiments in town planning, either by speculation or by decree.

Aberdeen's set-piece of town planning has two axial streets, the mile-long Union Street and King Street going off almost at a right angle

Plate 3. Robert Adam's proposed South Bridge buildings with ground floor shops (Soane Museum, vol. 34; reproduced by permission of Sir John Soane's Museum).

(plate 4). This basic architectural infrastructure, underpinned by the Union Bridge which levelled the uneven geography of the city, was incrementally 'monumentalised' with key public and commercial buildings. The first city architect, John Smith, set an architectural standard of great refinement achieved in his St Nicholas Graveyard Screen (1829), recalling Robert Adam's celebrated Admiralty Screen and the equal of contemporary work in London such as Decimus Burton's screen at Hyde Park Corner of 1825. But Smith did much more than set an elevated tone. He took granite almost to the limits of its sculptural capabilities, unsurpassed until Marshall MacKenzie's Marischal College of 1891. As city architect, Smith designed solid Schinkel-*esque* monuments such as the single-storey Town School (1830) as well as the more predictable but nevertheless powerful agglomeration of Greek Revival sources, the North Church (1829–30).

Smith's less obvious achievement was as adviser on the planning matrix for Archibald Simpson's personal Greek Revival in the city. Simpson's Athenaeum or 'Union Buildings' (from 1819) was something of an Adam-type multi-function megastructure. It was a building that could not be forced easily into a temple format. Thrusting dynamically, awkwardly, with its great *in antis* entrance front, into a gushet site on Union Street and Castle Street, it addressed rhetorically the square around the newly focussed Mercat Cross. Whilst Adam's work in Glasgow and Edinburgh bore traces of the inward-looking side of the Baroque, Simpson's Aberdeen monuments are fully neo-classical, occupying crucial spaces within the Union Street/King Street axis, binding the city stylistically together, but lending it also an unfinished,

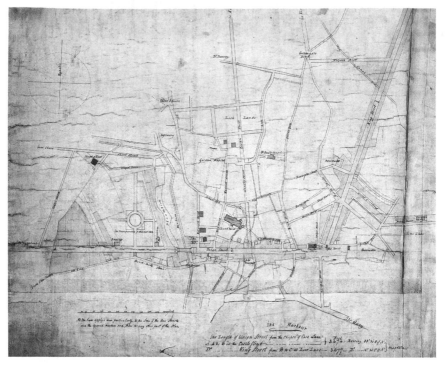

Plate 4. Union Street and neighbouring streets surveyed by Thomas Fletcher, 1807 (reproduced by permission of Aberdeen Art Gallery).

infinite quality. His Northern Bank at 1–4 King Street (1839–40), with its curved portico set on the corner, is the pivot at which the successful transition from Union Street to King Street occurs. The Royal Infirmary (1833) on Woolmanhill is firstly a romantic object in the landscape – seen looming over the tenements of the Denburn Valley viewed from the heights of Union Bridge – and only secondly an exceptionally dry essay in strict, economical Grecian.

Smith and Simpson are the Hamilton and Playfair of Aberdeen, but perhaps Simpson lacked, if lack it was, the freedom and the confidence of Playfair to break the rules. As a result much of Simpson's work is derivative at a time when it was no longer original to lift details straight from Stuart and Revett's *Antiquities of Athens*. However, there are exceptions: the staggering, stripped monumentality of the New Market, an early shopping mall; and the Germanic romanticism of the Triple Kirks (1843) – a masterly amalgam of three churches built (largely of brick) in three weeks, for congregations who had previously occupied

St Nicholas prior to the Disruption.

But underpinning this assembly of great public buildings is Union Street. And the key to Union Street as an idea and as the centrepiece to the whole designed city is the Union Bridge. It was constructed at a crucial time for bridge design when the engineer was beginning to take over from the architect, a period that was paralleled in the 1930s with loss of 'architecture' in the sense of applied ornament from bridges altogether. The eventual design was widely approved in an age that took a huge interest in engineering construction; engravings of the bridge were published in all the guide books to Aberdeen and in general topographical works such as *Scotia Depicta*, illustrated on page 27. More recently, since the street itself and its public buildings have been developed, the Union Bridge as a (now altered) structure has much less prominence. Originally, the bridge served almost as a viewing platform for the city's dramatic geography and for its monuments.

In the eighteenth century the focus for the concern with set-piece bridge engineering and city planning was Europe, and particularly those continental countries which had a centralising state authority able and willing to invest in public architecture. Advances in bridge design, often linked explicitly by the planners with the science of political economy, met up with a propensity for monumentality in architecture to produce the great bridging schemes of the late eighteenth and early nineteenth centuries. In France, for example, bridges and bridging schemes were an essential part of the growth of towns; and these utilitarian structures came to be linked to houses and public buildings in the rapidly growing provincial towns such as Aix, Marseilles and Montpellier – all of which became stopping-off points for Grand Tourists on their way to Italy, among them Robert Adam and (making the journey in more modest style) Robert Mylne.

The stylistic linking of bridge- to building-design, which is of course central to the Union Bridge idea, most probably had its origins in the eighteenth-century French government department, the Ecole des Ponts et Chaussées. This had been founded by Colbert in the time of Louis XIV, but had been expanded and transformed in the eighteenth century under Perronet, so that many other architectural projects besides bridges were carried out by the Ecole's engineers, usually in the current Parisian style. There existed, then, a unity of style and purpose in the 'command economy' of centralised France, which lavished money on the 'provinces' in a way that the new state of Britain did not lavish it – nor indeed did it spend at all – in Edinburgh or

Aberdeen. The result, in France, was an incredible uniformity of high architectural and engineering achievement, such as was achieved only by edict at other European centres such as St Petersburg or Stockholm.

The debate concerning London's Blackfriars Bridge and the eventual construction of that bridge – designed by Robert Mylne, fresh from his triumph in winning the Concorso Clementino in Rome – gave tremendous impetus to bridge building, as did the construction of Perronet's immensely influential Pont de Neuilly in Paris. Hundreds of bridges were built in the 1760s and 1770s, Robert Adam himself making sketches or fully worked-up designs for more than a hundred and fifty in Scotland and in England, and possibly entering the Blackfriars competition himself. But in Scotland, and for Scottish architects abroad, the bridge as a structure was only the departure point for more ambitious ideas: along with his elder brother John, Robert Adam had produced a scheme for the North Bridge in Edinburgh in 1751 which united a bridge with a multi-purpose structure. And eventually, he developed the multi-function idea, commercially and architecturally, to such heights of ambitiousness that his Leith Street scheme was pronounced 'impossible to build'. This tendency was bound up with the European urban norm of dense, horizontally layered agglomerations.

Bridges – along with quays – were the architectural parvenus of the eighteenth century. However, to an extent, they came to be regarded as the very symbols of economic progress and political power. In England, John Gwynn campaigned for improvements of this kind, as did Chambers in the *Treatise on Civic Architecture*, where he associated the issue with national and international trade. The French theorist Abbé Laugier's celebrated *Essai*[5] on architecture had a section devoted to utilitarian and commercial buildings which dealt with the, by now familiar, political economic aspects of the argument. But unlike Gwynn and Chambers, Laugier also dealt with the architectural issue involved, since the form of these 'necessary structures'[6] was still not fixed by the rules of architectural propriety. For Laugier, harbours, quays, and bridges ought to 'give strangers a great idea of our country'[7] by applying 'architecture' to those buildings that were to become the stock-in-trade of the engineer. Blondel's 'Cours d'Architecture' included bridges and other utilitarian structures, and it had been in Paris that the Ecole des Ponts et Chaussées was set up to study and systematise this whole new area. Perronet's Pont de Neuilly (1768–72), with its regular arches, narrow piers, and flat profile, might be said to be the

first truly 'modern' bridge. It was widely admired and became an international exemplar. Perronet's designs were published and bought by architects throughout Europe.

It was precisely because bridge building was in its technical and aesthetic infancy, however, and not yet taken over by the nascent civil engineering profession, that architects, creating stylistic hybrids out of the confusion, might take up the challenge to dress these utilitarian structures in whatever way their genius demanded. Sir James Clerk had commented that William Mylne's North Bridge was, architecturally, wholly unsuitable since it was built as if it were a bridge over a river, rather than simply a way across a valley. Clerk thought that a viaduct 'after the manner of the Romans'[8] would have answered the purpose in a more appropriate way.

Aberdeen's Union Bridge was effectively criticised in the same way by Thomas Fletcher who had been appointed 'superintendent' of David Hamilton's winning three-arch design. Fletcher instead proposed a very wide single-arch structure similar to Adam's Cowgate arch, and contrary to the conditions of the brief. Having been conceived therefore by its promoters as a multi-arch, North Bridge type of structure, the Union Bridge was converted to a single-arch South Bridge type, an altogether more modern and constructionally daring scheme. The sources of the Union Bridge, and of the scheme are complex, but I want to try and separate some of the strands of these sources and thereby identify the exemplars for Union Street, to investigate the European and the Scottish context in which it was conceived.

Union Street is, of course, a 'great street' in the same tradition as Grey Street in Newcastle or Nash's later Regent Street in London, but, looking at the plan of Regent Street, we can see that its main distinction lies in the way it winds from the town to the 'rus in urbe' – the artificial 'country' – of Nash's development at Regent's Park. Union Street, however, is resolutely neo-classical. The axis, the materials and the idea of an infinitely long monumental street is strictly in keeping with a national tradition of town planning. Like Edinburgh, Aberdeen having decided on grandiose town planning, stuck to it: Edinburgh had five, arguably even eight, new towns. Nash's Regent Street is an escape route from the now problematised city, whereas Union Street is typical of the Scottish tendency to celebrate monumental urbanism – the glory of the planned town.

For many outsiders of course, Union Street *is* Aberdeen, so that is has developed an iconic quality. Just as Edinburgh's New Town seemed

to be rationalism and enlightenment mapped out in stone and lime, so Aberdeen's Union Street has stood, many would say very appropriately, for Aberdeen: a straight, clean, uncomplicated idea made real. Such notions, alas, do not withstand the investigation of the historical facts. Edinburgh beautified itself because it was affronted by its decline as Scotland's capital. The town council's *Proposals* of 1752 were framed in the strong rhetoric of Scoto-British patriotism against a background of the absence of state patronage. And Aberdeen did not invent Union Street at all: it had Union Street thrust upon it by the roads commissioners.

During the second half of the eighteenth century, Aberdeen had improved its harbour. But it was in need of an inland gateway, and out of this came the decision of the County Road Trustees to employ Charles Abercrombie, whose soon-to-be-famous document offered three possibilities:

1. a road from Bridge of Dee which followed the banks of the river to the foot of Marischal Street;
2. a road continuing Marischal Street over to Torry;
3. 'Union Street', with a bridge over the Denburn.

The town council were astonished by such a radical third option.[9] The proposed bridge street was immediately suggestive of the Edinburgh improvements, but the Aberdeen Council's reaction was in sharp contrast to Edinburgh's pro-active role in city improvements. It was the ratepayers of Aberdeen rather than their representatives who insisted on the Union Street solution, a solution which necessitated compulsory purchase on a large scale. The citizens loaned their money in large amounts and on 12 February 1799 the Aberdeen New Streets Act was passed, with New Streets trustees established to supervise the work. Half of the street from what is now Adelphi Court[10] to Diamond Street is an artificial creation raised at the lowest level of the ground and carried on a series of arches with a bridge at the Denburn – designed by Thomas Fletcher with modifications sought from the great Thomas Telford. Work began in 1802 and was finished in 1805. The new street cost in all £114,000. Then the burgh became bankrupt. Buildings were cleared and the ground was laid out, but there were no new buildings. Aberdeen had been a city with no entrance; now it was an entrance with no city.

Abercrombie estimated £6,493 and £30,000–£40,000 for acquiring property, but the eventual cost was £225,000. And on top of everything else, this was an act of faith in granite, the material for the stripped

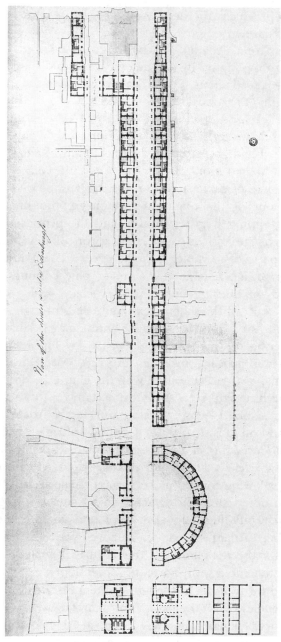

Plate 5. Robert Adam's plan of the South Bridge, Edinburgh, 1785 (Soane Museum, vol. 34). In this first scheme the existing university buildings are not replaced but simply fronted by a screen and flanking professors' houses. Opposite is a crescent of shops. (Reproduced by permission of Sir John Soane's Museum.)

neo-classicism in which Aberdeen was to specialise. But what were the sources of this daring design?

Like Union Street, Adam's South Bridge in Edinburgh linked the lower level with the higher by means of a graduated scheme of private housing and terraced shops. Like Edinburgh, Aberdeen also had a difficult topography, the awkwardness of which it is now difficult fully to appreciate. Whereas, for example, Glasgow's first 'new town' could develop in a relatively flat river plain prior to that city's move westwards, Aberdeen had grown up on a series of hills. Road transport and the associated penetration of Aberdeen's hinterland was set on a spectacular course of expansion, immeasurably improved by the effective levelling out of the town. In Edinburgh, monuments such as Adam's vista-stopping Register House, and the proposed aggrandisement of the college with its associated apron of development, were conceived as parts of a whole, a 'great street'. The Edinburgh South Bridge/North Bridge scheme was a remarkable commercial development founded on housing but now – crucially – also on shopping (plate 5). The roots of the scheme can be traced through earlier Adam projects at Bath, Ayr, and the Adelphi; and it may be that shopping – now also entering the modern phase of its development of purpose-built parades and malls – provides the link with David Hamilton's scheme for Union Street. Hamilton won the Union Bridge competition with a three-arch design. He was almost certainly a former assistant of, or surveyor for, Robert Adam, possibly working as Adam's man in the west of Scotland on jobs such as the Glasgow Infirmary and the Trades House. His undertaking of the Union Bridge works was abandoned when it became clear that he had miscalculated. Hamilton's scheme was set aside, allowing for the more elegant single-arch solution. However, although other surviving schemes do not include shops, the earliest Union Street buildings allow for them, and this too was the key to some of Robert Adam's great speculative work. In Glasgow even Adam's plan for the re-building of the Tron Kirk included re-fronting the site with a tenement with shops at ground floor.

The demand for housing in the late eighteenth century grew steadily throughout Scotland with the growth of manufactures, and the migration to the towns. It has been shown that in Aberdeen's case this increased population was coming largely from the immediate rural hinterland.[11] In a sense, housing for middle and higher-middle income groups, along with town housing for the aggrandized gentry, was required to establish social relations in a novel, urban setting. People

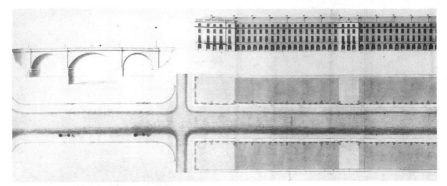

Plate 6. James Young's design for Union Street and Bridge, 1807. The proposed arcaded shops echo Adam's South Bridge. (Reproduced by permission of Aberdeen Art Gallery.)

were being brought together in an undifferentiated mass: now there had to be developed strategies of social zoning, through which an acceptable structure of urban life could be created.

In Edinburgh, the South Bridge was a road which was to be a continuation of the North Bridge, on the line that centred on Register House. The South Bridge Act was passed in 1785, permitting the construction of a gigantic viaduct across the Cowgate, linking the High Street and the proposed university. Like Union Street, the South Bridge was effectively to zone out of existence the decaying urban 'low life' of the Cowgate below and to introduce at a higher level – on a plane with the fashionable districts to the north and south – a new development of shops and housing, characterised by the fact that they were sited not in a new area, but on top of an existing one. A great street, like all open, geometrically planned town spaces is to a large extent self-policing; a place where the 'gaze' of the police can penetrate every corner, and this aspect of town planning should not be forgotten.

Adam's design for a new bridge for the town council at Ayr[12] had a similar character. Here the architect seems to have proposed a bridge with flanking housing at higher level and terraced quays at the lower, all within the usual monumental framework. His Bathwick scheme had also employed 'palace fronting'[13] subjugating the individual houses to the design of the whole, which posed problems for a gradualist feuing strategy. This may at least partly explain why James Young's very grandiose scheme of palace-fronted blocks (plate 6) was not successful in the Aberdeen competition, although we should bear in mind that

[37]

Plate 7. Union Street c. 1875 (reproduced by permission of Aberdeen Art Gallery).

palace-fronted schemes such as Charlotte Square and Moray Place were individually feued. The 'row house' solution finally adopted for Union Street has more in common with Edinburgh's first New Town, and is in contrast with the daring Edinburgh-inspired bridging solution on which the scheme as a whole depended. The architectural scaling down of the Union Street houses was unfortunately characteristic of much town-planning in eighteenth- and nineteenth-century Scotland, where ambition often outstripped financial viability or entrepreneurial daring. Examples of this tendency can be found in places as different as Edinburgh, Skye (the Lochbay fishing station), and Ardrossan.

Union Street was conceived within the context of direct municipal action, predicated upon a road improvement. Clearly, its principal exemplar was Edinburgh's bridge-street scheme, South Bridge, although it differed from the scheme in one important respect. The trustees clearly preferred their bridge to be, and to be seen to be, a bridge, in a way that the South Bridge Trustees did not. The Aberdonians required that Union Bridge should be narrower than Union Street, so that the separation between the two would remain apparent. Clearly, the architects and engineers bidding to build the bridge did not share this vision. James Young's unsuccessful scheme (plate 6), for example, is a hybrid, with a conventional three-arch bridge and terraced axial carriageways, but the bridge is the same width as the

street, giving a modern impression of seamless progress across the gap. Although Union Street never really shook off its humble origins as a road improvement, with continued undue emphasis on the Union Bridge, the similarities with Edinburgh's South Bridge are too great to ignore. Both schemes were – or became – highly imaginative commercial and engineering adventures; and both, it may be argued, suffered in the end from a tentativeness in execution. Union Street, nevertheless, provided the essential armature for the creation of the monument-studded neo-classical city of Aberdeen.

Notes

1. John Betjeman, 'Aberdeen Granite', in his *First and Last Loves* (London, 1952), p. 33.

2. Francis Groome, *Ordnance Gazetteer of Scotland* (London, 1882), vol. 1, p. 6.

3. See John Fleming, *Robert Adam and His Circle* (London, 1962), pp. 204–07: fig. 10.

4. See Brian Edwards, 'Glasgow improvements, 1866–1901' in Peter Reed (ed.), *Glasgow: the Forming of a City* (Edinburgh, 1993), pp. 84–103.

5. Abbé Laugier, *Essai sur l'Architecture* (trans. S. Wale, London, 1755).

6. Laugier, *Essai*, p. 227.

7. Laugier, *Essai*, p. 232.

8. Scottish Record Office: GD 18/5832 – letter to the lord provost of Edinburgh from Sir James Clerk concerning the style of the proposed bridge.

9. See Frank Farmer, 'The early history of Union Street' (Dissertation, Scott Sutherland School of Architecture, 1974).

10. Adelphi Court seems to have been named after the Adams' spectacular housing and warehousing complex in London which embanked the Thames for the first time.

11. See A. A. MacLaren, 'Class formation and class fractions: the Aberdeen bourgeoisie 1830–1850' in G. Gordon and B. Dicks (eds), *Scottish Urban History* (Aberdeen, 1983), pp. 112–29.

12. See the version of the Adam scheme drawn by another hand, Carnegie Library, Ayr.

13. Sir John Soane's Museum, *Adam Drawings*, vol. 38, nos 1, 6–9; and vol. 10, nos 79–82.

3

Advertising Made a 'Fine Art' in Victorian Aberdeen

Edward Ranson

The history of Union Street over the last two hundred years would be incomplete without some reference to the merchants and traders who made their living offering a wide variety of goods and services to the general public of Aberdeen. The story told in these pages relates to the career of a man who occupied the same premises, at 34 Union Street, for nearly half a century, 1838–1885, and who, by virtue of his penchant for publicity, achieved more than local fame as the self-styled 'Hatter to the People'. Any biographical sketch of Samuel Martin is, however, more than just an interesting and amusing tale of a local shopkeeper who indulged his own eccentricities, it is also an insight into the business practices of the mid-nineteenth century and the growth of advertising techniques. Indirectly, Martin's comments on international, national and local affairs, which he freely made in the advertising columns of the *Aberdeen Herald*, shed a good deal of light on contemporary events and attitudes. Indeed, it may not be going too far to describe him as a weather-vane of public opinion and even as the *vox populi* of the granite city.

In fact, Samuel Martin was not an Aberdonian, nor even a Scot, by birth, although his father, William Martin, was a native of Hamilton in Lanarkshire, who joined the army and rose from the ranks to be appointed a cornet in the 6th Dragoon Guards in July 1812. Continued in service after the end of the Napoleonic Wars William Martin was

placed on half pay in 1822 and died in 1825. At some point he had married an Irish girl, Rosina Wilson, who bore him seven children, three girls and four boys, including Samuel who was born in 1814 in Preston, Lancashire, where his father's regiment was stationed at that time. According to one source all Samuel's brothers entered the army, but less is known of his sisters although his twin sister apparently died aged only three years.

At all events there was certainly a strong military flavour to Samuel Martin's background, and had not his father died in 1825 he would have joined the army himself. Throughout his life Samuel was always interested in and knowledgeable about military affairs, and intensely proud that his father had been an officer. Samuel Martin was later to claim that because of his English birth, Irish mother and childhood, and Scottish father, he really belonged to three kingdoms and might, therefore, be pardoned for not doing things in the normal style. [1]

As family circumstances demanded that he follow a more peaceful calling, he was apprenticed to the hat trade in Glasgow in about 1826 or 1827 when he would have been twelve or thirteen years old. He worked for some time as a journeyman in Stockport before returning to Glasgow where he and one of his brothers entered business as hatters, but he received medical advice to live and work further north. Samuel Martin chose Aberdeen as his future home, making the journey to the north-east sometime in 1837, and in his own words 'he never regretted the selection.' He arrived in Aberdeen as an enterprising young man looking for a business opportunity, and in February 1838 he opened a modest shop at 34 Union Street in what was then the most frequented part of the town. Although Aberdeen was at that time a community of about 65,000 people, the pace of life was placid and he closed his shop every day for an hour for lunch remarking that any customer would just have to wait till he returned. [2]

Both the *Aberdeen Herald* and the *Aberdeen Constitutional* published the announcement on Saturday, February 10, 1838, that a new hat establishment was to open that day at 34 Union Street, and in the conventional language of the day informed readers that, 'SAMUEL MARTIN respectfully intimates to the Public of Aberdeen and its vicinity, that he will Open the above Establishment THIS DAY . . . with a large Stock of HATS, Caps, &c., and his system of doing business being to sell a good article at the smallest possible profit, for CASH, he trusts by a strict personal attendance, with a wish to please, to merit a share of public favour.'[3] What note Aberdonians made of the arrival of this

MARTIN'S STOCK OF HATS, CAPS, &c.,

Is more than unusually LARGE at present, this
being MARTIN'S busy season. MARTIN has
lately got to hand A LARGE ASSORTMENT of SATIN
HATS and DRAB SHELL HATS, the New
Shapes, beautiful goods.

Also TWEED, SHOOTING, and FISHING
HATS, Splendid New Patterns ; STRAW HATS,
SATIN and GLAZED LIVERY HATS, GOLD,
SILVER, and MOURNING LIVERY BANDS,
COCKADES, GLAZED (HAT) COVERS,
STABLE CAPS, &c., &c., &c., all at moderate
prices.

SEE MARTIN'S
ATTRACTIVE ESTABLISHMENT
AND HANDSOME WINDOWS.

Observe !

SAMUEL MARTIN,
HATTER TO THE PEOPLE,

34, UNION STREET (WAREHOUSE ABOVE SHOP),
ABERDEEN.

ESTABLISHED 1838.

EVER THANKFUL FOR THE
SUPPORT OF "THE PEOPLE."

17th *July*, 1875.

Figure 1. Aberdeen Herald, *17 July 1875.*

newcomer in their midst is impossible to say, especially as the town
seems to have been well provided with hatters. As a result competition
was fierce, even though in the nineteenth century a hat was regarded
as an essential part of the male attire. In consequence the promotion
of one's own goods and services, and the denigration of rivals, appears
to have been standard practice among those in the hat trade.

[42]

Samuel Martin was adept at attracting attention and apparently thrived on competition, including that of the established firm of Craig & Anderson, 85 Union Street, who claimed that:

> for goods of equal quality, our prices are lower than those of any vender of Hats in Aberdeen. We state again that, both as Manufacturers and Importers of Hats, we can afford to sell, are selling, and will continue to sell, goods of a superior quality, and at a cheaper rate than the common-place articles offered for sale by those Shops who depend for any little trade they can pick up on the Day & Martin system of puffing. [4]

The reference to 'puffing' relates to Samuel Martin's early reputation as someone who appreciated and exploited the power of advertising. As was later noted Martin 'was the first shopkeeper who made advertising a fine art in the north of Scotland: he "woke up" the inhabitants to a sense both of the merits of his goods and his own smartness. . . . Mr Martin nonplussed his neighbours. They shook their heads and said it "would never do in Aberdeen" – he was only "wasting his money." They changed their minds in a year or two.'[5] Martin replied to his critics with the unashamed claim that his shop placed all others in the shade as he offered the cheapest and best hats in town and was able to do so because of his full knowledge of his chosen trade. His 'Small Profit and Ready Money System' enabled him to undercut and outsell all rivals.[6]

In October 1841 there began a new rivalry, one that was to be long lasting but essentially friendly, when Steele & Co., Hat and Cap Manufacturers, opened a shop at 20 Union Street, at the corner of Union Street and Broad Street. Steele & Co. were also prepared to advertise, and on February 5, 1842, published an announcement, which ran for several weeks, praising the 'NEW PATENT WASHABLE BEAVER HATS' they were offering for sale.[7] Martin replied on February 19 by placing an advertisement alongside Steele & Co.'s offering for sale 'SUPERIOR BEAVER HATS . . . which . . . never require WASHING.' This was also the first time Martin referred to himself as 'HATTER to the PEOPLE'.[8] By January 1846 he was calling himself the 'HATTER KING OF THE NORTH', nine months later 'THE INVINCIBLE HATTER', and by Christmas 1847 'Hatter to the People, AND ADVERTISING HATTER'. [9]

A rash of new hat shops opened in Aberdeen in the years 1842–45, including William Thomson, 131 Union Street, who tried to persuade customers to purchase not only headgear but also 'Biggs patent HAT

YOUR HEAD! YOUR HEAD!!
TAKE CARE OF YOUR HEAD!!!

AT all times this is a good advice; for, in going through the world, the troubles caused by neglecting the head are so numerous, and so often met with, that comment upon the subject would be superfluous; but, from the position of the head, it is more likely to be affected by the seasons (particularly winter) than any other part of the person. The truthfulness of these remarks will at once be admitted by keeping in mind the many complaints which affect the head from colds—viz., Rheumatism, Erysipelas, Toothache, &c.—and who that has been annoyed with any one of these complaints, would not like to avoid the cause?

MARTIN,
HATTER
TO
THE PECPLE,
ABERDEEN,

Has no hesitation in stating that a thorough Waterproof, proper fitting HAT is the best article extant for protecting the head from the effects of the weather, and on the present occasion, at the beginning of another year to Father Time, MARTIN thinks himself justified in enlarging upon "The article, the HAT." It is a remark sometimes made, that a HAT is a very inconvenient article of dress, from its bulk, &c. the reasons given being, that yon cannot take a HAT into a crowded hall, or even into a parlour conveniently; but individuals who make such remarks should keep in view the purpose for which a HAT was originally intended, and, by so doing, they will find that it is not the *use* but the *abuse* of the HAT that causes the inconvenience. As to the bulk of a HAT. The circumference of a man's head being about half the circumference of his shoulders, the height of crown, &c. of the HAT is *required* to correspond to a reasonable extent with the size of the body under it, and HATS, like many other articles, being intended for a particular purpose—viz., an article of dress for out-door wear, to protect the head from the weather, &c.—they never were intended to be taken into crowded halls or parlours. Else it may be asked, What were anterooms or pegs in lobby walls intended for? But to expect a HAT to be a convenient article under all circumstances and in all places, would be equally absurd as to expect a *Plough to be useful in a Drawing room*, or to attempt to *wind up your Watch with a Coal Scuttle*. Dress Coats were not intended for sleeping in, else you might expect

Your Hat to be useful as a Night Cap.

But the fact is, that the HAT of the present day, if put to its *legitimate use*, is really and truly a very useful article, as it protects the head from damp, and, being properly *ventilated* and manufactured upon true scientific principles, it allows free egress to the warm air generated, thus keeping the head in a healthy state; and, from its admirable formation, has the pleasing effect of keeping the hair as arranged and in good order.

In short, if the HAT was so inconvenient an article as some people think, how is it that, amidst the genius, talent, and inventive powers of this great nation, no article has hitherto been brought out to supersede the HAT? Simply because a HAT, put to its legitimate use, is the most comfortable, useful, and becoming article that can adorn the head of man.

MARTIN's Stock of HATS are particularly attractive at the present season. SATIN HATS, splendid shapes, 6/6, 7/6, and 8/6, and the New Style of SATIN HATS, with Cloth Underbrims, 10/6, 12/6, and 15/6. MARTIN's HATS

LOOK WELL,
WEAR WELL
FIT WELL,
SELL WELL,
AND
PLEASE WELL.

Magnificent Stock of GLENGARRY CAPS (the New Shapes), TWEED and CLOTH CAPS, &c. which will be found very useful, if put to *their* legitimate use

PORTMANTEAUS, COAT CASES, Carpet and Leather TRAVELLING BAGS, Leather HAT CASES, UMBRELLAS, &c. &c.

OBSERVE!—SAMUEL MARTIN,
Practical Hatter and Hatter to the People,
34, UNION STREET,
ABERDEEN.

ESTABLISHED 1838.

THE CASTLE STREET
SO-CALLED IMPROVEMENT.
A FEW LINES ON THE MATTER
(WITH NO WISH TO OFFEND)
BY SAMUEL MARTIN.

Water, blessed Water,
Yet, all must agree
Water may be put
Where Water need not be.

THE ARISTOCRACY IN THE BACKGROUND.
A HORSE TROUGH
UNDER A DUKE'S NOSE.
WHAT NEXT!

Shades of Departed Dukes and other great Gordons what think ye of this!

Has this thing been done
In too great haste,
Or placed where it is
For want of taste!

Or is it indicative that the *Stone* DUKE is dropsical.
Oh! Surely not.

Then why this trough
Where it is laid,
And, lamps put up
The "DUKE" to shade.

Methought I heard the *Stone* DUKE say
Oh! pray take this vile trough away,
Councillors might very well suppose
'Twould spoil my view and offend my nose.
Truly, if I could get away,
I would no longer near it stay;
'Tis most unseemly to the eye—
Remove it quickly let "The People" cry.
Oh! 'twould surely be a pity
To insult my memory in the "Granite City."
In good "old times" 'twas plainly seen
I was much respected in Aberdeen.
What! a Knight of "The Thistle and the Garter"
To associate with every passing Carter—
Oh, shame! the matter's out of place—
Remove "this trough" from before my face—
Top of Castle Street there's lots of space.
Behind me would be its *proper* place;
I've often drawn my Sword in Battle—
Could I draw it now, I'd make it rattle
Upon this "trough" and paltry lamps,
Which want of taste *their* position stamps;
I thought at first the whole a myth
Till I heard the working of a *Smith*.
But, take the "trough" from me away,
That is what I mean to say;
To leave it and me in our present place
Would *Bon-Accord* and *me* disgrace.
So hold a Council on the matter *specially*,
And I will loudly shout Long Life to PROVOST LESLIE.

MARTIN would politely suggest that "The Horse Trough" be placed midway between the *back* railing of "The Duke's" monument and the front railing of "The Round House," a neat *granite* pedestal to be placed in the centre (say from 5 to 6 feet high) and "the trough" to be about 6 feet long on *each* side of "the base," the iron pillar supporting the lamps, not Globes, to be placed on the apex of the granite pedestal, and the *top* lamp to be higher than at present, so that it would blend its *light* with the lower lamps, which, returning the compliment, would throw out a *combined* glare of light that from height, &c., would well

LIGHT UP CASTLE STREET.

Then, not forgetting "The DUKE" (we're not very rich in monuments), put around him a *handsome* Railing, Gilt, &c., something like the corner of "St. Nicholas Street," and a *handsome Large Lamp* at each *side*, with extra large burners; *of course, taking away the present puny Lamps, which appear more suitable for the useful house at the top of Castle Street.*

MARTIN would therefore further suggest that the Provost take the opinion of *five* (himself being one) of our most scientific townsmen, all of course acting gratuitously, to take into consideration the Site that MARTIN suggests, as to its being the best as to SPACE, CONVENIENCE, and GENERAL EFFECT; and if the *majority* or all approve of MARTIN's suggestions, then let the matter be gone into by THE COUNCIL at once. The extra expense to the TOWN of doing the thing *properly* may very possibly in the end be highly satisfactory to THE COUNCIL themselves and TO THE PEOPLE.

MARTIN'S idea is that the HORSE-TROUGH (or to call it by its genteeler name *Drinking Fountain*) should be made A CONVENIENCE AND AN ORNAMENT TO THE CITY, NOT AN *IN*CONVENIENCE AND *NO* ORNAMENT.

HURRAH! GO-AHEAD MARTIN!
RIGHT AGAIN!

MARTIN's Stock is very large at present with FANCY GOODS his WINTER TRADE. PRICES MODERATE. See his
SHOWY WINDOWS.

Observe SAMUEL MARTIN,
HATTER TO THE PEOPLE,
34, UNION STREET
(WAREHOUSE ABOVE SHOP),
ABERDEEN.
ESTABLISHED THIRTY-FIVE YEARS.

EVER THANKFUL FOR THE SUPPORT OF "THE PEOPLE."

23d *January*, 1874.

THERE IS NOTHING THAT ELEVATES
OR ADDS MORE TO THE
STABILITY OF A NATION
THAN TO SEE
HER EMINENT MEN
HONOURED AND RESPECTED;

PARTICULARLY by a nation, in the highest scale of civilization, with all the attributes that makes her the leading power of the world, and however high the social and political position of such men may be, it cannot but be highly satisfactory to them to see that their talents, attainments, and position are appreciated by their countrymen.

GREAT
PREPARATIONS FOR THE
PRINCE OF WALES' TRIP TO INDIA.
"HAPPY PRINCE,"

A trip to India and all expenses paid.
That's the way to do it. HURRAH!
O! that MARTIN THE HATTER had been born a PRINCE, but it is perhaps better as it is as the "PEOPLE" enables MARTIN to enjoy many trips that cost much less than

£142,000.

The preparations for the trip are nearly ready, and MARTIN hopes that the results will be highly beneficial. Many might suppose that it would have been more complete, and

A GRACEFUL ACT ON THE PART OF
"HER MAJESTY" TO HAVE
KNIGHTED MARTIN,

and appointed him to accompany the PRINCE OF WALES to India. His advice and presence might have been of much service to the PRINCE, as in many parts of India MARTIN'S name might be as well known to some of the NATIVE CHIEFS as the PRINCE's. But this is a matter that has evidently been neglected on the part of the "QUEEN," so that

MARTIN'S KNIGHTHOOD AND OTHER
HONOURS

Are yet to come, and the sooner the better. MARTIN cannot say that he is wearying, but, nevertheless, he is anxious; but hope keeps him up wonderfully, which might be well supposed from his philosophic mind.

Hope!
Oft relieves the mind
When other remedies fail.

MARTIN'S STOCK OF HATS, CAPS, &c.,

Is more than unusually LARGE at present, this being MARTIN'S busy season. MARTIN has lately got to hand A LARGE ASSORTMENT of SATIN HATS and DRAB SHELL HATS, the New Shapes, beautiful goods.

Also TWEED, SHOOTING, and FISHING HATS, Splendid New Patterns; STRAW HATS, SATIN and GLAZED LIVERY HATS, GOLD, SILVER, and MOURNING LIVERY BANDS, COCKADES, GLAZED (HAT) COVERS, STABLE CAPS, &c., &c., &c., all at moderate prices.

SEE MARTIN'S
ATTRACTIVE ESTABLISHMENT
AND HANDSOME WINDOWS.

Observe!
SAMUEL MARTIN,
HATTER TO THE PEOPLE,
34, UNION STREET (WAREHOUSE ABOVE SHOP),
ABERDEEN.
ESTABLISHED 1838.

EVER THANKFUL FOR THE SUPPORT OF "THE PEOPLE."

17th *July*, 1875.

Figure 2. Various advertisements in the Aberdeen Herald.

GUARD, a contrivance at once simple and efficacious for keeping the hat FIRM on the Head in the highest wind – combining at once SAFETY TO THE HAT, SIMPLICITY OF APPLICATION, AND COMFORT TO THE WEARER.' Other entrants into the trade were Francis Bell, 38 Queen Street; Mrs Bennet, 10 Union Street; D. Burge, 38 & 40 Broad Street; the Central Hat Mart, 26 Union Street; and the London Hat Company (Millar Brothers), 31 Union Street. [10]

Undaunted by these challenges, Samuel Martin claimed his experience and business methods permitted him 'to keep all attempts at competition by less extensive houses entirely in the Background.'[11] By 1845 he was no longer satisfied merely to praise his own stock while disparaging his rivals' taste and abilities; he adopted the ploy of extolling the medical advantages, particularly in warm weather, of a light, durable, and properly fitting hat in order to avoid headaches. [12]

Samuel Martin survived his first decade in business at 34 Union Street despite the problems of what appeared to be an overcrowded line of trade and cut-throat competition. His willingness to advertise undoubtedly helped to promote his image and to boost his sales and profits. As he wrote in July 1848, 'I am sure it is no fault of MARTIN'S if the Public don't hear enough about his Hats!'[13] However, it was the early visits of Queen Victoria to Aberdeen and Deeside, closely followed by the Crimean War, that really provided him with the chance to combine fervent loyalty and patriotism with a keen eye for business.

In anticipation of Queen Victoria's arrival in Aberdeen in September 1848 *en route* for a vacation at Balmoral, Martin published an announcement a few days prior that referred to the city's opportunity 'on this momentous occasion, of showing the national feeling by receiving our illustrious queen, and amiable mother of Britain's future Sovereigns, with that loyal, enthusiastic, and genuine good feeling, which she so justly deserves.' He called for a popular reception that would become a matter of history, but went on to suggest, in view of the fact that a hat was the most conspicuous part of a man's attire, the propriety of appearing on that day wearing a good one:

> Martin's idea is, that all should have Good Hats on this occasion; and, notwithstanding that Hats will, as a matter of course, be taken off as the Queen passes, Martin wishes the Public to avoid what *might* be an *unseemly* sight to Royalty – viz., to be received by the *Waving of Thousands of Old Hats*, which individuals can easily avoid by purchasing one of MARTIN'S beautiful

SATIN HATS, with nice showy Linings, pleasing to the eye, and which MARTIN is Selling at very Moderate Prices.

As the Queen was understood to be an early riser, and might pass through the streets of Aberdeen at an early hour, Martin recommended to potential customers his Wide Awake Hats. [14]

Martin's wish that Aberdeen should make the most of the royal visit was fully granted as the newspaper accounts of both Victoria's arrival and subsequent departure after a three weeks sojourn reveal. The *Aberdeen Herald* noted that no expense or labour was spared to make the illuminated display that marked her departure memorable, 'The flare of the light from Union Street was seen reflected on the sky many miles around . . . Mr. Martin, hatter, displayed a fiery hat, in the shape of the latest fashion.' [15]

The early 1850s saw the usual comings and goings in the hat trade, and Martin continued to espouse his own cause in the columns of the *Aberdeen Herald*. The budget of 1853, therefore, brought good news for him with the proposed reduction of the Advertisement Duty from 1s. 6d. to 6d., which, as he pointed out, 'will enable MARTIN at a cheaper rate to remind the Public of the advantages of Purchasing at his Establishment.' [16] Even better tidings followed when the government bowed to pressure and repealed the Advertisement Duty completely. Thus, in January 1854, Martin was able to make the point that he had prospered for fifteen years by close personal attention to his business and by his efforts at salesmanship:

> And although his advertising propensities may possibly not have pleased all, yet MARTIN would, in the most polite manner remind that portion of the public who do not approve of advertising, that, from the march of intellect, the old prejudiced opinion that advertising is not respectable, is fast wearing out; and that the legislators of this Great Country having taken off the Advertisement Duty, have thus countenanced advertising as both respectable and legitimate – these prejudices should therefore no longer exist. [17]

From mid-1853 Samuel Martin's attention was increasingly focused upon foreign and military affairs, especially the likelihood of war between Britain and France on one hand and Russia on the other. Should hostilities commence, Martin, whose attitude reflected the Russophobia of the day, was confident that British broadsides and

SHAKEN, AND TAKEN TOO!
FALLEN AT LAST!!

Three times Three Cheers, and One Cheer more!—Hip, hip, hurrah!!
Let every true-born Briton hurrah! Let the Nation be glad!!
Let every true-born Briton rejoice, with heartfelt enthusiasm!!!

GLORIOUS NEWS, INDEED!

SEBASTOPOL IS TAKEN!!
NO MISTAKE THIS TIME!!!

THE Lion of Britain and Eagle of France are floating over its ruins! The Bombardment reopened on the 5th, and the Assault was made on the forenoon of Saturday the 8th instant. The Allies attacking four points simultaneously, and after a struggle fearful to contemplate, the French obtained possession of the Malakoff—the British fighting bravely, *as they ever do*, were nevertheless twice driven back from the Redan, being mowed down in hundreds by the Russian Artillery, ramparts being, it may be said, formed by the bodies of their comrades ; but the THIRD and FOURTH time they came FEARLESSLY on,

DETERMINED TO CONQUER OR DIE!

on which the Russians, as if thunderstruck at such indomitable courage (far beyond their powers to comprehend), though themselves fighting well, were gloriously driven from their Stronghold with fearful carnage, blowing up their Magazines, Ships, &c. and leaving hundreds of Prisoners—suffering a

Total and Ignominious Defeat.

Thus fell Sebastopol, that has been nearly HALF A CENTURY in preparing to defy the World, but which the

VALOUR, COURAGE, & PERSEVERANCE

of the Allies has completely destroyed, after an investment of little more than THREE HUNDRED DAYS. 'T will now be merely a matter of Time, and that comparatively short, on the part of the Allies, to reduce the North side of Sebastopol, and thus thoroughly humble the Power of Russia, hitherto the scourge and disturber of the Earth, henceforward to be classed as a Third or even Fourth Rate Power.

Great Anxiety--List of Casualties expected daily.

Meantime, 't is reported that the Allies have lost Ten Thousand Men in Killed and Wounded. But, however, this IS and OUGHT TO BE a matter of regret, yet the Country could not but expect serious casualties in obtaining so glorious a result.
Happy Britain! Surely there breathes not a British Subject whose heart does not expand with Delight, Enthusiasm, and Endearment to his Country, on hearing this Glorious News!! Oh, how Proud, how Happy, how Delighted should all be, who can place their Hand on their Bosom, and exclaim—Britain, the Pride of the World! Britain, the Enlightened Power of the Earth!! And Britain,

MY NATIVE LAND!!!!

Oh, what a thrilling feeling of satisfaction to all British Subjects, on hearing of this Great and Glorious Victory. But what words can convey thanks sufficient to their Brave Brothers in Arms who have thrust this great

HONOUR UPON THE BRITISH NATION!

No, no. Words fall short to convey the enthusiasm and good feeling of the Nation to her Brave Soldiers. 'T is deeds that must stand forth in bold relief, showing to the European Nations of the earth that, as British Soldiers ever fight well, and where they fight they ever conquer, so Britain, shows her just appreciation of her Brave Sons, by REVERING the Memory of the Dead,

HONOURING THE LIVING,

And providing for the Widows and Orphans of those who have died for her on

THE BATTLE FIELD!

Thus there need be no false delicacy—the Widows and Orphans of those Brave Men who have died in the Crimea HAVE A RIGHT to be provided for, the WOUNDED and MAIMED MUST be cared for and made comfortable in their latter days. 'T is common sense, 't is justice ; as the Country that forgets properly to recompence the Power that PROTECTS and DEFENDS her, deserves to be ruled by the iron hand of Despotism, and her subjects to be treated like Slaves. But,

BRITAIN'S BELOVED QUEEN,

Ever, even at her lovely Highland Home at Balmoral, has apparently her mind's eye upon the Deeds of her Soldiers ; and her NATURALLY GOOD and AMIABLE Disposition will remind her ever truly to appreciate and recompence the

Brave Defenders of her Crown.

SO THINKS

MARTIN THE HATTER,

Who is able and determined to continue selling his far-famed Hats at very Moderate Prices, and thus try to please all who purchase at his Establishment.

Observe!—SAMUEL MARTIN,
HATTER TO THE PEOPLE,
34, UNION STREET, ABERDEEN.
ESTABLISHED SEVENTEEN YEARS.

LONG LIFE TO BRITAIN'S BELOVED QUEEN,
And One Jolly Good Cheer for her Brave Defenders---Hurrah!!!

Figure 3. Martin celebrates the fall of Sebastopol in the Aberdeen Herald.

French bayonets would ensure victory.[18] In fact, the British and French declarations of war against Russia and in support of Turkey came at the end of March 1854. This news was, of course, carried prominently in the next number of the *Aberdeen Herald* on April 1, as was Martin's enthusiastic support. By the end of April 1854 Martin was using a technique he favoured frequently in the future, namely a visually deceptive headline:

MARTIN, THE HATTER

Does not expect

TO BE MADE A FIELD MARSHAL

Nor, he added did he expect to receive a naval command or even to be consulted on matters of moment. He considered it his duty to attend to his own business and to continue to sell first-rate hats at moderate prices.[19]

During the war, 1854–56, Martin's increasingly lengthy advertisements appeared regularly, proffering comment and advice which revealed surprisingly detailed knowledge of diplomatic manoeuvres and military developments. Approximately every three or four weeks Martin changed the text of his announcements, and though they concentrated heavily on the war he still found time to welcome Queen Victoria on her annual visits to Balmoral.[20]

Martin's combination of patriotism and humour was appreciated not only in Aberdeen, but also wherever copies of the *Aberdeen Herald* were to be found. William Carnie, a reporter and editor with the paper, later recalled that Martin's high opinion of the British Army was reciprocated, and that, 'During the weary anxious winter of the Crimean War – 1854 – letter after letter from soldiers in the Highland Brigade to friends in Aberdeenshire was brought to the Herald Office, dwelling fondly on general things happening at "home", but all declaring that the first portion of the paper read around the snow-encompassed camp-fires was that containing the poetical patriotic advertisement of the "Practical Hatter".'[21]

Throughout the early months of 1855 Martin looked forward to military success in the Crimea, the fall of Sebastopol and an honourable peace. However, for many Aberdonians the major news on May 5 that year was, no doubt, the absence from the columns of the *Aberdeen*

Herald of any announcement by Martin. Their curiosity or concern was abated the following Saturday when his regular advertisement re-appeared under the headline:

CONSTERNATION!

WONDER!! AND AMAZEMENT!!!

Martin explained that his advertisement had somehow been over-looked, and reassured his readers that he had not been offered a polit-ical or military post, had not been unwell or away from home, and had not been the object of an assassination attempt. [22]

During June, July and August 1855 Martin ran a series of advertise-ments full of patriotic sentiments, describing events in both the Crimean and Baltic theatres of war and looking forward still to the fall of Sebastopol. Finally, Martin's optimism and repeated predictions regarding the surrender of the city were rewarded, when on Sep-tember 9, after a siege of 339 days, the Russian garrison abandoned the town. Martin's response was an outburst of joy and patriotic pride tempered only with regret for the heavy casualty lists and a plea for generous help for the widows and orphans of the fallen and care for the wounded. Even by his own standards Martin's advertisement was brazenly chauvinistic, and was spread across two columns with many headlines.[23] Half a century later A. S. Cook in his *Old-Time Traders and Their Ways* remembered this particular advertisement. Cook recalled that Martin was very particular about the exact lay-out of his notices in the *Aberdeen Herald*, and that any departure from the copy was a serious matter for the compositor.[24]

Martin now looked forward to a peace that would leave Russia pros-trate, and he viewed the negotiations in Paris in early 1856 with suspi-cion. The *Aberdeen Herald* announced the news of the signing of the peace treaty on April 5, noting the reservations felt by Martin:

> The coming Peace having cast its shadow pretty intelligibly before, the news of the actual event, when it arrived on Monday, did not create that burst of enthusiasm which it other-wise might have done. During part of the day, however, the bells rang out merrily – flags and bunting of various hues were displayed – and the laddies made a terrible noise at night in

Union Street, threatening destruction to porters' hurlies and merchants' barrows of every description, in their endeavour to raise a beacon fire of rejoicing. On Tuesday most of the schools obtained a half-holiday; and every person apparently was glad except Martin, the practical hatter, who, doubtful in his wisdom of the 'honourable' terms on which Peace had been arranged, and jealous for the credit of his country, filled his principal window with white beavers clothed in sackcloth. [25]

Although the excitement of the Crimean War subsided by mid-1856 Samuel Martin was never at a loss to find a topic on which he could lecture his attentive public. From late 1856 until 1860 there was the Arrow War in China, a localized conflict arising out of the arrest at Canton of the crew of a junk, or lorcha, flying the British ensign. Naturally, Martin applauded all efforts designed to avenge such an insult to the national flag. [26]

The Indian Mutiny of 1857–58, which for a time threatened the rule of the East India Company and of Britain, produced some bloodthirsty remarks by Martin. He demanded 'no imbecile philanthropy' be shown toward the mutineers whom he characterized as beasts in human form and the 'murderers of defenceless women and helpless children', who deserved to be blown to atoms from a canon's mouth for their diabolical and demoniacal acts. The readers of his advertisements in the *Aberdeen Herald* at this time were treated to Martin's patriotic assessments of the situation and to his praise of the bravery of the British army in general and the Scottish regiments in particular.

Even such stirring deeds as those in China and India did not absorb Martin's attention entirely. In September 1857 Queen Victoria and her entourage paid their annual visit to Deeside, and on October 15, en route back to London, the Queen and the Prince Consort made a ceremonial visit to Aberdeen. The town was *en fête* for the occasion and, as the processional route passed immediately in front of 34 Union Street, Samuel Martin could be relied upon to make his mark. The local newspapers covered the royal visit in detail, including long descriptions of the decorations. The *Aberdeen Herald* gave particular attention to Martin's personal and ornamental demonstrations of loyalty:

But hark! what's that? by our veracity, if it is not our trusty friend, Mr. Samuel Martin, energetically sending forth from a French horn or cornopeon, the well-known notes of – No; yes

it is, he's got it again – 'God Save the Queen'. Nor was that all, for we were told though, unfortunately for ourselves, not until some time after – that, Mr Martin observed the good old custom of 'open table,' and made all and sundry who liked to call, welcome to cake and wine. While we have our own notion of the music, and have no doubt but the wine was capital, we can have no hesitation in asserting that, for pure chasteness and simple beauty, the decorations of Mr. M's establishment were unmatched in the city.[28]

By the late 1850s Samuel Martin had achieved local celebrity, and, indeed, on public occasions it became part of the accepted scene for him to stand at his open window above his shop, 'which was gaily decorated, clothed in a red jacket and wideawake hat, in Garibaldi costume, playing on a silver bugle "God Save the King," to the great enjoyment and amusement of the onlookers.'[29]

The marriage of the Prince of Wales to Princess Alexandra of Denmark in March 1863 was just such an occasion, when, according to the *Aberdeen Herald*:

Samuel Martin, Hatter to the People, again attracted numbers to look in at his upper window, in front of which he had a neatly assorted collection of flags; and, just seen inside, was the gentleman himself, dressed à la Garibaldi, lustily blowing loyal tunes out of a bugle.[30]

The return of the 93rd Sutherland Highlanders to Aberdeen in March 1870 after an absence of fourteen years was another opportunity for Martin to demonstrate his patriotism and martial zeal when he 'waved a flourish with his sword and welcomed the Highlanders with a blast from his trumpet, as well as by appropriately emblazoned sentiments.'[31] Fifteen months later, in June 1871, when the regiment left Aberdeen for Edinburgh, the route of the troops to the railway station took them past 34 Union Street:

On passing the premises of Mr. Samuel Martin that gentleman appeared at one of the windows, waving a banner in his hand, bearing the friendly expression 'Good-bye,' 'Haste ye back,' the officers as they passed bowed an acknowledgement to Mr. Martin's compliments, and a cheer burst forth from the crowd on the street.[32]

However, it was not only royal and military occasions that caused Samuel Martin to decorate his shop and to entertain passers-by with his musical repertoire. Although he never took a particularly active role in local politics, and never ran for office, he was intensely interested in civic improvements and campaigned via his advertisements on such diverse issues as street lighting, the siting of cannon captured in the Crimean War, the position of a horse trough, and the removal of what he considered to be unsightly iron railings to St Nicholas Churchyard in Back Wynd. If not an active party member he never disguised his support for the Liberals at the city, county or national levels. He made it clear that he favoured extending the franchise and he supported social and economic reforms to help the lower classes. His hero was Lord Palmerston, whom he praised effusively in his advertisements, and he celebrated the success of Liberal candidates in his announcements in the *Aberdeen Herald* and by suitable window displays.

As early as 1841 Martin was listed as a member of a committee to secure the election, as a member for Aberdeen, of Mr Bannerman, and in July 1865 he endorsed the Liberals and Lord Palmerston in the general election at that time, taking the opportunity to display his poetical talents as well as his political preferences with the rhyme:

> So, go-ahead Liberals, you're gaining the day,
> Keep up the steam, your talents display,
> Aberdonians, as usual maintaining their rights,
> Their duty have done and returned Colonel Sykes. [33]

In 1866, when a by-election was held for the county, the *Aberdeen Herald* reported on May 19:

> Among other displays yesterday, Mr. Samuel Martin, hatter to the people, showed his zeal for the Liberal cause by having several neat little banners floating from his windows, and a larger one commending the county voters in these words – 'Well done, Aberdeenshire'. Hurrah!' From the other window shot a poll with a bunch of crape at the end, and a black cloth depending from it with an inscription expressive of mourning for the Tory cause – now presumed dead in the county. Mr. Martin himself appeared occasionally at the window with a curious shaped hat – something after the fashion of a Parsee's head cover with 'Reform' painted over the front. [34]

" Since every man who lives is born to die,
And none can boast sincere felicity,
With equal minds what happens let us bear,
Nor joy, nor grieve too much for things beyond our care,
Like pilgrims to the appointed place we tend ;
The World's an Inn, and death the journey's end."

DELAYS ARE OFTEN DANGEROUS.

THE REFORM BILL DEBATE A SLOW AFFAIR.

THE MINISTRY EVIDENTLY GETTING A FRIGHT.

POSSIBILITY OF THEIR RESIGNING—MIGHT DO WORSE FOR THEMSELVES AND THE COUNTRY.

EARL RUSSELL is doubtless anxious to please the People, and, with more firmness, might drive the Political Coach nicely, but he'd better keep his Whip-hand firmer, as from political foes and luke-warm friends he'll be fortunate if he avoid an upset, indeed, he looks rather Shakey already, still he is enabled to retain Office, MARTIN THE HATTER would say tighten the reins. Lord John, tighten the reins. The Statesman that's most likely to govern the Country at present, and carry a really useful REFORM BILL, is a PRIME MINISTER that in going a-head keeps his Leaders straight. Leaders know good driving, Lord John, and work accordingly. As the Debate has progressed the Ministerial chance of a great success has been gradually diminishing and growing beautifully less. But it is to be hoped that the WORKING CLASSES of the Country are fully Cognisant of their mercies, for really they have had the "Butter" laid on tremendous thick of late ; indeed, if all the Compliments that have (during the Reform Debate) been lavished upon them by many Members of the House, be thoroughly and honestly believed in by the Speakers and the House of Commons generally, then are

The Working Classes of the Country

SOCIALLY, MORALLY, AND JUSTLY ENTITLED TO A PREPONDERANCE OF POLITICAL POWER, when it is so manifest by present M.P.'s own showing, that they appear to have a preponderance of governing abilities, Intellectuality, and TAXATION. Thus it might well be considered an advantage to the country if a few of the Working Classes were at present M.P.'s, so that they might be at Mr. GLADSTONE'S elbow when he's bringing out the BUDGET. But alas !
" Words are like leaves, and, where they most abound,
Much fruit of sense beneath is rarely found."
But as the Working Classes have had the butter laid on so evenly, 'tis to be hoped that they are fully aware (as doubtless they are) of how disinterested M.P.'s speak in their apparent anxiety to protect some of the Working Classes M.P.'s. Well ! better late than never. Yet, their disinterestedness would doubtless be more apparent and better understood if they would show a shade less anxiety to retain their own seats and preponderance in the House, for, to use a homely saying, they stick to their seats through thick and thin, their visionary organs being apparently often affected by the different positions of being IN and OUT of Office. Perhaps they may think
" 'Tis often constancy to change the mind."

" 'Tis often constancy to change the mind."
Thus, rather than lose their seats without an effort to retain them, and knowing that EARL RUSSELL was in a manner pledged to bring forward a REFORM BILL, they hurriedly (and to say so may be considered a compliment to them) bolstered up the present abortive-looking production. Thus, as the Working Classes have for years had a good deal of political power in THEORY, they are apparently to remain enjoying it in that sense rather than in PRACTICE.
Pshaw ! there's a deal of farcical nonsense about Reform Bills now-a-days. It often looks as if M.P's. merely brought in such measures to be baulked because so framed as not to be interesting to or appreciated by the parties that should be most interested in their becoming the Law of the Land, notwithstanding their being so often fluently advocated, and eloquently enlarged upon by what is called the Liberal side of the House of Commons.

To the Winds with Political Powers that merely waste the Public Time,
Showing up the best part of measures, and telling the people what they are honestly and justly entitled to, and then baulking such measures by paltry differences of opinion among themselves upon matters of no moment whatever to the people generally, whose comfort and Political Status, 'tis said, it is their anxiety to protect and enlarge.

BUT LEGISLATORS OF BRITAIN WILL DO WELL TO KEEP IN MIND THAT AS EDUCATION AND POLITICAL KNOWLEDGE PROGRESSES, NATIONS MUST, AND WILL BE GOVERNED IN ACCORDANCE WITH THE INTELLECTUAL IMPROVEMENTS OF THE AGE, AND AS THE PEOPLE SHOW ABILITIES TO GOVERN, THEY MUST BE PROPERLY AND INTELLIGIBLY GOVERNED. THE RIGHTS, PRIVILEGES, AND WELFARE OF THE PEOPLE BEING THE TRUE FOUNDATION STONES OF

NATIONAL GREATNESS.

SO THINKS

MARTIN, THE HATTER.

MARTIN'S Stock of HATS, CAPS, &c. &c. is very large at present.
Best Quality, London-made SATIN HATS, 18/ each.
SPLENDID SATIN HATS, NEW SHAPES, Light, Durable, and Easy-fitting,

6/6, 8/6, 10/6, 12/6, 13/6, 14/6, 15/6, 16/6, and 17/ Each.

TWEED and FELT HATS, NEW SHAPES, BEAUTIES, PORTMANTEAUS, SHOULDER BAGS, UMBRELLAS, &c. &c. very Cheap.

Observe !

SAMUEL MARTIN,

HATTER TO THE PEOPLE,
34, UNION STREET (WAREHOUSE ABOVE SHOP), ABERDEEN.

ESTABLISHED TWENTY-EIGHT YEARS.

Figure 4. Martin advertises his political thoughts as well as hats in the Aberdeen Journal.

Again, in June 1872, in a city election, the *Aberdeen Herald* reported that Samuel Martin featured a large card in each window of his shop with the message 'Vote for Mr. Leith', and he also exhibited a photograph of the candidate. At the close of the poll he displayed a board with the word 'Victory' upon it in large letters. Mr Martin himself appeared in fancy dress and blew his trumpet. [35]

Martin's devotion to the royal family in general and to Queen Victoria in particular was revealed in his frequent attestations of loyalty in

his advertisements and his numerous ventures into verse on the subject. When, in early 1864, the idea of erecting a statue of the queen was mooted, Martin was an enthusiastic supporter of the scheme as his advertisement on March 5 clearly showed:

> NEVER was there a QUEEN on the British Throne that deserved the Love of her Subjects more than GOOD QUEEN VICTORIA.
>
> NEVER was there a QUEEN on the British Throne that's done more to please her people by her kindly, amiable, and QUEENLY, aye, womanly feelings and conciliatory considerations for their welfare than good QUEEN VICTORIA.
>
> NEVER was there a QUEEN on the British Throne who apparently more appreciates the knowledge that her Subjects are aware that their comfort and well-being are among the greatest Solaces to her bereaved heart.
>
> NEVER was there a QUEEN on the British Throne who so well deserved the Love and Respect of the *People of Aberdeen* than good QUEEN VICTORIA.

Accordingly a statue raised by public subscription was no more than she deserved and Aberdonians should do their duty by proceeding with the project. Martin then offered his readers six indifferent verses on the subject, the brevity of which they might well be thankful for, since he was capable of a dozen stanzas or more on many occasions. This particular poem is quoted in full merely as a sample of his work, not for any intrinsic merit:

> Up with the Statue to Britain's loved QUEEN;
> Let it be handsome, complete, and well seen;
> Let the site be well chosen, the best that's in town,
> For a more beloved QUEEN ne'er wore a crown.
>
> In choosing the Site there should be no delay,
> For on that much depends both style and display,
> But there's no occasion to choose it in haste,
> If a little delay shows 'The People's' good taste.
>
> Somewhere in Union Street would be the best place,
> If about there could be got a good space;
> But it must be conspicuous and easy to view,
> Without these essentials it may please but a few.
>
> St. Nicholas Street corner really would be
> A very nice Site, 'The People' may see,
> Couldn't be better, tho' they give a small bounty,
> And would likely be pleasing to THE TOWN AND COUNTY.

And tho' not made of Granite there's no need to garble,
T'will look very well of Sicilian Marble.
THE QUEEN, God bless her, is a nice canty bodie,
And the *Statue* may please if done by *A. Brodie*.

So up with the Statue, let all Scotland see
There's spirit and taste on the banks of the Dee;
Little more need be said on this pleasant matter,
But up with the Statue, says MARTIN THE HATTER. [36]

Samuel Martin had every reason to be pleased with the finished statue unveiled by the Prince of Wales on September 20, 1866, since the artist was, indeed, the local sculptor, Alexander Brodie, the material Sicilian marble, and the site the corner of St Nicholas and Union Streets. In describing the scene on that occasion the *Aberdeen Herald* noted:

The appearance of Union Street was especially good – gay and jubilant but without anything meritricious. . . . Mr. Samuel Martin, hatter to the people, was also prominent in his loyal demonstrations. There was not much in the ordinary way of display. There were flags; and a banner hung down the wall above the shop window appropriately announced – 'Glad to see your Royal Highness. God Bless the Queen.' There was a sort of bower of bliss in the first floor window, in the shape of a cluster of 'Ladyes fair,' – and in the centre Martin himself stood ready to proclaim his loyalty. [37]

Such loyalty deserved reward, or so Martin seemed to believe, and for many years a standing joke in Aberdeen were his tongue-in-cheek recommendations in his advertisements that he be granted a knighthood. As Martin was, apparently, a close friend of Queen Victoria's personal servant, John Brown, there is reason to believe that the royal party at Balmoral were aware of, and amused by, Samuel Martin's suggestions. Eventually, these included the idea of a statue of himself in Aberdeen.

Not only was Martin proud of Britain, her sovereign, her armed forces, her empire, and her democratic institutions, he was also immensely attached to Aberdeen and to Deeside. He rarely missed a chance to praise Scotland's beauty in general and Deeside's attractions in particular, which he compared favourably to Switzerland and the Alps. Queen Victoria's visits to Balmoral in May and September 1868 brought forth from Martin numerous verses flattering the monarch,

LOOKING

At the Prudential Political Policy, and the Ponderous Preponderating Peculiarly Pleasant Prosperous Position of the Progressive Parties in Politics, Prompting and Pointing to the Palatial Positions of the Powerful, and to the Penetrating Propensities of a Prominently Prudential People, Pertinaciously Performing Perilous Performances, with Persuasive Prudence and Pertinacity, without Perturbation, Petulance, or Pomposity, Philosophically Portrays a Philanthropic Picture of a Peaceful Persevering People, Prodigiously, Pungently, Potentially, and Proverbially happy in being Providentially Placed under the Protection of a Pre-eminently Pure Potentate.

Figure 5. Martin shows his alliterative skills.

Deeside and a number of local hostelries. The following is but a sample of his feelings:

'Tis well to visit foreign lands,
      And see all sights that's rare –
Then return to Scotia's hills,
      And distant scenes compare.

With Deeside's bonnie banks and braes
      Its winding silvery streams
Its Valleys like those fairy spots
      We picture oft in dreams.

But 'tis no dream, 'tis nature pure,
      In her attractive phase –
Oh, who need care for foreign scenes,
      Who on Deeside can gaze. [38]

Space does not permit a discussion of the many other causes and events that Samuel Martin felt compelled to comment upon. Hardly a foreign crisis or war in the period from the late 1850s to the late 1870s, and even into the 1880s, escaped his attention, while at home he offered gratuitous advice to the nation's leaders on a range of military, political, economic, religious and other subjects. His comments were nearly always contained within the advertising pages of the *Aberdeen Herald*, even extending on some occasions to a full column of a broad-

sheet newspaper, at what must have been a not inconsiderable cost. When, in 1876, the paper passed into new proprietorship, Martin expressed his satisfaction with the polite attention he had received from, and the advertising charges made by, the old management. He denied that his advertisements had been inserted free, but would not object if the new management adopted that idea. [39]

Martin was, in fact, a pioneer of advertising techniques. He knew how to catch and to retain the eye and interest of his readers, and was a master of the art of the misleading headline. He also made imaginative use of alliteration, as on July 22, 1865,[40] when he headed his advertisement with an unusual comment on the state of the nation (figure 5).

In January 1868 he began the new year with acrostic verses:

M any pleasures in Dress we often may find,
A s articles vary in cut and in kind;
R eally well pleased with people we meet,
T o see how well dressed from the head to the feet.
I n Dress there's philosophy, no doubt about that,
N o article so nice as a good-looking Hat.
H ow pleasant to view, so smart and so neat,
A man with a good Hat looks on the street;
T is pleasing to think the people all know
T hat to buy a nice Hat they've not far to go;
E very one's well aware no need to flatter –
R esort to 34, Union St, mind MARTIN THE HATTER.

For many years Martin inserted an advertisement in late December bidding farewell to the old year and in early January welcoming the new year. These particular advertisements often contained a review of the past twelve months as regards political and other events and a comment on Martin's business fortunes, plus a wealth of information regarding his health, eyesight, hearing, digestion, rheumatism and other personal details. On January 4, 1873, he wrote:

At this, the beginning of a New Year, MARTIN thanks 'THE PEOPLE' most heartily and sincerely for their kind support during the past year, a year of MARTIN'S business prosperity thoroughly up to his expectations. MARTIN has pleasure in thinking that 'THE PEOPLE' will be delighted to hear that his physical and mental energies are as lively as they were twenty

years ago, thus he is enabled to move about in that graceful and polite manner that so well becomes him; he is blessed with a good appetite *and dinkitite*, both of which he enjoys in moderation. . . .

FATHER TIME HAS LAID
HIS HAND GENTLY ON MARTIN.

His grey hairs are certainly in the ascendant, and he finds more hair on the *sides* than on the *top* of his head, from which it might be inferred that he has lately been growing through his hair. His moustache is fierce as ever, and his beard comely. His teeth of *youthful growth* are not too plentiful, but answer all the purposes of mastication, and sharpen up wonderfully with a glass of good 'Old Port.' He occasionally wears spectacles, perhaps because they are becoming fashionable; however, they suit him admirably, and his nasal organ holds them up nobly. There is an old saying that old age brings its troubles it *has brought MARTIN a great many comforts that he could not get at in his youth*, THANKS TO THE SUPPORT OF 'THE PEOPLE.' [42]

One of Martin's most interesting advertisements was published in April 1877, when he had been in business at the same address for nearly forty years, and was taking a retrospective and nostalgic view of his own career and the changes in the town:

Forty years; 'tis a long time. Yes! NO Railways at Aberdeen at that time. NO beautiful Market. NO magnificent Municipal Buildings. NO Bank Buildings like Noblemen's Mansions. NO splendid Post-Office. NO attractive Houses and Villas as are now to he seen in the West-End. NO Tramway Cars. NO Cabs and Few Carriages. NO Lorries. NO Wet Dock. FEW, if any Plate Glass Shop Windows. NO School Boards or Schools like Palaces (yet good solid education at a cheap rate). NOT as many churches, but better filled. NOT nearly as many BOBBIES, but more soldiers. THE same Barracks (for which those that are inclined may thank all the Governments that have been in power up to the present time). AND Last though not Least. NOT as many Grey Hairs in Martin's Head (he had

no moustache at that time). Oh! the changes of time. Forty years ago Martin was a dark-haired comely youth, with lots of philosophy and the world before him; and though now a trifle older his temperament is lively as ever, with a fine eye to business. . . .[43]

Unfortunately, Martin's health did deteriorate, and he may have had a stroke in the mid-1870s from which he never fully recovered. Thereafter his advertisements became much more routine. Already, in November 1871, John C. M'Leod, 'About 30 Years with Mr. Samuel Martin, Hatter', had opened a new hat shop at 46 Union Street, and in September 1885 there appeared Martin's last advertisement in the *Herald and Weekly Free Press*, followed by the announcement the following month in the *Aberdeen Journal* that John C. M'Leod 'has taken the Shop, Stock, and Good-will of Business at 34 UNION STREET, belonging to Mr SAMUEL MARTIN, so long known in the trade.'[44]

Martin's retirement, due presumably to advancing years and ill health, certainly marked the end of an era. Under his proprietorship 34 Union Street had become an Aberdeen institution and, if to call him 'The Mad Hatter of Union Street' is to exaggerate his eccentricities, he was certainly a local character renowned for his humour and practical jokes. Martin died in January 1888, but, ever unconventional, he had erected his own memorial stone eighteen years earlier in 1870, gaining some notoriety by so doing. On that occasion he had entered the office of his friend and legal adviser, James Collie, and announced 'I am buying an estate and I want you to act for me.' Martin then explained he was actually buying a lair in Nellfield Cemetery that amounted to only a few square feet. This time, however, his lawyer had the last laugh, as after taking down the details he enquired dryly, 'And when is the intended date of entry?' Fittingly, the inscription on the memorial stone reads, 'The Last Resting Place Of Samuel Martin, Hatter To The People, Aberdeen.'[45]

NOTES

1. Most of the details relating to Samuel Martin's family background and early life are derived from his obituary notices published in the *Aberdeen Journal*, Monday, 9 January 1888, p. 4, col. 6, and in the *Daily Free Press*, Monday, 9 January 1888, p. 4, col. 6.

2. *Daily Free Press*, Monday, 9 January 1888, p. 4, col. 6.

3. *Aberdeen Herald and General Advertiser for the Counties of Aberdeen, Banff and Kincardine*, Saturday, 10 February 1838, p. 1, col. 4, (hereafter cited as *Aberdeen Herald*);

and the *Aberdeen Constitutional, and General Advertiser for the Counties of Aberdeen, Banff, and Kincardine*, vol. 1, no. 22, Saturday, 10 February 1838, p. 1, col. 2.

4. *Aberdeen Herald*, 25 August 1838, p. 133, col. 4.
5. *Aberdeen Journal*, Monday, 9 January 1888, p. 4, col. 6.
6. *Aberdeen Herald*, 15 September 1838, p. 145, col. 3, and 15 December 1838, p. 198, col. 3.
7. *Aberdeen Herald*, 9 October 1841, p. 185, col. 7, and 5 February 1842, p. 22, col. 2.
8. *Aberdeen Herald*, 19 February 1842, p. 29, col. 5.
9. *Aberdeen Herald*, 10 January 1846, p. 6 col. 1, 24 October 1846, p. 170, col. 3, and 25 December 1847, p. 201, col. 7.
10. *Aberdeen Herald*, 12 March 1842, p. 41, col. 8.
11. *Aberdeen Herald*, 11 February 1843, p. 22, col. 1.
12. *Aberdeen Herald*, 14 June 1845, p. 94, col. 1.
13. *Aberdeen Herald*, 8 July 1848, p. 110, col. 1.
14. *Aberdeen Herald*, 2 September 1848, p. 141, col. 5.
15. *Aberdeen Herald*, 30 September 1848, p. 158, col. 3.
16. *Aberdeen Herald*, 7 May 1853, p. 4, col. 3.
17. *Aberdeen Herald*, 7 January 1854, p. 4, col. 2.
18. *Aberdeen Herald*, 16 July 1853, p. 4, col. 2.
29. *Aberdeen Herald*, 29 April 1854, p. 4, col. 3.
20. *Aberdeen Herald*, 19 August 1854, p. 4, col. 1, and 23 September 1854, p. 4, col. 1.
21. William Carnie, *Additional Aberdeen Reminiscences. Social, Civic and Personal Pencillings of the Granite City*, vol. 3 (Aberdeen, 1906), p. 273.
22. *Aberdeen Herald*, 12 May 1855, p. 4, col. 2.
23. *Aberdeen Herald*, 16 June 1855, p. 4, col. 2, 30 June 1855, p. 4, col. 1, 21 July 1855, p. 4, col. 4, 28 July 1855, p. 4, col. 3, 18 August 1855, p. 4, col. 1, 1 September 1855, p. 4, col. 1, and 15 September 1855, p. 4, cols 2–3.
24. A. S. Cook, *Old-Time Traders and Their Ways* (Aberdeen, 1902), p. 76.
25. *Aberdeen Herald*, 5 April 1856, p. 5, col. 4.
26. *Aberdeen Herald*, 10 January 1857, p. 4, col. 2, 7 March 1857, p. 4, col. 2, and 24 September 1859, p. 4, col. 2.
27. *Aberdeen Herald*, 18 July 1857, p. 4, col. 2, 5 September 1857, p. 4, col. 2, 24 October 1857, p. 4, col. 2, 21 November 1857, p. 4, col. 2, and 5 December 1857, p. 4, col. 2.
28. *Aberdeen Herald*, 17 October 1857, p. 5, cols 2–6. The *Aberdeen Journal*, 21 October 1857, p. 6, col. 4, also described the decorations in detail but selected Martin's contribution for special comment.
29. Cook, *Old Time Traders*, p. 20.
30. *Aberdeen Herald*, 14 March 1863, p. 6, col. 1.
31. *Aberdeen Herald*, 2 April 1870, p. 3, col. 3.
32. *Aberdeen Herald*, 17 June 1871, p. 5, col. 5.
33. *Aberdeen Herald*, 3 July 1841, p. 129, col. 4, and 22 July 1865, p. 4, col. 2.
34. *Aberdeen Herald*, 19 May 1866, p. 5, col. 4.
35. *Aberdeen Herald*, 29 June 1872, p. 5, col. 4.
36. *Aberdeen Herald*, 5 March 1864, p. 4, col. 2.
37. *Aberdeen Herald*, 22 September 1866, p. 5, col. 3.
38. *Aberdeen Herald*, 23 May 1868, p. 4, col. 2, and 19 September 1868, p. 4, col. 2.

39. *Aberdeen Herald*, 6 May 1876, p. 4, col. 2.

40. *Aberdeen Herald*, 22 July 1865, p. 4, col. 2.

41. *Aberdeen Herald*, 4 January 1868, p. 4, col. 2.

42. *Aberdeen Herald*, 4 January 1873, p. 4, col. 2.

43. *Herald and Weekly Free Press*, 7 April 1877, p. 4, cols 2-3.

44. *Aberdeen Herald*, 18 November 1871, p. 4, col. 1, *Herald and Weekly Free Press*, 12 September 1885, and *Aberdeen Journal*, 21 October 1885, p. 8, cols 2-3.

45. *Aberdeen Herald*, 5 February 1870, p. 5, col. 6.

4

Aberdonians Abroad: Two Centuries of Human Exports from North-eastern Scotland

Marjory Harper

Despite its relative geographical isolation, the city of Aberdeen in the eighteenth and nineteenth centuries was by no means a remote backwater, bypassed by the questions and events of the day. On the contrary, it had its finger firmly and consistently on the pulse of regional, national and international issues, and was alert to both the problems and the opportunities created by the Union of 1707. A notable part of Aberdeen's involvement with the wider world took the form of emigration, as a steady trickle of people from both the city and its hinterland participated in a nationwide phenomenon which grew in size, significance and controversy as time went on. The aim of this study is to investigate the ways in which the limitations and opportunities of the emigrants' Aberdeen origins fashioned their decisions to emigrate, their ambitions, their destinations, and their achievements in new surroundings.

STATISTICAL EVIDENCE FOR EMIGRATION

It is impossible to determine the precise extent of emigration even from Scotland as a whole, far less the exodus from the narrower confines of a city or region. In the eighteenth century the compilation of

emigration statistics was the exception rather than the rule but, even in the more closely documented nineteenth century, inaccuracies and distortions were commonplace for returns were still not compiled specifically for the study of emigration.[1] Recent estimates of eighteenth-century Scottish emigration range from 33,000 for the entire period 1760–1803 to 40,000 for the years 1760–75 alone, with Scots probably making up a small proportion of the 4,500 emigrants reckoned to have left the British Isles in the earlier period 1700–60.[2] The much greater exodus of the nineteenth century was recorded more systematically, first by the Customs Department and from 1873 by the Board of Trade, producing a figure of 1,807,659 emigrants from Scotland between 1825 and 1914.[3]

Aberdeen's involvement is largely suppressed within these national statistics, and has to be deduced from other sources. Between 1825 and 1872, however, thanks to a detailed breakdown of ports of embarkation in the Colonial Office returns, it is possible to identify, at least approximately, the extent of the overseas passenger trade from Aberdeen and other ports in the region. In that period, a total of 16,055 passengers embarked at Aberdeen, of whom 14,662 were bound for British North America, 1,073 for the United States, 212 for Australia, and 91 for the West Indies. Virtually all the 479 passengers who embarked at Banff, and the 310 from Peterhead, were also travelling to British North America.[4] These figures clearly do not give a comprehensive picture of north-eastern emigration, for even before steamships eclipsed sailing vessels and embarkations became centralised on Glasgow and Liverpool, an unknown but substantial number of Aberdeenshire emigrants travelled south to embark. Yet evidence of local passenger shipping movement gives a solid statistical foundation to the argument that Aberdeen itself was a not insignificant centre of emigration activity. That quantitative foundation can then be enhanced by qualitative evidence, in order to demonstrate not only the fact but also the form of the exodus from the city of Aberdeen.

ABERDEEN'S STRATEGIC LOCATION

Probably the most voluminous and varied local source of information about emigration is the press. For a century after its inception in December 1747 shipping advertisements in the *Aberdeen Journal* indicate that transatlantic emigration, harnessed to trade, was an established fact of life in the port and city of Aberdeen. Although it is well

known that the Union of 1707 opened up unprecedented opportunities for Scotland to trade with the American colonies, it is sometimes assumed that these opportunities were confined to the west coast, notably to Glasgow. Aberdeen's experience indicates otherwise, for while the city clearly could not claim anything like the volume of business transacted between Glasgow and the Americas, its merchants were not shut out of the Atlantic trade entirely, and dockside street names such as Virginia Street bear testimony to the direction of the trade. More concrete testimony is found in the *Aberdeen Journal*'s record of shipping movements at the port of Aberdeen, while the link between trade and emigration is demonstrated in the newspaper's regular advertisements for indentured emigration. In 1749, for example, the *Aberdeen Journal* recorded ten vessels leaving for or arriving from Virginia and the West Indies. On three occasions in that year local merchants also offered passages to 'men-servants of 12 years old and upwards' to go to Antigua and Virginia, with the proviso that 'no persons of bad characters [were] to be received'. [5]

After the American Revolution, business with the former colonies declined, while the French Revolutionary and Napoleonic Wars in the 1790s and 1800s brought further disruption to both trade and emigration. Yet the conflict with France indirectly helped Aberdeen, like many other British ports, both to refocus overseas trade and to stimulate emigration. Particularly after the Napoleonic embargo on Baltic trade in 1807 had cut off essential supplies of lumber, Britain redirected its custom to New Brunswick and the St Lawrence, and the imports of timber from these areas were coupled with an increasingly significant export business in human freight, in a reciprocal transatlantic trade which endured almost until the imperial preference on Canadian timber was removed in 1860. Continuously until about 1850, and sporadically for a year or two thereafter, up to sixteen timber ships were advertised each year in the *Aberdeen Journal*. They were enthusiastically patronised, largely by people from Aberdeen and its hinterland, although some passengers came from further afield to embark, not only from the counties in closest proximity but also from the more northerly mainland and the Northern Isles. It was even more common for the Aberdeen ships to call at northerly ports such as Cromarty and Scrabster to pick up extra passengers before setting off across the Atlantic. [6]

By the 1850s and 1860s Aberdeen's days as an emigrant port were numbered. As steam rapidly overtook sail, the increasing size and

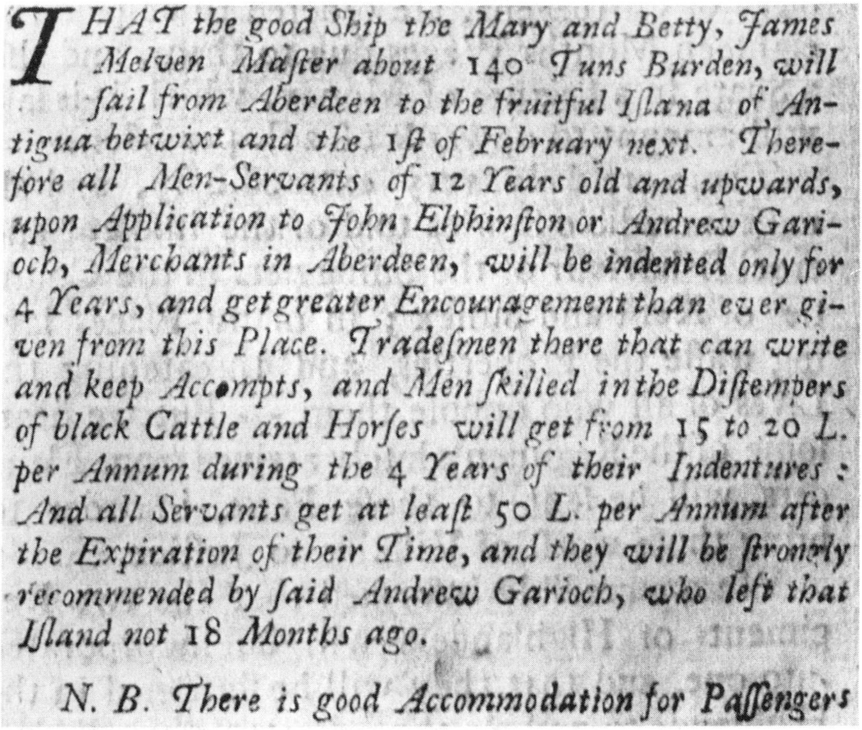

THAT the good Ship the Mary and Betty, James Melven Master about 140 Tuns Burden, will sail from Aberdeen to the fruitful Island of Antigua betwixt and the 1st of February next. Therefore all Men-Servants of 12 Years old and upwards, upon Application to John Elphinston or Andrew Garioch, Merchants in Aberdeen, will be indented only for 4 Years, and get greater Encouragement than ever given from this Place. Tradesmen there that can write and keep Accompts, and Men skilled in the Distempers of black Cattle and Horses will get from 15 to 20 L. per Annum during the 4 Years of their Indentures : And all Servants get at least 50 L. per Annum after the Expiration of their Time, and they will be strongly recommended by said Andrew Garioch, who left that Island not 18 Months ago.

N. B. There is good Accommodation for Passengers

Figure 1. Advertisements for indentured emigration were a regular feature of the local press in the second half of the eighteenth century; this early example is from the Aberdeen Journal, 10 January 1749.

sophistication of vessels led to the concentration of emigrant shipping on a few major ports, notably Liverpool and Glasgow, and to the replacement of small, locally based shipping agencies with large, highly capitalised and centralised companies which laid on custom-built emigrant vessels. But Aberdeen was still strategically placed to take advantage of the new opportunities, for the advent of the railway to the south in 1850 simply meant that the action shifted from the docks to the station. By the turn of the century special 'colonist carriages' were regularly attached to south-bound trains, and leave-takings at the Joint Station were major public events. One such in March 1913, when almost 300 emigrants were seen off to Glasgow by an even larger crowd, seemed to pose a considerable threat to public order. According to the *Aberdeen Journal*:

> The railway officials were ready for all emergencies. The barricade gates were closed, and a posse of police . . . was on the

spot. About half-past 7 o'clock the station area was crowded, there being a sea of faces from one end to the other. None but ticket-holders were allowed through the gates. The crowd became denser every minute, and it required all the skill of the police officers to keep order. As the time for the departure of the train came on, the situation became somewhat alarming. A rush was made at one of the gates, but police reinforcements were at hand, and, along with the railway porters, drove the intruders back. In other quarters things were kept lively by a number of young men attempting to jump the railings, and those who did get over were speedily turned back by the police. Crowds came trooping in from the Denburn direction. These, however, were led through the gateways, and when the gong for the departure of the train sounded order prevailed.[7]

Another dimension of emigration that was made possible as a result of the way in which the technological revolution in transport had shrunk the world was the increasing trend towards episodic, or temporary, emigration, particularly across the Atlantic. Aberdeen was well placed to capitalise on such opportunities, for in the half-century after the American Civil War her skilled granite tradesmen were in great demand to train an indigenous labour force, particularly in the easily accessible granite-producing states of New England, and most notably in Barre, Vermont. In the 1870s and 1880s it was not unusual for around 200 granite tradesmen to be lured away from Aberdeen each spring by the high wages offered in the American quarries and stone yards. Some of these emigrants settled down permanently and became manufacturers, opening yards which often became a source of employment for their more transient townsmen. Others stayed in New England for a few years, accumulating savings which they subsequently invested in establishing their own granite yards back in Aberdeen. But many quarriers and stone masons became long-term seasonal emigrants, crossing and re-crossing the Atlantic annually, and often encouraging their Aberdeen workmates to join them in the spring exodus to New England. As with the tobacco and timber traffic, emigration and trade went hand in hand, and the Aberdeen granite industry's flourishing export trade with the United States in the late nineteenth century was both a cause and a consequence of the presence of local granite workers in the American establishments.[8]

Figure 2. Shipping facilities for emigrants, often linked with imports of North American timber, were extensively advertised in the Aberdeen papers (Aberdeen Journal, 18 March 1835).

STIMULATING AN INTEREST: THE ROLE OF AGENTS

Such a steady and multi-faceted exodus from Aberdeen did not come about by accident. The city was certainly strategically placed to despatch permanent settlers and temporary wage labourers alike, directly by sea or indirectly by rail, but strategic location would have counted for nothing if the emigrants had not been encouraged to leave, or advised on where to settle. In the complex mosaic of influences which made up every individual's decision to emigrate, Aberdonians seem on the whole to have been swayed more by positive inducements than by expulsive factors, although the latter were by no means absent. Agents, who operated in many different guises, were crucial catalysts in stimulating emigrants' interests in overseas opportunities, and their activities therefore merit detailed analysis.

The merchants and ship owners who advertised freight and passages to Virginia and the Caribbean in the eighteenth century were recruiting agents for indentured emigration, a system whereby emigrants sold their labour for a period of up to seven years in return for a free passage, employment, and upkeep during the period of the indenture. Although such facilities were clearly particularly attractive to those without money, many indentured emigrants were skilled tradesmen, who were handpicked by the Scottish agents at the request of their merchant and planter contacts in the colonies. In much the same way, a century later, skilled granite tradesmen were often recruited by visiting American agents when they came to Aberdeen to place orders for locally manufactured stone.

After the demise of indentured emigration, the ship owners and agents who advertised passages on Canadian timber ships in the first half of the nineteenth century competed with each other in keeping prices down, the average steerage fare from Aberdeen to Québec hovering around £4 for most of that period. Although the business was dominated by a few recurring names such as Donaldson Rose, Robert Duthie and Provost George Thomson, no one agent had a monopoly of Aberdeen's emigrant trade, and in some years the number of agents advertising vessels was almost as great as the number of ships on offer.[9]

By the end of the nineteenth century, ticket sales were largely in the hands of firms with names recognisable to the late twentieth-century holiday-maker – H. W. J. Paton and MacKay Brothers, each with high-profile Union Street offices. These firms did much more than simply

[68]

sell tickets; encouraged by the commission they received from shipping lines and colonial governments for recruiting eligible categories of emigrants, they organised lectures and recruiting interviews in their own city-centre offices and in the surrounding rural areas, at which they deliberately targeted the farm labourers and domestic servants on whom they could claim a bonus. Their own representatives were sent overseas, not only to accompany emigrant parties and supervise their settlement but also to seek out employment opportunities for subsequent recruits.

By 1900 the practical organisation of emigration from north-eastern Scotland was largely in the hands of an army of almost 200 ticket agents, although only about 100 were active. The most important, along with Paton and MacKay, were W. T. Moffatt and R. & J. Davidson, also in Aberdeen, supplemented by busy regional offices such as those of William Maitland in Longside and John Sinclair in Elgin. Canada was the destination which generated most of their business, not so much on account of their own efforts to secure bonuses (which were offered by Canada later than by Antipodean destinations) but because of a remarkable public enthusiasm for the Dominion in the north-eastern area. Some of that enthusiasm was simply the result of a public perception of familiarity with Canada harking back to the days of the timber trade and even the late eighteenth century. Canada was certainly the destination most frequently and sympathetically referred to in the Liberal *Aberdeen Free Press*, a service which did not go unnoticed by the Dominion authorities. In 1911 the Canadian government's London-based assistant superintendent of emigration advised his superior in Ottawa that John Bruce, editor of the *Aberdeen Free Press*, should be given financial help with the publication of occasional special issues advocating emigration, on the grounds that 'there is no better friend to Canada than this newspaper, and it has an enormous circulation throughout not only the North, but extending to the Southern parts of Scotland.'[10] The request was granted, and eight years later W. D. Scott, head of the Canadian Immigration Department, categorically endorsed his British superintendent's opinion:

I do not think there is a single paper in the British Isles which has been more friendly towards Canada than the *Aberdeen Free Press* and there is no doubt but that the publicity already secured through this paper has been highly advantageous to Canada.[11]

Probably even more advantageous to Canada by the early twentieth century, however, was the work of professional agents employed by the Dominion and provincial governments and the transcontinental railway companies to harness and increase the existing public interest in Canada. After confederation in 1867, the Dominion government began to pour money and manpower into promoting settlement, partly in order to woo immigrants away from the United States; and this campaign reached its zenith between 1896 and 1906, when the Dominion's immigration budget escalated from $400,000 to $4,000,000 per annum. A crucial aspect of Canada's positive immigration policy was the appointment of resident territorial agents at strategic locations across Britain and (to a lesser extent) Europe. These men rapidly became the linchpins in a complex agency-network, not only developing aggressive promotional campaigns of their own but also co-ordinating the sometimes competitive activities of provincial agents, visiting delegates, and representatives of the Canadian Pacific and Canadian National Railway Companies. [12]

Aberdeen was granted its own resident Canadian government agent in 1907. Until then the whole of Scotland, along with northern England, had come under the umbrella of a Glasgow office which had been established in 1872, and whose resident agents, temporary sub-agents and visiting delegates had all paid regular visits to the northeast. By 1907, however, the Glasgow office could no longer cope with the increasing volume of enquiries from all over Scotland, so a separate agency was created to cover the north, with headquarters in Aberdeen, and responsibility for an area covering all mainland and island parts of Scotland north of Perth. The first northern agent was John Maclennan, a Gaelic-speaking Canadian of Highland descent, who arrived in Aberdeen with his wife and two children on 4 February 1907 to open his new office at 26 Guild Street.

Maclennan's workload was enormous. In his first week he conducted 258 interviews with prospective emigrants, 114 of them in one day alone. His office hours were 8.15 a.m. to 9.30 or even 10.30 p.m., six days a week, and after the initial burst of interest, the office saw an average of 25–30 visitors a day. He was also responsible, with the assistance of a clerk and a typist, for answering an average of 100 letters per week, although one record-breaking week in 1910 saw the receipt of 1,299 letters. Other important duties included distributing promotional literature to schools and booking agencies, inspecting the booking agents, and forwarding their bonus claims to Ottawa. Mac-

lennan was frequently absent from his office, particularly in the summer, for one of his main duties was to travel round his district, delivering lectures, mounting exhibitions and putting in regular appearances at feeing markets and agricultural shows. From time to time special itinerant agents were attached to his office to assist with the lecturing campaign, the most successful of these probably being Hugh McKerracher of Paisley, Ontario, whose wife was a native of Aberdeenshire.

The appointment of an Aberdeen-based Canadian government agent seems to have been timely, for John Maclennan's superior in London, J. Obed Smith, subsequently calculated that 3,000 emigrants had left Aberdeenshire for Canada in the first year of the northern agent's appointment, an exodus amounting to almost one per cent of the county's population.[13] None of the other major emigrant destinations had resident agents in Aberdeen, and it showed, for interest in the United States, Australia, New Zealand and South Africa was much more sporadic and specialised, often coinciding with visits to the city by itinerant agents, whose business was not infrequently to recruit tradesmen for specific contracts.

SUSTAINING A TREND: PERSONAL CONTACTS AND EMIGRANT NETWORKING

Agents clearly had a formative role in generating and shaping patterns of emigration from Aberdeen and its hinterland, and on the whole they seem to have maintained a remarkably good reputation. Yet agents were usually just professional propagandists, whose assurances lacked the seal of personal recommendation. One of the main reasons they were so successful in north-eastern Scotland, particularly in the Canadian context, was because their work was often underpinned by the more crucial encouragement – and sometimes the tangible assist- ance – given by pioneer emigrants to friends, relatives and acquaint- ances who were willing to follow their example. The Aberdeen area yields numerous examples of the persuasive influence of personal cor- respondence.

Sometimes the encouragement was offered publicly and indirectly, as in the case of the settler in Australia who in 1851 told his brother in Turriff to have his letter published in the *Aberdeen Journal*, so that 'all our friends on the Dee, the Don, the Spey and the Deveron, will then have an opportunity of seeing that I am living and liking the Antipodes

well.'[14] More often correspondence remained unpublished, although it might well be passed around the extended family and the local community, where it not infrequently precipitated secondary movement, particularly if a remittance or a prepaid ticket were enclosed as an added inducement. On a few occasions an individual or a delegation was sent overseas by family or friends with a specific remit to investigate and report back on the prospects for emigration before a final decision was reached by the larger group.

One example of delegated investigation comes from Aberdeen in the mid-1830s, when a group of friends who had been debating for some time the pros and cons of emigration took the decision to settle in Southern Ontario. Their attention had been directed to that area by the publication of Adam Fergusson's notes on his two visits to North America, in which the Perthshire land speculator and emigrant had strongly advised Scottish farmers to emigrate to upper Canada.[15] In 1833 Fergusson and his Scottish partner bought 7,367 acres in Nichol Township, and so glowing was his description of his new settlement of Fergus that the Aberdeen coterie decided to send one of their number, George Elmslie, on a reconnaissance trip. If Elmslie judged that the land matched up to Fergusson's account of it, he was authorised to purchase a suitable tract on which the friends could establish an Aberdeenshire colony.

On 14 August 1834 Elmslie reached Toronto, where he met up with an old friend, Alexander Watt of New Deer, who had newly arrived in Canada with his two sisters and brother-in-law. Elmslie and Watt joined forces and proceeded to Fergus, only to find so much of Fergusson's land had been sold that there was not a large enough block left for them to purchase. But since they liked the location, they set their sights a couple of miles further down the Irvine River, where more land was available. Elmslie recorded his impressions in his diary:

> I was now satisfied. We had found a block suitable in all respects for our projected colony. The quality of the soil, as indicated by the trees and their size, was equal to any we had seen; watered in such a manner as we had nowhere seen; . . . the society was superior to what we could have anticipated – the newer settlers almost entirely Scotch, the older, around and in the neighbourhood of Elora, respectable, intelligent Englishmen; the block bordering on the new and rapidly rising settlement of Fergus, with the immediate prospect of having a Church and Schools. [16]

Elmslie and Watt purchased 1,200 acres and 800 acres respectively at Elora. Elmslie then began to clear the sites of his own home and those of his friends who were to join him later. According to plan, in spring 1835 a party of around twenty emigrants came out from Aberdeen on the timber ship *Brilliant* to take up the holdings which Elmslie had bought on their behalf, in a settlement which was named 'Bon Accord' in recognition of their place of origin.

These arrivals laid the foundations of a significant pattern of emigration from Aberdeen to Nichol. Two further contingents came out later in 1835, two of Elmslie's sisters being included in one of these parties, and the exodus continued unabated throughout the 1830s, most of the emigrants travelling on timber ships from Aberdeen to Québec. Other emigrants from north-eastern Scotland put down roots in Bon Accord township after initially settling in other parts of Canada, thereby creating a community which preserved and continually reinforced the emigrants' original regional identity. Newcomers made use of informal ethnic networks as a means of gaining access to land, accommodation, employment and capital more easily than if they had gone to an entirely new environment, and these networks could be manipulated from Aberdeen as well as in situ. Elizabeth Connon, an Aberdeen shopkeeper who knew several of the Bon Accord pioneers, never went to Canada herself, but on at least two occasions she made use of her Canadian contacts to help first her nephew, and then a family friend, to establish themselves. Her shop was also a port of call for departing emigrants from the north-eastern hinterland as they passed through Aberdeen, and these emigrants were often entrusted with letters or parcels for the nephew.[17]

In Canada, as – to a lesser extent – in the Antipodes, emigration from Aberdeen was sustained by a combination of personal recommendations and agents' propaganda. But there was one part of the world where a significant influx of north-eastern manpower and capital in the nineteenth century seems to have come about almost entirely by word-of-mouth recommendation, family connections and private patronage. The island of Ceylon offered no schemes of assisted passage or settlement, no agents advertised land, employment or transportation, and few letters from emigrants were published, yet settlers from Aberdeen had an enormous influence on the economic development of Ceylon, an influence that was felt throughout most of the century, and which manifested itself primarily in the development of the coffee industry.

Pre-eminent among the pioneer planters was Robert Boyd Tytler from Peterhead. He arrived in the island in 1837, via Jamaica, where he had spent three years learning about tropical agriculture on the sugar plantation of a family friend. Two of his brothers were already in the service of the East India Company, and he came to Ceylon on the invitation of a maternal relative who was a partner in a firm which was in the process of establishing several coffee estates. Tytler worked his way up from a plantation manager to become, ultimately, one of the biggest private estate-holders in the island, as well as chairman of the Planters' Association, a member of Ceylon's Legislative Council, and a respected mentor for the second generation of planters. A disproportionate number of these men came from Aberdeen, and they included two of Tytler's sons and his brother-in-law. In 1875 Tytler himself was guest of honour at a dinner of over 100 planters and ex-planters held in Aberdeen,[18] and in 1922 Sir John Fleming, after encountering several Aberdeen planters and merchants during a visit to Ceylon, estimated that when plantation work had begun on the island '50 per cent of the overseers were Scotsmen, and of these 50 per cent were Aberdonians.' [19]

THE EXPORT OF CAPITAL AND IDEAS

It is clear that capital, as well as manpower, was being exported from Aberdeen to Ceylon. Both places benefited as a result, for in developing Ceylon's plantation economy, the planters imported machinery and supplies from Aberdeen, as well as repatriating much of their income, often investing it in the purchase of retirement properties in Aberdeen's select suburbs.

Ceylon was not unique, however, in offering an outlet for the surplus capital that was available in Aberdeen in the mid-nineteenth century. In the 1840s commercial sheep farming in eastern Australia was developed largely through the formation of two Aberdeen-based investment companies, the North British Australasian Company (founded 1839) and the Scottish Australian Company (founded 1840). Most of the shareholders in those companies were residents of Aberdeen and its hinterland who had no intention of emigrating to the Antipodes, but were confident enough to invest on a small scale because of successful sheep farming undertaken by pioneers such as the 'surplus younger sons' of William Leslie of Warthill, Old Rayne. [20]

Aberdeen money was also invested in North America, perhaps most notably by the seventh Earl of Aberdeen, who in the 1890s poured

Figure 3. Guisachan Ranch, British Columbia. This 480-acre property in the Okanagan Valley was purchased by Lord Aberdeen in 1890 (photograph reproduced by permission of the Earl of Haddo).

large sums into the establishment of commercial fruit-farming in the Okanagan Valley in British Columbia. The venture was undertaken mainly at the behest of Lady Aberdeen, who wanted her younger brother Coutts to leave behind the financial mistakes and bad company associated with his position as a 'remittance man' ranch manager in North Dakota to take up more respectable employment in western Canada. Lord Aberdeen, for his part, was eager to encourage small investors from north-eastern Scotland (and elsewhere) to settle on the compact orchard units which he carved out of his 14,000–acre ranches, but although he was successful in attracting some such settlers, and is still remembered as the Okanagan Valley's most visionary pioneer, his enterprise was a financial disaster. After more than a decade of deficits, he sold his first ranch in 1903 and incorporated his remaining properties in a company which was finally dissolved in 1921. [21]

On a much smaller scale, the Aberdonians who settled in the Bon Accord Township in the 1830s were also exporting capital. George Elmslie had been a merchant in Aberdeen, two of the 1835 arrivals, Alexander Dingwall-Fordyce and David Chalmers, came from wealthy Aberdeen families, and many of the other Bon Accord settlers were able to purchase large tracts of land without delay. Some bought their

farms unseen before leaving Aberdeen, others came out to take up land bought for them by their parents, and some employed contractors to clear and prepare their properties for cultivation.

The Bon Accord settlers also exported ambitions and ideas. It is significant that although several had been merchants, tradesmen or professional men at home, their goal in emigrating was to acquire land. This ambition characterised the vast majority of Aberdeenshire emigrants throughout and beyond the nineteenth century, embracing not only those from rural areas but also city people and those of more lowly income than Elmslie and his friends, and it had come about because of unwelcome innovations in farming policy at home. Throughout north-eastern Scotland, as in other parts of the rural lowlands, the implementation of new agricultural policies since the mid-eighteenth century had seriously eroded the prospects of both farm labourers and small tenant farmers. Smallholdings were swept away relentlessly, absorbed into larger units, as new theories demanded the creation of bigger and bigger farms in order to maximise production. As a result, not only did provident and ambitious farm servants find it increasingly difficult to rent a holding but many tenant farmers also faced an uncertain future, as landlords refused to renew their leases or imposed such large rent increases that it became impossible for them to stay on. In addition to those who responded to their straitened circumstances by emigrating straight from the country areas, many first-generation migrants to the towns also hankered after a farming life, and all alike were susceptible to the constant propaganda which promised them an agricultural El Dorado overseas, where they could enjoy independence and security as owner-occupiers of their land. While Elmslie and his friends were clearly neither disappointed farm labourers nor hard-pressed tenant farmers, their desire to take up land overseas was by no means an uncommon trait among north-eastern businessmen in the nineteenth century, many of whom subsequently harnessed professional or industrial pursuits to their colonial farming ventures. That craving for land further reinforced the image of emigration from Aberdeen as an exodus of practising and prospective agriculturists, and also guaranteed the continuing popularity of Canada, which was perceived as the destination where the ambition to acquire land could be achieved most easily.

Canada's popularity was further guaranteed by the emigrants' perception that it offered a friendly and familiar, rather than an alien, environment. For some emigrants, not least the Bon Accord settlers, the prospect of owning land was insufficient by itself. Many also required

[76]

the reassurance that emigration would not entail major social disloca-
tion, a concern reflected by George Elmslie when he expressed his
satisfaction at the social calibre of the settlers already established in
Elora, as well as the area's agricultural prospects. There is a telling
phrase in a novel by Frederick Niven in which an unwilling Highland
emigrant comforts himself and his family with the assurance 'We'll take
Scotland with us – a kingdom of the mind',[22] and a similar attitude
characterised many non-fictional emigrants from Aberdeen, who craved
the assurance that their relocation would not cast them adrift from the
most treasured associations of the homeland. For that reason, they
sought destinations to which they believed their lifestyles and institutions could be transplanted most readily; and Canada, with its long
history of Scottish settlement, was the obvious choice.

What institutions did the emigrants transplant or seek to re-estab-
lish? Perhaps the most treasured emblems of Scottish identity were the
church and the school, and when George Elmslie was sent out to
Fergus, he was specifically instructed to ensure that both these institutions were within reasonable distance. The parent churches at home
were usually just as anxious to meet the spiritual needs of their flocks
overseas as the settlers were to secure such support, and several ministers went out from the north-east to serve emigrant congregations both
in Canada and in other parts of the empire. There were also secular
means through which emigrants could demonstrate their identity and
sometimes offer tangible assistance to their fellow-countrymen – Burns
clubs, sporting and piping associations, and St Andrew's societies, as
well as regional organisations such as the Aberdeenshire, Kincardineshire and Banffshire Association of Winnipeg, which in 1911 had a
membership of 200.[23]

UNSUCCESSFUL EXPORTS

While the documented history of emigration from Aberdeen generally
suggests an exodus of willing exiles, the picture was not entirely
positive. Eighteenth-century emigrants included a number of convicted
criminals sentenced to banishment,[24] as well as victims of kidnapping.
Aberdeen's most famous kidnap victim, Peter Williamson, subsequently
made sure that the city magistrates' connivance in 'that villainous and
execrable practice' was broadcast to the wider world.[25] Other emigrants
were fugitives from the consequences of debt or sexual misdemeanour,
while others, notably those from fishing communities, emigrated as a

Figure 4. The State Capitol, Austin, Texas. Most of the Aberdonians who cut stone for this building in 1886–87 never saw the finished product (photograph reproduced by permission of Robert Baumgardner, Jr.).

last resort in the face of financial hardship and unemployment.

Even those who left with high hopes could easily meet with disaster. A glance at the obituary lists in the press reflects the frequency with which emigrants succumbed, particularly in the fever-ridden West Indies. Some did not survive to reach their destination, for a voyage in a sailing ship, even across the Atlantic, was a major test of endurance and stamina, not a luxury cruise. Steerage accommodation in timber ships was frequently crude and squalid, and although the Aberdeen trade had a good reputation, disasters could still occur. [26]

Agents also came in for criticism, including local shipping agent Alex Cooper, convicted in 1855 of issuing fraudulent tickets, and the Canadian government agent, John Maclennan, criticised half a century later by large farmers and the Conservative *Aberdeen Journal* for draining the north-east of its best agriculturists.[27] At the same time the booking agents, paradoxically, were accused by the Canadian Immigration Department of recruiting emigrants indiscriminately, simply in order to secure the bonus payments, and the department periodically revoked bonuses on emigrants who had proved unsuitable. [28]

More commonly, however, it was the emigrants themselves who were

the victims of sharp practice by agents. One of the most notorious deceptions of emigrants from Aberdeen involved the recruitment in 1886 of 86 stone cutters and blacksmiths to work on the construction of the new Texas State Capitol in Austin. These men were recruited in Aberdeen by a visiting American agent, George Berry, who neglected to tell them that the need for their labour had arisen because the American Granite Cutters' Union had boycotted the job in protest at the use of cheap convict labour in the stone quarries. By the time they heard this news on disembarking at New York, most were unable or unwilling to change their plans, and all but twenty-four proceeded to the stone yards at Burnet, seventy miles from Austin, where they were put to work in searing heat, with no prospect of pay until their employers had recouped the cost of their passage. After eighteen months they were dismissed to seek re-employment in an American granite industry whose union had blacklisted them as untouchable strike-breakers. [29]

CONCLUSION

Despite these cautionary tales, Aberdeen's human exports during the two centuries under review were generally driven by ambition rather than despair. That ambition was fed by a potent cocktail of personal recommendation and professional propaganda, mediated through private correspondence, public lectures, newspapers, and a vibrant, if sporadic, market in locally published emigrant pamphlets and guidebooks.[30] Independence through land ownership was the clarion call of the bulk of the propaganda, reinforced by assurances about the preservation of social and cultural amenities overseas, a combination which helped to establish Canada as the favourite destination of generations of north-eastern emigrants.

Was there anything unique about Aberdeen's contribution to the mosaic of Scottish emigration? Probably not, except perhaps in the ready availability of surplus capital seeking opportunity for investment, or the enduring quest, even of town-dwellers, for land overseas. But Aberdeen's part in the overall picture cannot be discussed with confidence until much more comparative research has been done, not least into the papers of the professional emigration agents, and in neglected regions, such as Fife and the Borders. What is clear, however, is that emigration is both a significant part of Aberdeen's own history and a challenge to the traditionally negative view of Scottish emigration as a flight of unwilling paupers.

Notes

1. Before 1853 passengers' nationality was identified by port of departure rather than place of origin; until 1863 masters were not legally required to include cabin passengers in the returns; and only from April 1912 were emigrants and passengers differentiated. For details of the source of emigration statistics and their deficiencies, see N. H. Carrier and J. R. Jeffery, *External Migration: a Study of the Available Statistics* (London, 1953), particularly pp. 137–40.

2. Ian Adams and Meredyth Somerville, *Cargoes of Despair and Hope: Scottish Emigration to North America 1603–1803* (Edinburgh, 1993), p. 209, and Bernard Bailyn and Barbara DeWolfe, *Voyagers to the West: Emigration from Britain to America on the Eve of the Revolution* (London, 1986), p. 26.

3. Carrier and Jeffery, *External Migration*, pp. 92–93. The statistics were published in the appendices to the annual land reports of the colonial land and emigration commissioners, 1841–72, and subsequently in the 'General statement of emigration from the United Kingdom' issued annually by the Board of Trade.

4. Parliamentary Papers 1830 (650) xxix 435; 'Returns of emigrants to the British colonies and the USA, 1830–1840' (Irish University Press reprints of British Parliamentary Papers, vols 19 and 20); appendices to the annual reports of the colonial land and emigration commissioners, 1840–1872 (IUP reprints, vols 10–18).

5. *Aberdeen Journal* (hereafter *AJ*), 10 Jan., 2 May, 19 Dec. 1749.

6. See, for example, *AJ*, 7 July 1847 for comments on passengers from the Northern Isles who embarked at Aberdeen; and *AJ*, 14 May 1845 for intimation of the departure of the Aberdeen vessel *Lord Seaton* from Scrabster Roads with a large complement of passengers from Caithness and Orkney.

7. *AJ*, 22 March 1913.

8. For further discussion of the seasonal emigration of granite tradesmen from Aberdeen to the United States, see Marjory Harper, 'Transient tradesmen: Scottish granite workers in New England', *Northern Scotland*, vol. 9 (1989), pp. 53–75.

9. George Thomson exemplifies the prosperous local merchant and politician. In addition to operating a fleet of Aberdeen vessels to Québec and later becoming involved in Australian shipping from Liverpool and London, he was Aberdeen's dean of guild in 1840, its provost from 1847–50 and its member of parliament from 1852 to 1857.

10. J. Obed Smith to W. D. Scott, 28 Nov. 1911 (National Archives of Canada (hereafter NAC), RG 76, C–10291–2, vol. 401, file 572933).

11. Memo, by Scott, 9 Jan. 1919; reference as note above.

12. For detailed discussion of the Canadian government's agency activity, see H. Gordon Skilling, *Canadian Representation Abroad: from Agency to Embassy* (Toronto, 1945), ch. 1.

13. J. Obed Smith, assistant superintendent of emigration, London, to W. D. Scott, superintendent of immigration, Ottawa: report on British agencies, 15 March 1909 (NAC, RG 76, C–10294, vol. 405, file 590687, part 1).

14. *AJ*, 12 May 1852.

15. Adam Fergusson, *Practical Notes on a Tour of Canada and Parts of the USA* (Edinburgh, 1833); *Practical Notes Made during a Second Visit to Canada in 1833* (Edinburgh, 1834).

16. John R. Connon, *Elora*, pp. 70–71. Elmslie's diary, preserved in the Wellington County Museum, Fergus, Ontario (A 984.15 MU 59), describes in full the pioneers' search for a suitable tract of land.

17. For further details about the community of Aberdonians in the Bon Accord township, see Marjory Harper, *Emigration from North-East Scotland*, vol. 1, *Willing Exiles* (Aberdeen, 1988), pp. 215-24. Elizabeth Connon's correspondence is preserved in the Connon Collection, Wellington County Museum.

18. *Aberdeen Herald*, 4 Sept. 1875.

19. Sir John Fleming, *Looking backwards for Seventy Years, 1921-1851* (Aberdeen, 1922), p. 185. Detailed analysis of Aberdeen's links with coffee planting in Ceylon is found in Ranald C. Michie, 'Aberdeen and Ceylon: economic links in the nineteenth century', *Northern Scotland*, vol. 4, no. 1 (1981), pp. 69-82. See also Harper, *Willing Exiles*, pp. 330-39.

20. Malcolm Prentis, *The Scots in Australia: a study of New South Wales, Victoria and Queensland, 1788-1900* (Sydney, 1983), p. 30. See also D. S. MacMillan, *The Debtor's War: Scottish capitalists and the economic crisis in Australia 1841-1846* (Melbourne, 1960), pp. 1-12. According to MacMillan, of the 416 shareholders in the Scottish Australian Company, 185 lived in Aberdeen, 87 in Aberdeenshire, and most of the others in the adjoining counties.

21. See Marjory Harper, 'A gullible pioneer? Lord Aberdeen and the development of fruit farming in the Okanagan Valley, 1890-1921', *British Journal of Canadian Studies*, vol. 1, no. 2 (Dec. 1986), pp. 256-81.

22. Frederick Niven, *The Flying Years* (London, 1935), p. 19.

23. *AJ*, 19 Apr., 27 Dec. 1911.

24. *AJ*, 30 May, 10 Oct. 1749, 2 Apr. 1751, 12 Sept. 1763.

25. Peter Williamson, *The Life and Curious Adventures of Peter Williamson, who was carried off from Aberdeen and sold for a slave* (Aberdeen, 1801).

26. See, for example, Marjory Harper, 'Voyage to disaster', *The Aberdeen Leopard*, Oct. 1989, pp. 4-7.

27. Harper, *Willing Exiles*, pp. 107-108; *Emigration from North-East Scotland*, vol. 2, *Beyond the Broad Atlantic*, pp. 12-13.

28. Harper, *Beyond the Broad Atlantic*, p. 241, describes the dispute between Paton's agency and the Canadian Immigration Department over an unsatisfactory domestic servant, Rose McIntyre, who, after leaving three placements in Toronto, had eloped to the United States, leaving a trail of debt behind her (NAC, RG 76, C-10627, vol. 538, file 803839, part 2: letter from J. Mitchell, inspector of employment agents, Toronto, to W. D. Scott, immigration agent, Dept of the Interior).

29. For further details of this incident, see Marjory Harper, 'Emigrant strikebreakers: Scottish granite cutters and the Texas Capitol boycott', *Southwestern Historical Quarterly*, vol. 95, no. 4 (April 1992), pp. 465-86.

30. Thomas Fowler, *The Journal of a Tour through British America to the Falls of Niagara* (Aberdeen, 1832); John Mathison, *Counsel for Emigrants* (Aberdeen, 1834), *Sequel to Counsel for Emigrants* (Aberdeen, 1834), 3rd edition (Aberdeen, 1838); David Burns, *The Way to Wealth, and How to Enjoy It* (Aberdeen, 1851).

5

The Added Values of Learning

John Hargreaves

The theme of this chapter was suggested by a lecture entitled 'Art Values and the Value of Art' which the late Mary McCarthy delivered in Aberdeen University about twenty years ago. It later became the seed of her novel, *Cannibals and Missionaries*. In the lecture McCarthy contrasted the intensely personal value which people derive from experience of an artist's work with the very large financial rewards which may be gained (not usually by living artists themselves) from sales of such work in the public market place. The novel takes up this theme in a scenario where a group of hi-jackers attempt to use the Vermeers and Cezannes owned by their wealthy hostages to secure political demands. Here (as in E. L. Doctorow's *Ragtime*) the moral equation is complicated because the lives and liberty of human beings are the principal stake, but the central irony remains the way in which the value of art changes when its original purpose, the enlargement of personal experience, becomes confused with the different value-scales of finance and politics.

In the opinion of many, during the 1980s traditional humane values of higher education were similarly hi-jacked. Universities and colleges which saw their fundamental purpose as the advancement of learning and the education of students through the liberal arts and the diverse scientific disciplines which have grown out of them were increasingly

required to justify their existence by financial criteria. The quality of learning came to be measured by its productivity. This was distressing to teachers and scholars who believed education to be, literally, of priceless value. But perhaps this was an elitist view? After all, students with careers to make, as well as public servants with budgets to balance, have always used different valuations. In the quincentennial history of the University of Aberdeen we have been anxious that economic, as well as cultural and institutional historians, should have their space. This chapter is a light-hearted and largely speculative exploration of some problems in drawing these different paths together.

In *Academe and Empire*,[1] my book about the overseas connections of Aberdeen University, I did not say much about financial values. Yet clearly these are relevant to the economic history of Aberdeen and its region. It is well known that during the nineteenth century north-eastern Scotland was an important exporter of both labour and capital to regions beyond the UK. Less has been written about the value added to both these factors of production by knowledge or expertise derived through education. Without presuming to any such sophisticated analysis as A. G. Kemp and Sandra Galbraith have attempted for recent decades,[2] this chapter considers what methods might be used to evaluate, not the total contribution of the university to the regional economy, but the value added by its growing involvement in the expansion of the British empire. It concentrates on the period between the union of the colleges in 1860 and the First World War, relying on evidence other than detailed measurement. Should future scholars want to attempt the relevant quantification, it would be necessary to find a way of incorporating relationships between north-eastern Scotland and other parts of the UK into their calculations.

There is, first of all, the economic benefit of attracting students from outside the region – the aspect which has governed official policy towards overseas students since 1979. Until recent times this was for Aberdeen overwhelmingly a question of medical students. After the establishment of the General Medical Council in 1858 the new combined medical school in Aberdeen University, whose rise has now been studied by Carolyn Pennington, became one of a limited number of centres where a medical qualification could be obtained in the UK.[3] A sample of those graduating MB ChB during the 1880s shows that rather more than one third gave addresses outside northern Scotland. About nineteen per cent came from England, Wales or Ireland; thirteen per cent gave addresses outside the UK; three per cent were from Scotland

south of Montrose.[4] Though as students most of them were no doubt far from affluent, collectively they represented a considerable market for local tradesmen, landladies and publicans. Until the Universities Act of 1889 they also made, through class fees, a substantial contribution to their teachers' incomes. Providing education for a profession which was growing both in numbers and in respectability brought modest profits into the local community.

Yet only the most myopic economist would use this standard to measure the total value of Aberdeen's growing medical school. This chapter deals neither with the value of their educational experience to the students themselves, nor with the contribution which those individuals subsequently made to health throughout the world. But from the viewpoint of the Aberdeen community, it was surely valuable that its horizons should be widened by the presence of young men from other parts of the UK and of the British empire. Although those students with overseas addresses were largely children of Scots working overseas, especially in India, the sample also includes students native to India, Ceylon, Sierra Leone, South Africa, and the West Indies. Apart from their expenditures in Aberdeen, such students must have brought ideas and experience to the city which cannot be evaluated in financial terms.

There has been much interest recently in the early history of overseas students in UK, but unfortunately we know little of their life in Aberdeen, which many must have found a coldly unfamiliar environment. Probably most of them put their heads down and got on with their studies; I have found no mention of overseas influence in the somewhat introverted accounts of student life in early issues of the magazine, *Alma Mater*. Perhaps their main contact with the civic community was through membership of city churches. Certainly one remarkable example of this can be cited.

Christopher Davis, a black Barbadian, who graduated in medicine in 1870, was an active evangelist of the Plymouth Brethren. The *Aberdeen Free Press* described him as 'a blyth, handsome-looking man with exceedingly frank and affable manners', who during his time in Aberdeen 'took a very earnest and active interest in the welfare of the poor and degraded classes.' On graduation Davis took a job at Bart's in London, where he had completed his clinical studies before coming to Aberdeen. But on the outbreak of the Franco-Prussian War Davis immediately left to do relief work in the area of Sedan, taking out 'a large sum of money contributed by himself and his friends of the same religious

persuasion.' For the next four months he worked tirelessly, treating Bavarian soldiers wounded in the battle of Sedan, and then providing soup kitchens for starving French civilians (which he financed partly by selling his prize gold watch). Tragically, Davis himself caught smallpox and died at the end of November. Both the French mayor of Sedan and the representative of the Prussian occupiers attended the moving funeral service of *le bon docteur noir*.[5] It is a very moving story. Yet, but for this sad end we would know nothing of this remarkable man. How many equally interesting careers went unrecorded?

As it is, we can only speculate about the social life, and the romantic entanglements, which overseas students enjoyed during their time in Aberdeen. One group of foreign students seems to have become assimilated fairly easily into Aberdonian society: the Dutch-descended Burghers from Sri Lanka. One of them, J. L. Scharenguiyvel (MB 1906), became a popular member of the Aberdeen cricket team. Intermarriage with Burgher families seems to have been quite acceptable socially. Emily Miller became the wife of E. L. Koch (MD 1876), a pioneer Principal of the Ceylon Medical College; Alice Palmer, daughter of the owner of the Holburn Brewery, married J. L. Van Geyzel (MB 1876), who was to enjoy a notable scientific career in the Indian Medical Service. Less respectably, a Sri Lankan opthalmologist, George Ferdinands (MB 1888, MD 1891), seems to have lived at Bishop's Gate, 78 Don Street, as 'life companion' of Isabella Mayo, minor novelist and Labour member of the Aberdeen School Board. A disciple of Tolstoy, Isabella later became interested in the philosophy of Gandi, so Ferdinands may have provided some trans-cultural input to the city's literary elite. Unfortunately he gets only a passing mention in the volume of rather diffuse *Recollections* which Isabella published in 1910. [6]

With only such scraps of anecdotal evidence to work on, I dare not suggest that there is a large hidden history of trans-cultural relations waiting to be discovered. Yet if we shift our attention to more recent decades it seems clear that the presence of a cosmopolitan student community – now including women as well as men – has been of value to the life of the city, and not merely in the economic sense. Scholars working on other aspects of nineteenth-century civic life could usefully be alert for references to this overseas presence.

To return to the search for financial returns and the vast majority of students in the educational institutions of the city who were natives of northern Scotland: not all of these could, or wished to, find profitable employment locally, or even in the UK. About thirty per cent of all

university graduates of the years 1860–1900 worked overseas at some point in their careers; for doctors, the figure was higher. It would be interesting, though very difficult, to discover what part of the value added to their earning power by their education was returned as re-mittances to their home region. But I would not expect any such figure to be large. My impression (and it is only that) is that the nineteenth-century rate of return on investment in an MA, and perhaps even in an MB, was not usually very high, and was not necessarily much increased by going to work abroad.

One small index of the return to the regional economy from gradu-ate migration may be found in the endowment of university bursaries. Alumni working in the reformed Indian services, it seems, could not afford to be as generous as their eighteenth-century predecessors. At least four alumni in the services of the East India Company had endowed bursaries in one of the colleges: George Smith in 1789; John Mather in 1807; John Milne in 1808; and Sir John Macpherson in 1817. Other such endowments included one from Alexander Moir of St Croix in 1769 and one from the Reverend James Stuart of South Carolina in 1809. But, apart from a small endowment by James Henry, a minister in New Zealand, the only post-1860 graduate to establish bursaries seems to have been Sir James Sivewright, a somewhat disre-putable associate of Cecil Rhodes. In the new empire of the late nine-teenth century, South Africa was most likely to foster a new generation of free-spending nabobs.[7]

Another clue to the scale of remittances might be found by counting how many of the substantial Victorian houses in and around Aberdeen were built or restored by retired members of the Indian services. Lt-Col. A. F. Milne of the Indian Medical Service (MB 1991), for example, bought and refurbished the house of Morkeu, at Cults. But striking examples do not come readily to mind. Senior imperial servants and military officers seem to have preferred to retire to warmer climates or more prestigious addresses in the south. Junior officials, or missionary clergy, rarely had much material reward to re-invest, and most of them would not have thought of evaluating their education in financial terms at all. Nevertheless, this may be one way in which returning graduates added material as well as cultural value to the Aberdeen economy.

Many graduates of course went overseas to start a new life, and pre-ferred to re-invest the value which education had added to their native talents in their new homes. Patrick Murdoch, son of a Free Church Minister from Pitsligo, was clearly seeking a new beginning when in

1884 he migrated to Melbourne at the age of 24. In rapid succession he became minister of a fashionable congregation, (where the young R. G. Menzies later sat at his feet), moderator of the Free Church in Victoria, and in 1905 moderator of the Australian General Assembly. As in many other cases, Patrick Murdoch's new family resources were not returned to Scotland but re-invested in Australia, where eventually they secured spectacular returns. Patrick's son Keith, having made his journalistic reputation as a reporter with the Anzac forces at Gallipoli, went on to found the most spectacular newspaper and communications dynasty of our time.[8]

In fact, it was men who had gone abroad without the benefits of extended education who returned most wealth to the north-east. The two most striking examples, George Stephen and Donald Smith (first Baron Strathcona), were products, respectively, of the parish school of Mortlach and of Anderson's Institution, Forres. The great American tycoon George 'Chicago' Smith (1806–99) had studied medicine at Marischal, but it is doubtful how far what he learned there contributed to the fortune of five million pounds which, assisted by his associate Alexander Mitchell from Ellon (1817–87), he accumulated by speculating in real estate, banking and insurance during the scramble to develop the American Mid-West. Chicago Smith made donations to the extension of Marischal College, as well as to education in his home parish of Old Deer. But his main claim to recognition in Aberdeen rests not on philanthropy but on the capital which he was able to provide for the manifold enterprises of his cousin, Sir Alexander Anderson.[9]

To return to our graduates: only a few pursued successful business careers during the nineteenth-century expansion of the empire. There are exceptions: J. G. Macgowan (MA 1866) seems to have been one of the first university men to enter the petroleum industry. But we must remember that only just over half the students in a typical mid-century arts class would actually proceed to graduation; as far as wealth creation is concerned those who did not do so are probably more significant than those who did. Some of those who went abroad after attending a few Arts classes, whom in *Academe and Empire* I called 'educated adventurers', had very interesting business careers. G. S. Yuill, a minister's son from Peterhead, an alumnus in 1864–66, went to China in the service of the Orient shipping line, became its Australian manager, and later founded his own business with branches in the main Australian cities. Unlike the Murdoch family, Yuill retained his attachment to Aberdeen, and in 1914 founded a scholarship to en-

courage the practical application of chemistry to industrial purposes. The Dey scholarships for educational research were also supported in part by John Dey (MA 1864), a former minister who invented and developed a time register in Syracuse, New York. Perhaps successful entrepreneurs were disposed to support post-graduate study directed towards the application of knowledge rather than student bursaries?

Many nineteenth-century professors and students shared this concern that education should have practical applications; others were disdainful of the idea that the university should accept responsibility beyond the traditional learned professions and services. When, in 1883, the university senate invited public support for a programme of developments, which included a chair of engineering, *Alma Mater* loftily declared 'We are not a Science College nor a Mechanics Institute.' Instead the student journal gave priority to a chair of history – 'Ancient if possible, if not Modern' – so that Aberdeen students should not be disadvantaged in the Civil Service examinations.[10] So it was that when in 1890 Robert Williams, whose application of practical engineering skills in the Transvaal goldmines had already made him one of the new nabobs, wanted to improve his scientific understanding of metallurgy, he had to go to Anderson's Institution in Glasgow.[11]

Nevertheless, the mathematical and philosophical education provided by the MA degree did provide some basis for successful engineering careers abroad, as no fewer than four members of the class of 1866–70 found. John Benton, who entered the Indian Public Works Department through its own college at Cooper's Hill, was later knighted for important achievements as inspector-general of irrigation. Andrew Jamieson had taken the class in natural philosophy before serving an apprenticeship with Hall Russell. As chief electrician to the Eastern Telegraph Company he was in charge of British naval communications during the Near Eastern crisis of 1877–78, and later became professor of electrical engineering at Glasgow Technical College. David Simpson became a railway engineer in Sydney, and James Stewart, a marine engineer. So, indirectly and against the instincts of traditionalists, the university did begin to contribute to technological development abroad and at home, and so to growth in the regional economy.

In another field of importance to imperial development, that of tropical agriculture, the university gradually took initiatives of its own. Few of the men from Aberdeenshire and Kincardine who established coffee plantations in Ceylon during the early nineteenth century had much university education, and, as Tom Barron has shown, they were

'conspicuously lacking in any kind of agricultural scientific expertise.'[12] But from mid-century some planters began to take the MA degree, or at least the courses in natural history and chemistry. Robert Boyd Tytler from Peterhead worked with Professor J. S. Brazier to develop and market a chemical fertilizer known as sombreorum. It did them little good. Science had no answer to the coffee-leaf disease which devastated Ceylon's plantations in the 1870s, still less to the competition on the world market offered by the virgin plantations of Brazil. After the foundation of the chair of agriculture in 1895 graduates and diplomates in agriculture did begin to go out to tea and rubber plantations in Ceylon, Malaysia and Indonesia; but now it was as managers for large capitalist companies, rather than as independent planters. Agrarian scientists were more likely to find overseas careers in multinational than in individual or family enterprise.

These examples, of engineering and agriculture, suggest that intellectual skills encouraged by the traditional Scottish Arts syllabus could add value to the services provided by those who went to seek their fortunes in the late-Victorian empire. How deeply such an evaluation should affect our view of university history is another matter. Most university teachers, then as later, would have regarded quality rather than productivity as the proper measure of value for their work. They might not have agreed on the proper definition of that quality, on the relative importance of transmitting a cultural inheritance and extending it by original research, but few would have seen any direct attempt to measure the economic return on investment in higher education as appropriate. If such an attempt were to be made, I suggest that any financial value added to the regional economy by Aberdeen University's involvement in the expanding empire would probably prove rather modest.

Does this tentative survey of Aberdeen's contribution to the export of education tell us anything of wider interest to historians of the modern empire, and of Scotland's place in it? In *Academe and Empire*, my conclusions about Aberdeen University's overseas connections are discussed in relationship to the important study of British imperialism recently published by P. J. Cain and A. G. Hopkins.[13] These authors identify the forces governing British imperial policy by the name of 'gentlemanly capitalism' – an alliance forged over three centuries between the landed wealth of old aristocratic families and the new financial power concentrated in the City of London. Communities in the provinces which lived by trade and manufacture certainly drew

many benefits from the expanding empire, but when policy makers had to arbitrate between the claims of finance and industry, Cain and Hopkins argue, it was the City which won out.

Their thesis will no doubt be fiercely debated. It may not, for example, do justice to the continuing strength of Edinburgh as a financial as well as a cultural capital. It is not, though it may sound like it, a simple thesis of English hegemony. Scots, Welshmen and people from the English provinces were not left out, they were continually being incorporated into the upper circles of gentlemanly capitalism. But to participate fully they had to establish a position in the metropolis – by acquiring an office in the City and a main residence in the Home Counties, and by sending their children to English-model public schools and then to Oxford or Cambridge.

As a consequence, Aberdeen University, which in the nineteenth century prided itself on educating worthy members of the heaven-born elite of the Indian Civil Service, in the twentieth became increasingly concerned with the lesser role of training for the specialised colonial services. As Cain and Hopkins might have put it, they were providing foresters, chaplains, tutors, factors, to serve the overseas households and estates of gentlemanly capitalism. During the first half of this century, over forty per cent of students in the university forestry department and in NOSCA (the North of Scotland College of Agriculture) – both of which were founded with an eye to special needs of the regional economy – went to work overseas. More consciously than before, universities and colleges were preparing men and women for careers which would improve the value of the colonial empire, both qualitatively and economically. It may be added that, since political decolonisation, this role has been extended in many directions, all related to some definition or other of the concept of international development.

How have these changes in the overseas orientation of our colleges and universities affected the regional economy? Much attention has in recent decades been consciously directed towards increasing the earning power of local alumni who work overseas. We must assume, therefore, that they are perceived to have at least the capacity to reinvest more of the product of their skills in Aberdeen. As far as overseas students are concerned, there is no doubt that, as a result of government policies imposed on reluctant universities during the last quarter century (particularly the huge rises since the mid-1970s in overseas students' fees), they do now make a greatly increased contribution to

the local, as well as the national, economy.[14] It is to be hoped that they – and those in much poorer countries who sponsor their education – feel that they are getting value for money.

NOTES

1. John D. Hargreaves, *Academe and Empire. Some Overseas Connections of Aberdeen University, 1860–1970* (Aberdeen, 1994). Evidence for statements not supported by specific references may be found in this volume.

2. Alexander G. Kemp and Sandra Galbraith, 'Contributions to the regional economy: expenditure and employment aspects', in J. D. Hargreaves and Angela Forbes (eds), *Aberdeen University 1945–1981: Regional Roles and National Needs* (Aberdeen, 1989), pp. 19–46.

3. Carolyn Pennington, *The Modernisation of Medical Teaching at Aberdeen in the Nineteenth Century* (Aberdeen, 1994).

4. Of 220 persons shown in *University Calendars* as graduating MB ChB during the sample years 1882–85, 29 gave addresses overseas or in the Services, 41 in England, Wales or Ireland, and 7 in Scotland south of Montrose. For the 92 MDs of the period, the respective figures were 17, 47 and 3; but this degree did not require residence.

5. *Aberdeen Free Press*, 9 December 1870.

6. Isabella Fyvie Mayo, *Recollections* (London, 1910). I am grateful to Brenda Cluer for drawing my attention to the work of Professor James D. Hunt of Shaw University, North Carolina, on Mrs Mayo.

7. I am grateful to Pat Booker for showing me the result of his valuable unpublished research on the university bursaries.

8. William Shawcross, *Rupert Murdoch: Ringmaster of the Information Circus* (London, 1992), pp. 20ff.

9. *Dictionary of American Biography*, s.v. Mitchell, Smith. Alexander Keith, *Eminent Aberdonians* (Aberdeen, 1984), 'Sir Alexander Anderson', pp. 1–4; 'The fabulous Chicago Smith', pp. 22–24.

10. *Aberdeen University Magazine (Alma Mater)*, vol. 1, 1883–84, pp. 255–56; *University Calendar, 1883*, pp. 187–91.

11. John D. Hargreaves, *Aberdeenshire to Africa* (Aberdeen, 1981), p. 42.

12. T. J. Barron, 'Science and the nineteenth-century coffee planters', *Journal of Imperial and Commonwealth History*, vol. 16 (1987), pp. 5–23.

13. P. J. Cain and A. G. Hopkins, *British Imperialism* (London, 2 vols, 1993).

14. John D. Hargreaves, 'African students in Britain: the case of Aberdeen University', in D. Killingray (ed.), *Africans in Britain* (Ilford, 1994), pp. 129–44.

PART II:

ISSUES IN SOCIAL, POLITICAL AND CULTURAL HISTORY

NEW PUBLICATIONS.

A. BROWN & CO.

RESPECTFULLY announce, that the following esteemed WORKS have been recently published, and may be had of them :—

Davy's Elements of Agricultural Chemistry, new edit. 16s.
Hayne' Tracts on India, maps and plates, 42s.
Stewart's History of Bengal, 65s.
Kerr Porter's Account of the Campaign in Russia, 16s.
Pitscottie's Chronicles of Scotland, 2 vols. 21s.
Duncan's Essay on Genius, 8vo. 7s. 6d.
Bioscope, or Dial of Life Explained, by Mr Penn, 12s.
Aikin's Manual of Mineralogy.
Sinclair's (Sir John) Account of the Husbandry of Scotland, 2 vols.
Vattell's Law of Nations, 18s.
Lord Byron's Poetical Works, 2 vols.
Walter Scott's Poetical Works, 4 vols.
Campbell's Poetical Works, 2 vols.
Orphans, or the Battle of Nevil's Cross, a Metrical Romance, 7s. 6d.
Waverly, or " 'Tis Sixty Years Since," 3 vols. 21s.
Ellis' Specimens of the Early English Poets, 3 vols. 31s. 6d.
Wanderer, or Female Difficulties, 5 vols. 42s.
Patronage, by Miss Edgeworth, 4 vols. 28s.
Queen's Wake, a Poem, by J. Hogg, 7s.
Anster-Fair, a Poem, by William Tennant, 7s. 6d.
Aphorisms, from Shakespeare, 7s.
Allison's Sermons, 12s.
Dean Kirwan's Sermons, 12s.
Poems, by Margaret Chalmers of Lerwick, Zetland, 8vo. 7s.
        As above may be had,
The NEW PUBLICATIONS, as they issue from the press, with WRITING PAPERS and STATIONARY of the best quality.
⁂ ACCOUNT BOOKS ruled and bound to any pattern, on the shortest notice.
☞ BOOKS BOUND in a very superior manner—specimens to be seen at the shop.
        Aberdeen, 2d August, 1814.

TENTH REPORT.

THE TENTH REPORT of the BRITISH and FOREIGN BIBLE SOCIETY is arrived at Baillie Brown's, and is ready for delivery to Subscribers, gratis.

AT a Meeting of the Presbytery of Fordyce, held at Portsoy, on the 28th day of April, 1813,—

THE Presbytery, in pursuance of a Resolution entered into at their last Meeting, took into consideration the expediency of addressing the Commissioners of Supply of the County of Banff, with regard to the PREVENTION of VAGRANT BEGGING, which has become so great a burden upon this part of the country, and is so injurious to good morals and to industry; when they unanimously came to the following Resolutions, viz.:
    RESOLVED,

HUSBANDRY OF SCOTLAND.

This day is published,
Sold by A. Brown & Co. Angus & Son, George Clark, and A. Stevenson, Aberdeen ; J. & G. Imlach, Banff ; Isaac Ford, Elgin ; and Clark & Co. Peterhead,
In two volumes octavo, with numerous Engravings,
Price 1l. 10s. boards,
The second edition, greatly enlarged,

AN ACCOUNT OF THE SYSTEM OF HUSBANDRY

ADOPTED IN THE MORE IMPROVED DISTRICTS OF SCOTLAND ; with some Observations on the Improvements of which they susceptible.

Drawn up for the consideration of the Board of Agricul with a view of explaining how far these systems are appli to the less cultivated parts in England and Scotland.
BY
The right honourable Sir JOHN SINCLAIR, Bart. P dent of the Board of Agriculture.

Printed for ARCHIBALD CONSTABLE and Co. Edinburgh; L MAN, HURST, REES, ORME, and BROWN, London; and CUMMING, Dublin.
☞ This is the most comprehensive practical work on culture ever published.

NEW COURT HOUSE AND JAIL ACT.

THE FIRST MEETING of the COMMISSION named by this Act, entituled, " *An Act for erecting* " *maintaining a New Court House and other Offices for th* " *and County of Aberdeen, and for providing and maintaini* " *additional Gaol for the said City and County, and for* " *purposes relating thereto,*" is to be held within the Laigh booth of Aberdeen, on Thursday the 4th day of August ne 12 o'clock noon, for the purpose of proceeding in the execut the Act. The Commissioners are the same as those named the Bridewell Act. This notice is given by the Clerk to the missioners of Supply of Aberdeenshire, as directed by th New Court House and Jail Act.
            THO. BURNETT, C
Aberdeen, 19th July 1814.

TO BE SOLD,
A Fashionable London-built SPORTING GIG, with of HARNESS, Brass mounted, and in good order.
To be seen at the New Coach Work, Queen-street.
Queen-street, Aberdeen, 19th July.

OAK BARK FOR SALE.

There will be sold, upon Friday the 12th of August er SCROGIEMILL, near Elgin,
ABOUT Ten Tons of excellent BARK, taken off the this season. For particulars, apply to Mr Lawson mills.
Credit to be given ; and the sale will begin at 12 o'clo

CONTRACTORS WANTED.

Figure 1. New publications for sale by A. Brown & Co. advertised in the Aberdeen Journal, 3 August 1814.

[94]

6

'All New Works of Interest Received on Publication': Aberdeen and Its Access to the Printed Word, 1800–1850

Iain Beavan

'All *new works of interest* received on publication' was a slogan (with variations) commonly used in local booksellers' advertisements. In so far as it raises the questions 'of interest to whom?' and 'received how and by whom?' it provides a convenient entry point for a survey of some aspects of the supply and availability of the printed word in Aberdeen.

In August 1819 Robert Southey visited Aberdeen, where he paid homage at the last resting places of James Beattie and his sons, bought a couple of second-hand books, and made the acquaintance of Alexander Brown, whom Southey subsequently described as the 'chief bookseller in the place'.[1]

Brown had been in business on his own account for thirty years, had made a speciality of book-auctions, ran the Stamp Office, and had built up the largest circulating library in Aberdeen. Brown also had the eminent good sense to marry well – and in 1795 became the son-in-law to James Chalmers (1742–1810), who was very much the town's printer and proprietor of the *Aberdeen Journal*.

By 1805 Brown had two premises: a bookshop and stationer's business in Broad Street,[2] and a circulating library with a reading room in the Castlegate opposite the old Town House.[3] The bookshop, seem-

ingly very impressive, with its external Corinthian pillars and its interior decorated with prints of Henry Dundas and the Tory leaders, became the 'showiest shop in town' and a 'fitting temple of literature'.[4] It would, however, be wrong to assume that Brown's shop was a quiet, solemn place. There is plenty of evidence (from Aberdeen and beyond) to indicate that bookshops served a useful social function. At the time, and long enough after, they were the meeting places of the local gossips and 'literary loungers' whose presence sometimes interfered with business.[5]

The Athenaeum Reading Room (subscription, a guinea and a half yearly) was established to supply 'the multifarious Productions of the Periodical Press, [so that] the man of much and the man of little Leisure, has an inexhaustible Source of Amusement and Information at all Times accessible to him'.[6] The prospectus suggests that information was uppermost in the proprietor's mind. Newspapers from London, Edinburgh, Glasgow, Dundee, Liverpool and Hull were subscribed to, as were various shipping lists. Commercial and shipping interests were further catered for by a large selection of nautical maps and pilotage charts (mostly northern European and Mediterranean). And for those concerned with the conduct of the Continental Wars, army and navy lists were available. The more reflective reader was not ignored however, and was supplied with a good range of periodicals and magazines. These included the *Monthly Review*, the *Anti-Jacobin Review*, the *Gentleman's Magazine*, the *Edinburgh Magazine* and *Edinburgh Review*, and Cobbett's *Weekly Register*, though presumably only before its politics became too radical. In short, the reading room reflected the preoccupations of the time. At this time, the majority of printed books were transported to Aberdeen by coastal shipping. But in order to get the latest news to Aberdeen as quickly as possible, Brown arranged for the reading room's magazines and newspapers to be brought up by mail coach. Glasgow and Edinburgh papers were available for consultation two days after publication, though Cobbett's *Register*, published in London on a Saturday was not available until the following Wednesday.

Those who wished for a wider range of reading matter could have joined Brown and Burnett's Public Library, a commercially run subscription library, then the only one of any size in Aberdeen, at a top rate of one guinea a year if the reader wanted first pick of the new arrivals on the shelves. And what was the lending stock like? Brown and Burnett seem to have struck the right balance for educated and

literary tastes in Aberdeen, with broadly a third of the stock given over to novels, the rest non-fiction.[7] James Johnston, on the other hand, got it completely wrong, when he tried in 1821 to set up a circulating library given over exclusively to books on religious and moral themes. The project was abandoned through lack of support, and he had to approach Alexander Brown & Co. to auction off his lending stock. [8]

Brown succeeded both commercially and in civic terms, and twice became a Tory provost of Aberdeen in the 1820s. Statistics suggest others fared less well. It was a tempting business for many, but more than half the firms that started in the early or middle decades of the nineteenth century in Aberdeen lasted less than four years. Indeed, over one third had disappeared in two. [9]

The local bookshops of course did not supply the totality of reading material: some of it was directly encountered on the street. Broadsheets (topicality was often the secret of their success) were quickly run off by local printers, and were sold by hawkers and other street sellers, at prices from 1d. upwards. They ranged from satirical poems to details of murders, confessions and executions, representing one form of popular publication, available for sale at very modest prices on the street, bought in large numbers, and by a wide range of readers, including many who would not have had the income or the inclination to enter a bookseller's shop. [10]

The town's insolvency, announced in early 1817[11] (the situation exacerbated, according to the council's detractors, by a total lack of public accountability), the subsequent expressions of regret that emanated from the council chambers, and the discomfiture attendant upon new council elections in September that year presented the local printers with a golden opportunity and numbers of song sheets found their way onto the streets. John Booth, printer of the *Aberdeen Chronicle*, enjoyed himself at the council's expense with his *Last Speech of the Town's Officers* (1817 or 1818) issued with a headpiece of death's head, crossed bones and hourglass put to grimly humorous use.

In 1818 there was much public sympathy for James Ritchie, who was executed in Aberdeen for sheep-stealing. There was a widespread feeling that Ritchie was the least deserving culprit to be made an example of, and the event was recognised by the printing of his *Last Speech, Confession, and Dying Declaration*. The broadsheet[12] noted the various petitions for clemency but adopted a tone of resignation at the irreversibility of the sentence, and recorded Ritchie's penitential statement. The local printing of broadsheets evidently went on throughout

[97]

much of the century, though very few have survived. In the 1840s Blin'
Bob (Duncan Mackinlay) used to make a quick profit by selling lists of
those present at the Aberdeen races – but with the initials of men and
women attending placed in intentionally provocative juxtaposition.
Sales seemingly went well until the printed stock was seized. [13]

And what of these hawkers? Other interests tried to exploit them.
The Aberdeen Religious Tract Society aimed to distribute (usually
without charge) the tracts of the London, Edinburgh and Glasgow
Tract Societies and to do it through the very hawkers who had hitherto
been selling broadsheets and similar publications. Shortly after 1811,
the local society proclaimed that it had supplied the tracts among the
lower classes of Aberdeen society, to the prison and infirmary, to the
soldiers and sailors based in Aberdeen, and as far north as Shetland.
How welcome the tracts were, must remain open to question, though
there can be little doubt that, for many, they were the most commonly
encountered form of printed word. In 1825 John Ferres joked that the
evangelicals even resorted to throwing tracts out of the windows of the
Aberdeen – Ballater stage coach. [14]

The statistics need to be viewed cautiously, but it is claimed that the
Aberdeen Tract Society distributed nearly 480,000 tracts in the ten
years after the society's foundation, which, if only halfway true, is still a
prodigious number. Moreover, by 1822 there were no fewer than
twenty-two organisations in Aberdeen given over to the 'general
diffusion of religious knowledge'. [15]

The more radical political press also appeared in Aberdeen.
Certainly in the 1790s Alexander Brown had been prepared to sell editions of Tom Paine (along with works critical of that author); on the
mood amongst some sections of the working classes in Aberdeen after
1815, William Walker has commented:

> A wave of political excitement passed over the country shortly
> after the peace settlement that followed Waterloo, and was felt
> with particular keenness in the great centres of manufacture.
> Loud and clamorous rose the cry for reform on every hand.
> Newspapers were costly in those days but workshops clubbed
> together for them. *Cobbett's Register* was a special favourite, and
> on Saturday afternoons its arrival was the signal for 'calling a
> bar' to hear the news of the week, and discuss whatever items
> called for special attention.

And beyond William Cobbett's *Political Register* we know that dedi-

cated agencies were set up for the distribution into Aberdeen of other London-produced radical periodicals, the *Republican*, and the *Black Dwarf*.[16] The established book trade would not touch them, for fear of obloquy or of prosecution.[17]

Until the late 1820s, book prices were high, and crossing a bookseller's threshold could prove an expensive business. Some books were published in parts, though even then they were not cheap, and even the least expensive reprints were likely to cost 6d or more.[18]

But assuming that disposable income was available, how would a reader find out what was available? The answer lay in the advertisement columns of the *Aberdeen Journal* or in the review columns of the monthly magazines. Alexander Brown's advertisement in August 1814 is typical, with an appeal to the learned and fashionable with a mix of novels, poetry, history and scientific works. Amongst the newly published novels appeared Maria Edgeworth's *Patronage*, and Burney's five-volume *The Wanderer; or Female Difficulties*, and poetical works included Byron, Tennant's *Anster Fair* and Hogg's *The Queen's Wake*. Scott appeared twice, with a two–volume set of his *Poetical Works*, and the first edition of *Waverley*. The cheapest book on the list cost 7s.

The local booksellers would not have wanted to supply all new publications. Best estimates suggest that by the end of the 1820s in excess of 5,000 books were being published in Britain each year.[19] Many of these were not relevant to the market for reading matter as judged by the local booksellers, who took into stock only works that they thought would sell, and were prepared to act as wholesale agents for titles that they thought would sell well. What was not in stock had to be ordered via the booksellers' agents in Edinburgh and London.[20] Unfortunately, the consequence of the booksellers' offers quickly to order material not immediately available was the occasional remark bearing on the cautious nature of their stock.[21]

The early 1830s mark the starting point of some new initiatives in the local book and periodical trade, with the appearance of the first mass market periodicals, and with them the rise of the specialist wholesale book and periodical seller. In 1832, two weekly publications, the *Penny Magazine*, and *Chambers's Edinburgh Journal* priced at 1½d. arrived at the local bookstalls and made an initial, though not lasting, impression. It should also be said that with one exception (Lewis Smith) the Aberdeen booksellers were initially slow to appreciate the business potential represented by these magazines, the immediate popularity of which may well have caught them by surprise.[22] William

Lindsay, later publisher of the Aberdeen edition of the *People's Journal*, commented on the popularity of *Chambers's Journal* and 'the great crowds that gathered at his [i.e. William Laurie, the bookseller's] door and compelled him to stand outside his counter and hand the journals out at the door with one hand, and take the price with the other'.[23] *Chambers's Journal* itself suggested that Aberdeen was taking in nearly 1700 copies a week, at least initially – nearly as big a circulation as the *Aberdeen Journal*.[24] Lewis Smith acted quickly and became the regional wholesale agent for both *Chambers's Journal* and the *Penny Magazine*, the popularity of which encouraged him, in particular, to seek out sales – not just to county bookshops – but also to general country merchants and stores. These sales trips stretched from Dundee to Cromarty.

The publishers of both journals had similar aims. According to Brougham, who was chairman of the Society for the Diffusion of Useful Knowledge (responsible for the *Penny Magazine*), its purpose was to impart 'useful information to all classes of the community, particularly to such as are unable to avail themselves of experienced teachers',[25] and went on to observe, 'Many of the poor are anxious for books of useful learning, but they cannot afford to buy them.'[26]

But the *Penny Magazine* finally failed late in 1845. At the time, and subsequently, it was accused of dullness (no fiction), irrelevance and abstruseness, and of prolonging political ignorance amongst its readership.[27] Moreover, it could be claimed that both magazines appealed to the already converted. Contemporary commentators noted that the magazines were selling to what they called the elite of the labouring community.[28] The *Penny Magazine* in particular failed to sustain the mass readership it hoped to create. The local Mechanics' Institute (part of a nationwide movement set up to provide adult education facilities for the working man and woman) was manifesting similar symptoms. Andrew Ramsay, who contributed to the *Aberdeen Working Men's Prize Essays*, reported that 'well-fed merchants, nimble clerks, sprightly boys' were using the institute, its library and reading rooms, 'but not the tired artisan after the labours of the day'.[29]

So how was this 'tired artisan' to be catered for? 'A city like Aberdeen', Ramsay felt, 'should have five or six reading-rooms on a large scale for the Working Classes. . . . A gratis reading-room might be tried in the most populous and crowded part of the town. . . . Money from the town's funds would be well spent on such an object.' However, it was not until the 1880s that these ideas saw some sort of reality in the adoption of the Free Public Libraries Act in Aberdeen.

The 1830s and early 1840s kept the local printers busy. The output of the local press in the 1830s was almost double that of the previous decade, and this increased activity was sustained into the 1840s.[30] It was also very much the period of the local periodical and newspaper, with about 45 titles launched between 1830 and 1845. They range from the stillborn *Aberdeen Universities' Magazine* (1838) and the short-lived *Aberdeen Patriot* (1839) to *The Banner* newspaper (1840–1851), which was founded to promulgate non-intrusion principles in the Church in Scotland, and which made a substantial contribution to this debate. The reformist *Aberdeen Herald* (1832–76, successor to the *Aberdeen Chronicle*), which provided stiff competition for the *Journal*, disagreed strongly with *The Banner* over its stance on the main ecclesiastical questions of the day. Tory interests were represented by the 'Tool of the Rotten System',[31] the *Aberdeen Observer* (1829–37), succeeded by the *Aberdeen Constitutional* (1837–44). The attempt of the *Constitutional* to achieve 'a better tone of thinking and feeling among the people' earned for it a weekly circulation of 900 copies. The circulation of the *Journal* at the time was about 2400 copies, the *Herald*, 1300. But at least the *Constitutional* was aware of the need to supply Aberdeen with the most up-to-date news by changing its day of publication to accommodate the altered time of arrival of the northbound mails.

Aberdeen also saw the appearance of a family of satirical and scurrilous magazines. The *Aberdeen Shaver*, monthly at 2d. (previously the *Aberdeen Pirate*, then the *Aberdeen Mirror*, both weekly at 1d., 1832) – the name and format were changed from weekly to monthly to avoid paying the newspaper tax – was a strong supporter of the Reform Bill and, by the very nature of its existence, an advocate of cheap instructional and political literature. Primarily, however, it covered local civic, political and administrative developments, with frequent comment on working conditions. Early in its existence, it claimed for itself a circulation of 1000 copies, 'more than double the town circulation of any of our newspapers'.[32] It thrived on controversy, and picked an argument with just about every other local newspaper, taking particular delight at any casualties. It danced with joy in February 1839 at the early mortality (cause of death, 'public contempt') of the *Aberdeen Patriot*, local organ of the Chartist cause.

The *Shaver* also set itself up as local moral censor. In September 1836 it was unhappy with activities in Carmelite Lane. 'We have got notice', said the *Shaver*, 'of a scandalous practice carried on by several married women in a house in Carmelite Lane. We bid them beware, as

Figure 2. The Aberdeen Shaver, *October 1837.*

we will make a call some of these dark evenings, and report.' This general stance was the Shaver's ultimate undoing, and in putting names to accusations, the proprietors faced and lost a number of libel trials, and went out of business in 1839. *The Quizzing Glass* summed up a body of opinion when it called the *Shaver's* printing house at 5, Long Acre, 'a scandal manufactory', and a 'charnal house from which was vomited forth nothing but impurity'. [33]

We do, however, have to be thankful to the *Shaver* for its paragraph on 'Anti-Cheap Knowledge' in which it exposed the Aberdeen Booksellers' Society, a highly effective cartel, formed in late 1829 on the instigation of Lewis Smith and James Lumsden (1778–1856), the latter a major Glasgow stationer and publisher. [34] The society was supported by all the local established booksellers as a means of protecting their interests by controlling retail underselling.

The *Shaver* and its predecessors also did a great deal of good. In

September 1832 the *Pirate* carried a piece advising the local population to beware of profiteering quack doctors descending on the city with their ineffective 'Cholera Medicines'. In October 1838 the *Shaver* castigated the local medical profession for drawing salaries for their presence at the Aberdeen General Dispensary but actually sending only their 'young blockheads of apprentices' to attend the patients.

Increasing political expression, the excitement of Reform Act elections, and the interrelated legal, constitutional and theological crises that led to the formation of the Free Church of Scotland were all issues that provoked the production of local pamphlets. Many of the local printers and booksellers, who would previously have been nervous about publishing such material, responded to the demand for its availability.[35] Not that any of these controversial pamphlets could in any way be called commercial speculations. They were not written for profit, but rather they served as vehicles by which developing and strongly felt feelings could be publicly and quickly expressed.

There were some splendidly vitriolic pamphlet wars, outstanding among them the series of letters attacking either of the two parliamentary candidates standing for Aberdeen under the 1832 Reform Act. The letters critical of Alexander Bannerman (reformist candidate, and subsequently elected unopposed) entitled *Mr Hadden Vindicated*, all written by a 'lover of facts', were counterbalanced by three open letters by a 'prospective elector' headed *Provost Hadden and His Friends Called to Account*, and the production of the whole set, for and against, was arranged by the same bookseller and publisher, Lewis Smith, who was kept busy, as at least three sets (for and against) were prepared in one month (July) that year (see figures 3 and 4 overleaf).

The debates were not limited to local pamphlets. The newspapers contributed, sometimes at a very personal level. The *Scots Champion and Aberdeen Free Press*, in its first and only issue, took aim at Joseph Robertson, whom it called 'the Provost's Prime Minister . . . a rank Tory . . . [who] has a mechanical facility in stringing sentences together, with little or no meaning. . . . He is allowed by all to be the author of the political letters published under the signature "A LOVER OF FACTS" in which . . . he manifestly betrays he has the false side of the question.' The *Scots Champion* had not finished, for in the same issue it recorded the then approaching demise of the *Aberdeen Magazine*. The magazine, a general miscellany published by Lewis Smith, had been under attack from various quarters. It was variously criticised as too radical, too Tory, or just inconsistent in its approach.

LETTERS

TO

ALEXANDER BANNERMAN, Esq.

By A LOVER OF FACTS.

" In this point charge him home, that he affects
Tyrannical power : If he evade us there
Tell that the spoil got on the Antiates
Was ne'er distributed."

" I pray you, who is he ?
" Why, he is the ' town's' jester,—a very dull fool : only his gift is in
devising impossible slanders."   SHAKSPEARE.

EPISTLE I.—PREFATORY.

MR. HADDEN VINDICATED.

ABERDEEN :

PRINTED FOR THE AUTHOR,

SOLD BY LEWIS SMITH, 66, BROAD STREET,

AND THE OTHER BOOKSELLERS.

1832.

PRICE THREEPENCE.

Figure 3. Mr. Hadden Vindicated, printed July 1832.

Smith himself had cause for complaint, for he had not been served well by the local printers. The printing of Smith's first major piece of periodical publishing, the *Aberdeen Censor*, (1825-26) had been turned away by John Booth of the *Aberdeen Chronicle* in spite of that paper's radical reputation and Smith's second attempt, the relatively more staid *Northern Iris* (1826), was rejected by David Chalmers of the *Aberdeen Journal*, both being rejected because of the 'bondage of the Aberdeen press' and the printers' fear of 'offending somebody who might be made the subject of criticism'. By the time of the *Aberdeen Magazine*, 1s. monthly (1831-32), commercial pressures and the press-

[**Fourth Edition.**]

PROVOST HADDEN AND HIS FRIENDS
CALLED TO ACCOUNT:

A LETTER

TO

THE ELECTORS

OF THE

CITY OF ABERDEEN.

BY

A PROSPECTIVE ELECTOR.

" How piteous then that there should be such dearth
Of knowledge: and that many should unite
To work against themselves such fell despite;
Should come in phrenzy and in drunken mirth,
Impatient to put out the brightest light
Of Liberty that yet remains amongst us."

" When looking on the present face of things
I see one MAN, of men the meanest too!
Raised up to sway the City—to do, to undo,
With men of character for his underlings,
The great events with which old story rings
Seem vain and hollow; I find nothing great,
Nothing is left which I can venerate:

* * * such emptiness at length
Seems at the heart of all men."
Altered from WORDSWORTH.

ABERDEEN:
Printed for the Author;
SOLD BY LEWIS SMITH, 66, BROAD STREET,
AND THE OTHER BOOKSELLERS.

MDCCCXXXII.

Price Twopence.

Figure 4. Provost Hadden and His Friends Called to Account, printed July 1832.

ing demand for political expression were such that Smith felt that 'any of the printers would now execute any work that may be offered to them . . . because they know that if they will not, others will.' With time came acceptance and success. Shunned at first as the producer of provocative and 'ultra radical' material, and regarded warily as the publisher for 'Young Aberdeen', Smith subsequently prospered, and by the time of his death in 1880 he had served on the town council for eighteen years, having filled a number of offices, including city

treasurer. It is said that he was even offered the provostship itself.

Events demonstrate that Lewis Smith's shop in Broad Street, near Marischal College Gate, had been the gathering ground for budding talent. Smith himself, in later life, was justifiably proud of his publishing efforts and of the friendships he had made. The Rev. J. B. Pratt's book, *The Life and Death of Jamie Fleeman*, of which over 100,000 copies were produced, started existence as an article in the *Aberdeen Magazine*. John Hill Burton, later to become an eminent historian, and John Ogilvie, later editor, lexicographer and teacher, first wrote for Lewis Smith. *The New Deeside Guide* by Joseph Robertson, pamphleteer, newspaper editor, historian and record scholar, was developed from an article in that same periodical and as a book had a publication life of over seventy years. Indeed this latter work, along with Robertson's famous *Book of Bon-Accord*, the anonymous *Guide to Donside* and *Smith's Pocket Guide to the City of Aberdeen* provided the basis of many advertisements for 'books for the summer season' or books for 'summer tourists'. [36]

By 1830 the character of much material in local booksellers' advertisements had markedly changed from that of fifteen years previously. The appeal was to cheapness, regularity and seriality, often further qualified, as with the periodicals of the time, with a notice of the works' contributions to 'useful knowledge'. There was a marked move to publishing books as parts of series or in parts – not in itself a new publishing ploy – but to do so primarily with newly and recently written texts. Brown's advertisement in late 1829 headed 'Periodical Works'[37] included *Constable's Miscellany*, a non-fiction book series, monthly, at 3s. 6d., monthly parts of the 7th edition of *Encyclopaedia Britannica*, the SDUK's *Library of Useful Knowledge* and Cadell's monthly 5s. issue of Scott's *Waverley Novels*. The arrival of these relatively cheap books marked the start of the lowering of prices, though the pattern was neither clear nor consistent. Prices often remained beyond the reach of many. It is hard to imagine many copies of the three–volume set of *The Highlands of Ethiopia*, 42s., selling other than to the circulating libraries in Aberdeen.[38] And a whole publishing economy was in place to maintain the production of novels in smart, three–volume editions primarily for these lending libraries. On the other hand, some publishers adopted the true periodical form for the publication of works of fiction, by issuing new novels in weekly or monthly parts. In 1846 subscribers were being sought by the booksellers, Alexander Brown & Co., for Dickens' *Dombey and Son*, to be published by Bradbury & Evans in twenty monthly parts, at 1s each.

And of reprints? In 1814 Walter Scott's newly published three–volume *Waverley* was advertised at a guinea. In 1841, the announcement went out that 'All canvassers and dealers who wish to interest themselves in the circulation of the Waverley Novels, as announced for weekly publication (the people's edition) within the circle of Aberdeen will be furnished with terms from Lewis Smith.'[39] Moreover, it is perhaps significant to note that the agency for this edition was entrusted by Cadell, the publisher, to the same person who was wholesale agent not only for the *Penny Magazine* and Chambers's publications, but also reprinted fiction serials as with the *Romancist and Novelists' Library*, and the *Novel Newspaper*. Walter Scott had come down market, to those who could manage 2d. for the weekly issue.

By the mid-1840s local booksellers' stock was reflecting middle-class Victorian values of respectability and domesticity. In 1845 G. and R. King took over the regional wholesale agency for the Edinburgh-published *Hogg's Weekly Instructor*, 1½d., a miscellany of essays, tales, biographical notices, topographical notes and book reviews, imbued with a strong religious tone. William Tait, in his advertisement for his publication of *The Edinburgh Tales*, weekly, 1½d., 'a series of stories and novelties', took care to emphasise that 'it is the aim and hope of the conductor to furnish literary amusement of a healthful and refined character'.[40] Such material on offer was far from being entirely Scottish-based: John Cassell's publications – the *Working Man's Friend*, the *Popular Educator* and his illustrated *Family Paper* – all had sales sufficiently high as to justify the setting up of wholesale agencies in Aberdeen. Even the 'trade' in Aberdeen attempted, in 1846, an illustrated *North of Scotland Family Journal*, produced explicitly for 'the domestic good or the benefit especially of families' (figure 5). It did not last long, and had faded by July of 1847. The 1840s and thereafter saw much activity on the part of the Scottish religious press in its various guises. *The Banner*, published in Aberdeen, had established itself as a leading advocate of Evangelical and, later, of Free Church principles. But Aberdonians could supplement their reading with the *Scottish Herald*, printed in Edinburgh and equally supportive of the Free Church. Copies could be ordered through Charles Panton in Broad Street, who seems to have specialised in the supply of religious papers for in 1851 he was appointed agent for the weekly anti-Catholic *Scottish Protestant*.

The population of Aberdeen was always well supplied with bookshops and by the 1850s had a greater number per head of population than did Glasgow or Dundee.[41] From seventeenth-century beginnings,

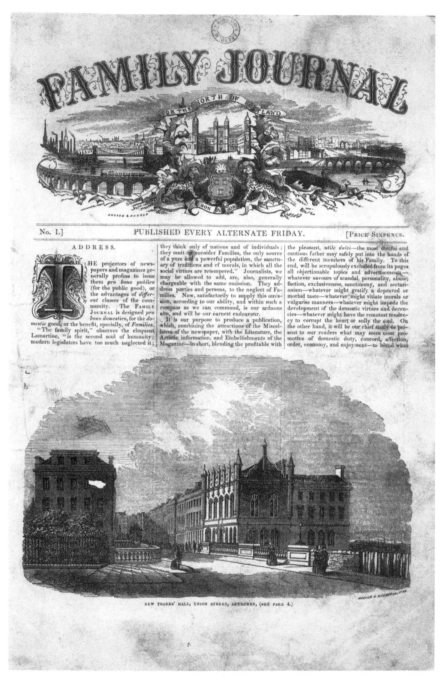

Figure 5. The North of Scotland Family Journal. *A revised reprint of the preliminary number, September 1846, published by Edward Ravenscroft, Aberdeen.*

there were, by 1750, five bookshops established in the city to supply both the town and county, and by 1801 some thirteen booksellers and four printers. And with the bookshops came lending libraries for various tastes and pockets, so that by the mid-nineteenth century the choice ranged from the three–guinea subscription library of David Wyllie (later to be in conjunction with Mudie's, the epitome of respectability), to the penny lending library and bookshop of James Vessie in the Gallowgate, who traded in penny dreadfuls, selling and lending numbers of *Paul the Poacher*, *Dick Turpin* and *Robin Hood*, which were frequently resold, second-hand, half-price, at ½d. Not that Vessie had the monopoly of the business: William Russel, and later George Middleton, lent and sold similar stock. Although self-conscious attempts to provide useful knowledge for the 'tired artisan' were only partially successful, for those desperate for news but not able to afford the price of a newspaper, enterprising citizens, like John Black, boot and shoemaker, hired out local newspapers at the rate of a halfpenny an hour. [42]

What was sold by the local booksellers? The markets in Aberdeen were substantial and various. Aberdeen, the business, administrative, legal, and educational centre for the north-east of Scotland offered the booksellers opportunities and potential customers not available in many other localities. Scientific, medical, legal and literary texts were all available, to match the interests of the professoriates and educated readers and, to complement these, many booksellers made a point of advertising the textbooks necessary for the universities' syllabuses. Appended to the list of 42 'books in medicine, surgery, physiology, and chemistry' available from John Rettie, Union Street, was the footnote that 'JR has received . . . an assortment of CLASS BOOKS used at the King's and Marischal Colleges, Grammar and English Schools'.[43] The majority of stock emanated from the two main publication centres, London and Edinburgh, but there was a local dimension as well, mostly local histories and guidebooks, books of poetry and sermons. [44]

By the end of the 1830s a number of Aberdeen booksellers had become major wholesalers, thus consolidating the city's position as the regional supplier of printed material. Indeed, William Booth, in setting up as a bookseller in Stonehaven in 1829, attempted to establish his business credibility by claiming that 'for the immediate supply of any article . . . which may not be in Stock, he has established a correspondence with one of the first houses in ABERDEEN, therefore, any order will be executed in the course of *One Day*'.[45] A progression can be seen as the century drew on. From being wholesalers for part-

icular titles, some booksellers moved to being wholesalers for particular series, e.g. *Chambers's Educational Course*, to being wholesalers for
an extended range of a publisher's output. In 1862 Lewis Smith drew
the attention of the local retail trade to the fact that he was wholesale
agent for fourteen publishers, including Chambers, Oliver & Boyd, and
Blackwood all of Edinburgh, Collins of Glasgow, Routledge of London,
and Milner & Sowerby of Halifax.[46]

There are also clear indications of local booksellers specialising in
certain topics.[47] The prosperity of Lewis Smith's firm was based on the
sale of 'useful knowledge' publications, having started in the 1820s
with the *Glasgow Mechanics' Magazine*. Under the managership of Forbes
Frost, Alexander Brown & Co. developed 'a wide clientele among the
Episcopal communion, print collectors, writers and editors on the staff
of the local and provincial press' and acted as local agent for the
Saturday Magazine, published in London under the aegis of the Society
for Promoting Christian Knowledge. George King, on the other hand,
always had to hand a large supply of evangelical tracts, and Archibald
Courage, described as Aberdeen's nearest equivalent to a 'Puritan
bookseller', had a stock of new and second-hand theology, classics and
poetry. For those seeking political comment, John Mitchell claimed he
was the sole local agent for 'the following Liberal Newspapers:- Nonconformist, 6d., Weekly Chronicle 5d., British Statesman 5d., Glasgow
Post 4½d., Edinburgh True Scotsman 4½d., &c.'

How does Aberdeen compare with other early- and mid-nineteenth-
century cities? No overall conclusion can yet be reached, but what evidence we have suggests that those magazines at one time popular in
Aberdeen – *Chambers's*, the *Penny Magazine*, and slightly later, the *Novel
Newspaper*, and the *Family Herald* – were popular elsewhere too. There
is a considerable body of evidence to suggest that many in mid-century
Aberdeen had succumbed to the mix of melodramatic stories and tales,
miscellaneous scientific facts, advice to correspondents, and recipes
found in the penny illustrated weeklies, *Reynolds's Miscellany* and the
less sensational *London Journal*. Contemporary observers have noted
that William Russel, bookseller, seller of '"Park's" small quarto pictures
of great actors . . . 1d. plain and 2d. coloured'[48] in their thousands, was
also wholesale agent for the *Family Herald*, the *London Journal, Cassell's
Working Man's Friend* and his *Family Paper, Reynolds's Miscellany* and,
later, *Bow Bells*, and the same commentators note that these same magazines had an extensive local sale. Further, there is evidence that, for
some, *Reynolds's* and the *London Journal* were the limits of their read-

ing. Ramsay in his essay adopted a disapproving tone towards *Reynolds*.

> In the cheap periodical line, there is a fearful amount of trash issued weekly, among the working men of our country. Horrible debasing tales, which never happened nor could happen . . . Mr. Reynolds, of London, has done his part towards giving the public a bad article. Let the readers of cheap weekly periodicals adhere to Chambers, Hogg, and Dickens.

It was a forlorn hope. In December 1860, readers throughout Aberdeenshire were accounting for 1920 copies of the *Family Herald*, 2600 copies of the *London Journal*, and 1300 copies of *Reynolds's Miscellany*. The 'quality' magazines were not selling well: the north-east was absorbing 70 copies of *Blackwood's Magazine*, and only 16 of *Fraser's*. However, the high initial circulation of the *Cornhill Magazine*, 1066 copies, surprised even the *Aberdeen Journal*.[49] *Chambers's*, initially so popular, had shrunk to a circulation of 208 copies in numbers, 114 copies in monthly parts.[50] Essentially, the relative popularity of these London-published mid-century weeklies in and around Aberdeen is entirely consistent with what descriptions we have from two other cities – Edinburgh and Manchester – and makes the arrival and considerable popularity of the local editions of the *People's Journal* all the more remarkable.[51]

Three opportunities and a challenge were to confront the local book trade in the decade of the 1850s. The challenge which the Aberdeen booksellers, along with the rest of the British book trade faced, was a sustained retail price-cutting war which, it is claimed, damaged the trade both nationally and locally. More positively, the local booksellers were presented in 1850 with the arrival of the railways in Aberdeen, which suggested not only new markets in the form of regular passengers and visitors either for the summer season or for day trips, but also a new mode of transport which was to offer a more efficient and speedier method of distribution for printed materials, particularly newspapers. Finally, in 1855 newspapers themselves benefited from the final repeal of the stamp duty and in consequence increased in both number and in circulation.

ACKNOWLEDGEMENTS

The author would like to thank the following for permission to use and quote from the various sources identified above:

The Librarian and staff of the City of Aberdeen Arts and Re-
creation Division, Library Services
Aberdeen City Archivist, Aberdeen City Archives
The Librarian and staff of Aberdeen University Library
The Librarian and staff of the Library of New College, Edinburgh.

Photographs reproduced by permission of Aberdeen University Library.

NOTES

1. R. Southey, *Journal of a Tour in Scotland in 1819* (London, 1929), p. 73.
2. For an analysis of the geographical location of booksellers' shops in nineteenth-
century Aberdeen, and of the evolution of libraries, see M. C. Head, 'Books,
readers and libraries in nineteenth-century Aberdeen' (unpublished MA dissertation, University of Strathclyde, 1984).
3. This circulating library (known as the Public or United Public Library) was initially
jointly owned by Brown and John Burnett (d. 1806), and at first shared the same
premises as the reading room known as the Athenaeum. The library can be seen
in Robert Seaton's 1806 painting of the Castlegate.
4. G. Walker, *Aberdeen Awa'* (Aberdeen, 1897), p. 140. Walker provides a discursive
account of the history of Brown & Co.
5. For a description of Wyllie's bookshop from 1815, see Lewis Smith's autobio-
graphy: Aberdeen University Library. MSS 945, 945². Also I. Beavan, 'The nineteenth-century book trade in Aberdeen, with primary reference to Lewis Smith', 2
vols (unpublished PhD thesis, Robert Gordon University, 1992), pp. 114-19.
6. Prospectus for the Aberdeen Athenaeum; or Literary Lounge, December 1803:
New College, Edinburgh: Alexander Thomson of Banchory papers, Tho 5(19), ff
36r-38r. 25 newspapers were listed.
7. For Brown's circulating library in 1795 see J. and M. Lough, 'Aberdeen circulating
libraries in the eighteenth century', *Aberdeen University Review*, 31 (1945-46), pp.
21-23; for his library in 1821, see Head, 'Books, readers and libraries', pp. 73-75.
8. *Aberdeen Journal* (hereafter *AJ*), 16 October 1822.
9. Beavan, 'The nineteenth-century book trade', pp. 152-56; 344-48; and for the
latter half of the century, Head, 'Books, readers and libraries', pp. 24-25.
10. Evidence for the sale of chapbooks in Aberdeen, 1800-50, remains frustratingly
indirect. J. Riddell, *Aberdeen and its Folk* (Aberdeen, 1868), pp. 118-19, 124-25,
notes street sellers of printed material and stationery. Very few chapbooks are
known to have been printed in Aberdeen at this time. The twelve-page *Origin and
History of Quack Doctors, Dr Lamert, & c. . . to which is Annexed, the Boat Race
Advertisement*, Cobban & Co., 1829 selling at 1d. is a late example. Within three
years a penny could have bought a magazine.
11. The city treasury was unable to meet the interest payable on loans taken out for
the development of King Street and Union Street.
12. Within William Walker's two-volume collection of broadsheets and squibs, as are
the 1817/1818 song sheets: deposited in Aberdeen City Archives.
13. W. Skene, *East Neuk Chronicles* (Aberdeen, 1905), pp. 48-49.
14. Anon., but by John Ferres, 'Letters from Pannanich and Ballater, no. I', *Aberdeen
Censor*, 12-13 (double issue) (August 1825), pp. 271-75.
15. For a survey of sources, see Beavan, 'The nineteenth-century book trade', pp.
188-91.

16. P. Hollis, *The Pauper Press* (London, 1970), map after p. 336.

17. William Walker's papers, Aberdeen University Library MS 2732/8/1, p. 156: it was said of William Laurence Brown, principal of Marischal College and University, that he

    Was a reformer at a time when to be such was to appear worse than an infidel. From these circumstances he could only read the radical publications . . . by stealth . . . Wᵐ Russel Confectioner took in Cobbetts Register, the Black Dwarf, and these were carefully made up, sealed & delivered to the Principals own hand, and if he was not at home the bearer did not deliver them. If he was in the bearer saw him [,] delivered the packet and recᵈ back the previous Noˢ of the secret and forbidden papers. The agent in this quasi-contraband business was Wᵐ Russel (son of the above) afterward Bookseller B ᵈ St, who gave a loan of these publications.

18. Many volumes in Cooke's 'cheap and elegant' Pocket Library of novels, classics and poetry were priced at 6d. a part. See Burnett's advertisement, *AJ*, 20 October 1800. The stamp duty on newspapers (after reductions, finally repealed in 1855) kept costs high. In 1800 the *AJ* cost 6d.; by 1818 the price had risen to 7d., and did not fall again until 1836, when the price was set at 4½d.

19. S. Eliot, *Some Patterns and Trends in British Publishing, 1800-1919* (London, 1994), pp. 110–11.

20. See Alexander Brown's announcement (*AJ*, 2 July 1806) requesting 'his friends to notice that his monthly order to London is sent regularly on the 24th; and that every Review, Magazine, and Publications of all kinds are forwarded by his correspondents the 1st day of every month; and that, from the regular conveyance by sea, they may be depended upon as nearly as soon as by post. A weekly order is dispatched to Edinburgh, and commissions for Music are also forwarded with the above'.

21. 'City of Aberdeen' in the *New Statistical Account* (Edinburgh, 1843), vol. 12, pp. 100–01, a sub-section on local newspapers and libraries.

22. The Aberdeen booksellers would appear to have been no different from those in other cities. On the resistance of booksellers to this 'cheap trash', see 'Johnstone's Edinburgh Magazine: the cheap and dear periodicals', *Tait's Edinburgh Magazine*, 4, (January 1834), pp. 490–99.

23. W. Lindsay, *Some Notes: Personal and Public* (Aberdeen, 1898), p. 291.

24. *Chambers's Edinburgh Journal*, 1 Feb., 1834, p. 1. The weekly circulation of the *AJ* in 1832 was claimed to have been 2231 copies. See 'The Aberdeen press: rise and progress of the "Journal"' in J. M. Bulloch's 'Aberdeen periodicals: [a collection of newspaper cuttings]' in Aberdeen University Library.

25. The objects of the SDUK, as cited in H. Smith, *The Society for the Diffusion of Useful Knowledge, 1826–1846* . . . (Halifax, N.S., 1974), pp. 5, 56.

26. H. Brougham (Lord Brougham and Vaux), review of 'Society of Useful Knowledge – Farmer's Series', *Edinburgh Review*, 50 (October 1829), p. 181.

27. See, for example, the preface to the first volume of the *Penny Magazine*: 'There have been no excitements for the lovers of the marvellous . . . and, above all, no party politics'.

28. *Chambers's Journal*, 25 January 1840, p. 8; Select Committee on Newspaper Stamps. *Report*, 1851 (Irish Universities' Press edition, 1969), qq. 3249, 3251. Although predominately marketed as cheap, weekly magazines, they were also available bound in monthly or annual parts, to appeal to more prosperous pockets.

29. D. Wright, A. Ramsay, et al., *Aberdeen Working Men's Prize Essays: Four Essays on the Elevation of the Working Classes* (Aberdeen, 1851), pp. 12–14, 32 (third sequence).

30. 1820–29: 186 locally printed books, pamphlets; 1830–39: 350; 1840–49: 359.

31. *Grand Reform Meeting on the Broad Hill of the Links* (Aberdeen, 1832). Broadsheet bound within the set of pamphlets, 'Aberdeen Trash', in Aberdeen City Libraries.

32. *Aberdeen Shaver*, 19 September and 17 October 1833.

33. As cited in Bulloch, 'Aberdeen periodicals'.

34. December 1835, p. 216.

35. The notable exceptions are David Chalmers and Alexander Brown, who contributed little to the production of political pamphlets of the time. Neither was a supporter of Alexander Bannerman.

36. For Smith's publishing activities, see Beavan, 'The nineteenth-century book trade', chs 5, 6, 9.

37. *AJ*, 25 November 1829.

38. *AJ*, 18 September 1844.

39. *AJ*, 5 January 1842.

40. *AJ*, 1 January 1845.

41. For ratio of bookseller to population, 1851–1901, see Head, pp. 23–24.

    Pop. of Aberdeen (rounded, thousands)/no. of book-selling firms

1801: 27/10?	1811: 35/14	1821: 44/18
1831: 57/41	1841: 63/45	1851: 72/36.

    Figures above derived from Beavan and Head. The basic statistics hide some important distinctions. Some booksellers, e.g. Samuel Maclean, held little stock of their own, and were supplied by their larger colleagues such as Brown & Co. See Aberdeen City Libraries, MS journals of George Walker, I, p. 56; others dealt in the 'overplus or faded stock of the regular booksellers': Walker, *Aberdeen Awa'*, p. 319.

42. Skene, *East Neuk Chronicles*, pp. 38–39.

43. *AJ*, 4 November 1829.

44. Throughout the nineteenth century, religious themes (including sermons), followed by local politics and administration, formed the largest subject groupings within the local printers' output in terms of separate titles and editions. Locally published literature in its various forms constituted c. 10%. Guidebooks and topographical works added up to c. 4%, but we know that certain titles sold exceedingly well, e.g. *New Deeside Guide*.

45. *AJ*, 7 October 1829.

46. A reference to their Cottage Library series, 1s. per volume, and presumably a good seller at railway bookstalls.

47. Beavan, 'The nineteenth-century book trade', p. 303 and ch. 10.

48. Skene, *East Neuk Chronicles*, p. 84.

49. George Walker's document (bound with his MS journals) was prepared for his lecture to the Aberdeen Philosophical Society. See Beavan, 'The nineteenth-century book trade' vol. 2, p. 838 for analysis. Walker's paper is discussed in *AJ* 6 March 1861, wherein is struck a disapproving attitude towards *Reynolds*. On the *Cornhill*, see R. D. Altick, *The English Common Reader* (Chicago, 1957), p. 359.

50. The tract societies' publications made the purely commercial titles look insignificant. The Scottish Monthly Tract Society's *Monthly Visitor*, 1s. per 100 copies, had a circulation of no fewer than 18,000 copies that December.

51. For Edinburgh, see J. Bertram, *Some Memories of Books, Authors and Events* (Westminster, 1893), pp. 138–40; for Manchester, see Abel Heywood's evidence to the Select Committee on Newspaper Stamps, qq. 2481 et seq. On the *People's Journal*, see W. Donaldson, *Popular Literature in Victorian Scotland* (Aberdeen, 1986), ch. 1.

7

'A Woman's Greatest Adventure':[1] the Development of Maternity Care in Aberdeen since the Eighteenth Century

Lesley Diack

In the life of a family today the birth of a child is regarded as an important event, which often fundamentally affects the attitudes and priorities of the parents. In most social histories, however, the study of the practicalities of childbirth is under-represented. This is perhaps because it is only relatively recently that such apparently mundane matters have begun to be taken more seriously: the advance of medical science and the existence of extensive social services have introduced elements of choice into a process previously seen as governed more or less by nature.[2] In Aberdeen since the eighteenth century, however, there has been a recurring interest in the technicalities of birth and how procedures could be made safer and easier. Although, in many respects, Aberdeen is on the periphery of Europe, and even of Britain, it has played an important role in the history of gynaecology and obstetrics from that time onwards.

Yet there is surprisingly little written about Aberdeen's contribution to the professionalisation of midwifery and the development of maternity care. And, while the approach of the millennium has encouraged an epidemic of 'anniversary seeking', important dates in the history of obstetrics in the city have been ignored. In 1994, Aberdeen could look back on a hundred years of continuous maternity care; 1995 was the

bicentenary of the publication of Dr Alexander Gordon's ground-breaking book on puerperal fever,[3] and the centenary of the first all-female medical practice in the city; and 1997 sees the sixtieth birthday of the Maternity Hospital at its present site next to Aberdeen Royal Infirmary at Foresterhill. This chapter attempts to redress the balance and to place Aberdeen's contribution in a national and international context – but it is not alone in doing so. In 1995 the Dugald Baird Research Centre was opened at the Aberdeen Maternity Hospital: it is dedicated to the recognition of the city's historic and continuing con-tribution in the fields of obstetrics and gynaecology, and named after one of the medical pioneers of the twentieth century. Baird, amongst his other achievements, was responsible for the establishment of a cervical screening service in the early 1960s.[4]

Attitudes towards public responsibility for childbirth are revealed most clearly with regard to the poor, whose intimate lives were most likely to be brought to the attention, and under the control, of the public administration. From the mid-eighteenth century onwards, there was a pattern of increased institutionalisation in the care of the poor, in Aberdeen as elsewhere. In the early 1740s, an infirmary was built and maintained by voluntary subscription at Woolmanhill, then a place of clean air and green spaces.[5] Perhaps significantly from the point of view of this chapter, Logie's map of the area, produced in 1742, marks the site of the infirmary as 'womanhill'.[6] To be admitted to the infirmary it was necessary to be recommended by someone in authority, such as a doctor or a minister. In an account of the Aber-deen Infirmary published in 1754, the reason given for the original establishment of the building was 'for the benefit of the diseased poor in all the north parts of the Kingdom':[7] for those with money, treat-ment would be in their own homes by their own doctors. About this time too, a Poor's Hospital[8] was built behind the Town House to take in the destitute – particularly the old, the very young and the infirm; and for a period this satisfied the city fathers' concern to establish improved public control over the care of the poor. What, then, can be learnt from the records of these institutions about the changing prac-tices within maternity provision?

The events surrounding the birth of a child had tended to be regarded as matters of exclusively female concern, but this was in part for financial reasons. Middle- and upper-class women, who could afford it, would quite often have had a doctor, who would be a man, in attendance. Pregnancy, in the eighteenth century and even into the

nineteenth, was considered to be such a natural function that there was no concept of antenatal care. Women would seek the aid of a local midwife or of an older female relative who had some experience, but only during labour. At that point males were excluded. By the middle of the eighteenth century, however, attitudes were beginning to change in Britain, and Scottish medical men, based in London, played a key role in this. During the 1750s, Dr William Smellie published his *Treatise of Midwifery*, which was to remain one of the main textbooks on the subject for the next century. In addition to his writings, he introduced several new types of forceps to be used in the delivery of children and developed rules for their safe usage. His teachings were to become even more widespread. Of the many students who passed through his classes, one of the most notable, William Hunter (one of the famous Hunter brothers from East Kilbride), became one of the leading obstetricians of his time.[9] The influence of such men was responsible, between 1739 and 1765, for the creation of two lying-in wards and four separate lying-in hospitals in London 'for taking care of poor women labouring of child.'[10]

From the point of view of Aberdeen, William Smellie's most important student was David Skene. Born about 1730 in the city, he was the son of the Andrew Skene who had played a leading role in the foundation of the infirmary. David was sent to Edinburgh to study medicine after a period at university in Aberdeen. He then furthered his studies with stays in both London and Paris. In London, he became Smellie's pupil and took part in the 'touching sessions' advocated by him to aid the diagnosis of pregnancy. The technique involved internal examination and was very advanced for its time. To gain more practical experience, Skene also studied midwifery with a *sage femme*, or midwife, in Paris.[11] Returning to Aberdeen in the mid-1750s, he began a campaign to professionalise midwifery in the area, and to introduce what was then 'male' expertise into this female preserve. In 1758, he wrote a letter to the Aberdeen kirk sessions asking for proper training to be given to midwives. In order that this could be accomplished, he proposed that the sessions should license the midwives, and that some form of examination, both written and practical, should be established.[12] As an aid to this he offered classes in midwifery, and these were periodically advertised in the *Aberdeen Journal* in the late 1750s. There is no direct evidence that these classes ever took place, but the fact that they were publicly proposed is itself significant: this was a very early example of formal training being offered in Scotland to mid-

wives. Elsewhere, things were different – notably in France, where Louis XV had appointed Mme du Coudray to travel throughout the country teaching midwifery.[13] In chapter two, Ranald Macinnes suggested that architectural innovation was more centralised in 'absolutist' France than in Britain, and the same point could be made about midwifery training. In Scotland, the organisational initiative, as well as the idea, for such training had to come from middle-class professionals, not from the state; and its incidence was much more local.

At the annual general meeting of the infirmary in 1758, a further extension of the building was proposed. This was to become the West Wing and was to contain 'wards for poor distressed lying-in women belonging to the town and country'.[14] An appeal for funds was placed in the local newspaper, with an advertisement to the effect that 'poor women are often in distress in labour, and many of them die for lack of proper care.'[15] Not surprisingly, one of the directors of the infirmary at this time was David Skene. In 1759, the infirmary minutes have a description of the second floor of the proposed new wing, which 'may be appropriated for lying-in women having two closets on each end.' They go on to say that 'there might be other closets with fire places which could contain two beds each.' And that there 'will likeways be two fire closets upon the turn of the stair, which may have chimneys and will serve for any useful purpose.'[16]

The ward for poor lying-in women was eventually opened in 1762, but was little used. There are records of under twenty women being delivered in the subsequent six years. From November 1762 to October 1767, a midwife, Jean Baird, was employed and paid a guinea per year 'for her trouble in bringing poor lying-in women in the infirmary to bed.'[17] She appeared not to have been re-employed, or replaced, and, in late 1768, a change of use was recorded for the ward. Since Baird treated women outside the infirmary, as well as those admitted, it seems reasonable to assume that her midwifery practice continued elsewhere. But the experiment of a lying-in ward had been short-lived, and a more profitable use was found for the space.

In June 1768 the infirmary minutes record that 'the state of the funds . . . was very precarious and uncertain'.[18] Fund-raising had continued from the opening of the infirmary and money had been raised from all over the world, from as far afield as Antigua and Trinidad – and even in London – as well as locally. Yet the constant need to raise funds was always a worry, and the directors felt that a more secure source was necessary. In September 1768, treatment of the military

appeared to offer a solution. An agreement was signed with General Righton, one of the military commanders, which brought in five shillings (25p.) per day, plus sixpence (2½p.) per day for every case treated. Furthermore, all funeral expenses were to be met by the regiment – a major consideration. The hospital would admit up to fifteen soldiers at a time as patients,[19] an arrangement that was financially more beneficial to the infirmary than a ward for poor pregnant women.

In any case, it is clear that women did not want to have their children in the infirmary and there had been little incentive for them to break with tradition and do so. A major part of David Skene's concern was to have 'specimen patients' under his observation and care; and he again resorted to advertising in the local paper, asking pregnant women in need to apply to him for help. He would meet their expenses before and after the birth if they came and lived under his care.[20] Thus Skene attempted to overcome the problem of the lack of facilities for 'hands on' clinical training for apprentice doctors, but there is no evidence that he was any more successful as a result of this advertising campaign than he had been in his attempt to get expectant mothers into the infirmary. His early death in 1770 ended his efforts to improve maternity care in the area.

The history of maternity care is not one of continuous growth, but more of sporadic advance. In 1781 the Aberdeen Dispensary was split from the Aberdeen Infirmary, in order to provide some form of outdoor medical relief to the poor. There are no records of birth under the auspices of this new organisation. In a history of Aberdeen medicine prepared for the 107th annual meeting of the British Medical Association, held in Aberdeen in 1939, however, it is stated that 'it is likely [that] medical advice was given to expectant mothers from the inception of the dispensary'.[21]

The career of Dr Alexander Gordon gives the next clear insight into the need for proper maternity provision. A list of the diseases treated by him in 1793 has survived and three births are listed.[22] Gordon was born in 1752 and, after his medical training, became a surgeon in the navy. In 1786 he was appointed physician to the dispensary, and until his return to the navy in 1795, he played a major role in the local development of maternity care. It has been argued that he was probably one of the greatest – certainly one of the most underestimated – figures in the history of obstetrics. The only public recognition of his achievement is a plaque in the Aberdeen Medical School.

Alexander Gordon's greatest work was *A Treatise on the Child-bed*

Fever, published in April 1795 by a London publishing company.[23] Puerperal or childbed fever had been at epidemic proportions in Aberdeen from December 1789 to March 1792. Dr Gordon's treatise recorded the names of all the women who had the disease, their ages, their addresses, dates of the illness, whether they survived, and the names of either the midwife or the doctor who delivered them. From his observations he found that the epidemic was spread by a lack of hygiene. Most midwives did not wash their hands before or after they attended a birth, thereby transmitting disease from patient to patient. This discovery was developed from his previous work, *Observations on the Efficacy of Cold-bathing in the Prevention and Cure of Diseases*, published in 1780 – but his contribution went largely unrecognised, and the discovery of the causes of puerperal fever is usually credited to a mid-nineteenth-century Austrian researcher. [24]

The foundation of the Medico-Chirurgical Society in Aberdeen in 1789 was also to prove of significance in the advance of maternity care. In 1827 attempts were made by the society to establish a Midwives Board which would register and certificate midwives – thus taking one of Skene's ideas a stage further.[25] Four years earlier, the dispensary had been redesignated the 'Aberdeen Dispensary, Vaccine and Lying-in Institution' – obviously the managers felt that this was a necessary step to take. Sadly there are no surviving records which would enable us to assess either the quantity or quality of the treatment given. These two initiatives in the 1820s may signify some revived consciousness of the need to improve maternity care, or possibly be a recognition that there already had been some piecemeal improvements that required co-ordination.

The eighteenth century had seen the introduction of men into mid-wifery, with the development of the 'man-midwife' – which some feminist historians have argued was a deliberate attempt by men to gain control in one of the few areas of medicine still traditionally in the hands of women. However that may be, the trend continued during the nineteenth century as obstetrics and gynaecology became more scientific. This culminated in the establishment of a Regius Chair of Midwifery (not, it may be noted, of obstetrics) at the University of Aberdeen in 1860.[26]

The history of the dispensary was in many ways integral to the growth of care in, and by, the community in Aberdeen. The town, the university and the infirmary all played their parts in its continuance and development. In the late-nineteenth century the dispensary was in

Barnett's Close just off the Guest Row,[27] and by 1872 portions of it had been fitted up as a branch of the lying-in institution with eight beds. However, by 1874, the ward was closed because it was not being fully used.[28] The births of forty-three babies in total were recorded. This situation was similar to that just over a hundred years before, when the lack of use of the maternity facilities meant that they were closed within a few years. On this occasion, one specific reason given for the failure of the ward was the ill-health of its guiding spirit, Andrew Inglis, professor of Midwifery at the university.[29] During the 1880s the rules of the dispensary still included one stating that 'lying in patients require to give a fortnight's notice'. In 1886 five midwives were appointed 'with the view of securing thorough efficiency in the midwifery department'.[30] But, even in a period when there was no ward in existence, midwifery activity did not stop. During the ten years to 1880, the average yearly number of midwifery cases was 151, and in the next ten-year period this had increased by nearly fifty per cent to 221. The cost of a maternity case at this time would have been about a halfpenny (just over 0.2p.).[31] By 1893 a house adjoining the dispensary was fitted 'for the lying-in department, where lying-in patients whose houses are too wretched for them to receive proper attention could be placed under thoroughly trained nurses and receive some comfort at a most critical and trying period.'[32]

A year later a maternity hospital with three beds was opened in Barnett's Close next to the dispensary, and the then professor of Midwifery, William Stephenson, gave his services free of charge.[33] Since then, Aberdeen has had continuous maternity provision. Stephenson, instrumental in the establishment of the hospital for sick children in the 1870s, has also been credited with being the main force behind the establishment of the Maternity Hospital, which was so successful that, by 1900, a building on Castle Terrace was acquired. It had two wards, and it was said that it occupied a 'high and sunny position in the heart of the city . . . [than which] no more favourable site for a maternity hospital could be found.'[34] The building had been a 'commodious family dwelling and a bank . . . the telling room of which was a ready made ward.'[35]

The twentieth century brought great advances in maternity care in Aberdeen, reflecting developments in the country as a whole. The building at Castle Terrace was extended by 'a commodious wing of two stories . . . [of which] the upper [contained] a full delivery room and a large ward for married women with other necessary rooms.'[36] The

lower floor had two small wards for isolation cases and for paying patients. In all there was a total of eighteen beds. By this time the attitudes of women had changed, and hospitalisation for delivery was no longer regarded solely as an option for the poor. If the tide of public opinion was turning, however, it was doing so very slowly. In the late-nineteenth and early-twentieth century, there were between about 3,500 and 4,500 babies born each year in Aberdeen. Only approximately ten per cent had any aid from the dispensary, and of these roughly half of the actual births were still taking place at home. A century ago, therefore, only a very small proportion of the city's babies were being born in hospital.

The change towards more general acceptance of hospitalisation for childbirth was assisted by the 'disjunction' of Aberdeen Maternity Hospital from the dispensary in 1912, so that it became formally established as a separate entity, meeting the growing needs of the city and the county. The reason given for this decision was that it would promote the provision of 'special medical aid to lying-in patients of poorer classes and to such patients as can afford to pay, either in the hospital or in their own homes.'[37] The hospital was also to function as a training centre for midwives and as an institution to 'assist medical students of the University to obtain the necessary midwifery experience'.[38]

The cost of maintenance of the hospital in the first year was £900, leaving a deficit of £450 to be obtained by subscription. The money to finance the hospital was received from many different sources – rents, grants from public bodies, fees from students, payments by patients, legacies and donations both in kind and in money. In 1912 it was stated that 'no progress has as yet been made with the matter of obtaining some financial assistance from the University.'[39] The cost of maternity care to the patient was ten shillings (50p.) if the child was delivered in the hospital and seven shillings and sixpence (37½p.) if it was born at home. As yet, most children, as we have seen, were born at home. This was especially the case if the mother was married: a disproportionate number of unmarried mothers had always used hospital facilities, presumably for the practical reason that the married poor were more likely to have at least some form of accommodation suitable for confinement.

A further reason for the establishment of a maternity hospital related to the passage, in 1911, of the National Insurance Act. Its implications for maternity provision were perceived as being far reaching, since

many prospective mothers, who had previously been in the hands of charities, might now be able to exercise choice about how to spend money available to them to assist with childbirth. And for several years it does appear to have led to a falling-off in the number of mothers who entered hospital. Administrators from all over Scotland held meetings to discuss this and to try to devise a solution. Fears of a long-term decline in demand, however, proved ungrounded.

A report presented to the British Medical Association, when it met in Aberdeen in 1914, remarked that, although the city's Maternity Hospital was 'small as it is compared with others . . . [it] is complete in its organisation and fulfils all the functions benevolent and educational, relating to pregnancy and labour.'[40] Thereafter, the system of childbirth used to this day was gradually put in place. One of the first steps along this road came with the Midwives (Scotland) Act, in 1915, which for the first time established formal training for midwives and arranged for them to be licensed – 150 years after the first attempts by Dr David Skene. This recognition of the need for proper training coincided with a Maternity Hospital report, stating that the mortality rate amongst mothers in Scotland was nearly fifty per cent higher than in England. The end of World War I saw the opening of the first 'prenatal cliniques' in Aberdeen – recognition at last that antenatal care was vital to safe and healthy childbirth. Such care was to be provided and financed by the local authority and not by the hospital; and the town council undertook to give £550 to adapt a tenement next to the Maternity Hospital for use as an antenatal annexe, with £350 a year for maintenance. A year later, in 1919, antenatal beds were provided in another adjacent building. This necessitated more fund-raising, the donations including £84 from Miss Esslemont of Esslemont and Mackintosh, the Union Street department store.[41] Next to be opened was a Mother and Child Welfare Clinic, providing much needed help and advice to the new mothers on such matters as nutrition and health care. State interest – or, as some saw it, interference – had taken a great leap forward, with pregnancy and birth now seen as of vital importance, and subject to all measures and every possible effort to make them easy and safe. One element at least in this change of outlook was, of course, the fact that the huge numbers of deaths in the war had created a concern to replace population.

The 1920s saw a burgeoning interest in maternity care and the opening of many small, private, maternity hospitals or nursing homes. At times there were at least fifteen maternity institutions of one sort or

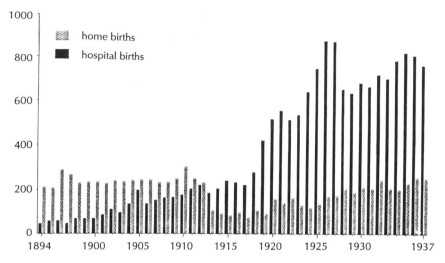

Graph 1. *Cases delivered each year for the period 1894–1937 at home and in the Aberdeen Maternity Hospital.*

another in operation. Some were little more than private homes with one or two beds for patients, but they did contribute to the quantity of care available. There has not yet been a comprehensive study of these institutions – when they were opened and closed, and how many people they took in. It should be stressed, however, that, even with these extra private hospitals, most mothers still had their children at home. The graph above shows the number of births in Aberdeen where the facilities of the dispensary and later the Maternity Hospital were used from 1894 to 1937.[42] In the mid-1920s institutional deliveries reached an historic high, yet they still accounted for less than a third of the total births in Aberdeen. Logistical, financial and other practical difficulties – such as the lack of facilities for the care of previous children – may, however, have been the deciding factors in the decision of expectant mothers to be delivered at home, rather than personal inclination.

With the opening of the new infirmary on a site at Foresterhill, it was hoped that an adjacent maternity hospital could also be built. The financial situation did not permit this immediately, although land for a new building had been gifted by the university. By 1934 an appeal for funds to build the new 'Matty' was launched; and three years later it was opened with thirty-five beds. The £52,000 cost was met entirely by public subscription. The new facilities included four single labour

rooms with their own equipment and a large operating theatre, all situated on the ground floor. On the first floor there was an isolation area for septic cases and space for lying-in accommodation. All four wards were equipped with Outram wirelesses; and the hospital as a whole had a steam heating system. There was no kitchen – food had to come from the infirmary[43] – but this was still a very modern hospital for its time. In 1938, 930 women gave birth there – 733 by appoint-ment and 197 as emergency admissions. This meant that, on the eve of World War II, nearly 30 per cent of all confinements in the area were in hospital.[44] In 1939, the British Medical Association, noting that the Maternity Hospital 'is remarkable for the varied and beautiful colour schemes of the wards' reported a change of attitude to home births. The 'function of a maternity hospital', it stated, 'has undergone a complete change. . . . From being a house to accommodate those whose home conditions were very bad it has come to be the central point for obstetrics in the area.'

The first year of training at the new institution, moreover, saw forty nurses presented for the Central Midwives Board examinations.[45] The changing attitudes to giving birth and to midwifery – already detectable at the turn of the century – seemed almost complete. The numbers of trained midwives, and the numbers giving birth in hospital were now rising commensurately.

The innovations were not to end there, however. A Special Nursery, to look after sick or premature babies, was set up in 1940; a year later, also at the Foresterhill site, the antenatal hospital was opened. In the period after World War II, the demand for obstetric care grew to such an extent that Fonthill, Queen's Cross and Summerfield nursing homes were all adapted for maternity use: in 1948 they became part of the National Health Service.[46]

In 1937, the appointment of Dugald Baird to the chair of Midwifery at the university helped to bring Aberdeen, once again, to the fore-front of progress in maternity provision. Baird came to the city from Glasgow where he had been 'deeply affected by what poverty did to women giving birth' and he was 'determined that Aberdeen should do better.'[47] His work on the sociology of childbirth was to earn him world-wide recognition and, in 1959, a knighthood. He was assisted by his wife, May, who was to become the chairman of the Health Board; and together they played a great part in the medical life of the city in the middle decades of this century. Baird was always to the fore on controversial issues such as contraception, sterilisation and abortion.

Despite the fact that he sometimes aroused controversy, his work was recognised by the Medical Research Council which, in 1955, funded a Medical Research Unit situated above the Maternity Hospital. Much of what was discovered by Baird and his colleagues, stated an obituary written in the late 1980s, is now 'part of the clinical and scientific judgement of every obstetrician in the country'.[48] For the citizens of Aberdeen, perhaps Baird's most important contribution was the achievement of the lowest perinatal mortality rates in Scotland. A World Health Organisation meeting in Geneva in the early 1960s was told 'Aberdeen's standards of antenatal care were . . . the best in the world'. [49]

By 1972 the city's *Report by the Medical Officer of Health* was able to comment that 'the swing from domiciliary to hospital confinement has reached the stage where almost total hospital confinement prevails, ensuring the optimum conditions of care for mother and child at that vital stage.' In 1962, 327 women had domiciliary confinements, with thirty-three being delivered in hospital by their own doctors. Ten years later there were only two domiciliary confinements, and four hospital deliveries by family doctors. This was, of course, against a background of a falling birth-rate, which was by then at its lowest recorded level in the city. Aberdeen's family planning services were now experiencing unprecedented growth, with a central clinic and five peripheral ones in operation. In the previous five years, the number of clients attending these clinics had trebled to 6,282.[50] This extension of birth control meant that the number of pregnancies in cases where the mother already had four or more children was now under a hundred, and that pre-marital conceptions were also on the decline.[51] Health visitor care for pregnant women was also developing – on average each patient saw their health visitor at least twice before the birth, and more frequently afterwards. Since the beginning of the century antenatal services had grown out of all recognition, so that by the 1970s over 90 per cent of all expectant mothers attended antenatal clinics, and puerperal fever had ceased to be a problem.[52]

Different methods of keeping statistics make it difficult to compare figures from the early part of this century with those of the 1990s. In 1928, however, the Maternity Hospital recorded that 656 children had been born there, and that it had had some involvement with 207 home births. It had, moreover, treated 233 patients in antenatal wards, making a total of 1,096.[53] In 1992 there were 8,583 in-patients and 17,747 out-patient attendances. This of course included some women attending more than once;[54] but the trend towards the institutionalisa-

tion is nonetheless clear, and has continued. Even new schemes, such as 'Domino' (Domiciliary Midwife In and Out),[55] allow women keen to remain at home the safety of admittance to hospital for the birth itself.

In the last decade innovations have continued with a neo-natal unit, ultrasound department, midwives' unit, and a new 56-bed ward all being opened. Aberdeen remains one of the safest places to have children, certainly in Scotland. And this tradition derives in some measure at least from a past during which the city has often been at the forefront of new methods and techniques of bringing the next generation into the world. It is a history which deserves to be better known.

A final point should be stressed. Over the last two hundred years male medical practitioners tried to improve the maternity care in the area with varied success. But it was not until women themselves felt that hospital care would benefit them that decisive advances were made. The change of attitude at the turn of the twentieth century, away from regarding maternity hospitals as places for the poor alone, was a major step. Allied to this development was the provision, since 1915, of better training for midwives and the increase in their numbers. Progress in obstetrics is often seen as led from above, by trained medical men, yet it could be argued that, in Aberdeen, such leadership has come only in response to the demand of ordinary women for safer labours.

NOTES

1. The quotation is from the speech of a councillor at the opening of the Maternity Hospital at its Foresterhill site in 1937 as reported by the *Aberdeen Press and Journal*: see press cuttings, held at the Northern Health Services Archive, hereafter cited as NHSA (formerly the Grampian Health Board Archives) at Woolmanhill.

2. For a recent account of the early history of midwifery in Europe, see H. Marland (ed.), *The Art of Midwifery: Early Modern Midwives in Europe* (London, 1993). In many respects Scotland was further behind in standardising her care than most of Europe.

3. Although Alexander Gordon has never been fully credited with the discovery of the role of hygiene in the control of puerperal fever, it was in this book that the links were first noted.

4. *Aberdeen Evening Express*, 3 April 1995.

5. F. Watson, *In Sickness and Health* (Aberdeen, 1988), p. 3.

6. This was a corruption of the abbreviation wo'manhill. Woolmanhill was the site of the former woolmarket.

7. NHSA: *Account of the Rise and Progress of the Infirmary at Aberdeen* – circulated in 1754 in a fund-raising campaign for the Infirmary.

8. Some explanation of the terms 'infirmary' and 'hospital' is necessary. Today the words usually refer to the same type of institution, but in the eighteenth century the infirmary was where the curable sick (who were also poor) would be treated; while the hospital was a charitable institution for the destitute which had the

function of educating the young, and housing vagrants and beggars, as well as being used as a workhouse. Many of the people within the hospital in Aberdeen might be sick, and would be treated by the doctors from the infirmary; but they were kept in the hospital because they were dying of old age, had incurable ailments, or suffered from contagious skin ailments such as 'skeirscald'.

9. In 1764 William Hunter (1718–1793) was appointed physician extraordinary to Queen Charlotte. He was behind the building of the famous Anatomical School in Great Windmill Street in London. As well as his work on anatomy in general, he is chiefly remembered for his research on the uterus.

10. See Helen Roberts (ed.), *Women, Health and Reproduction* (London, 1981), esp. chapter 2.

11. Letter from David Skene to his father from Paris, 12 May 1753: Aberdeen University Library Special Collections (AULSC), ms. 38 (Correspondence of Dr David Skene).

12. Old Machar Kirk Session Register has a copy of the letter, the original of which is in AULSC, ms. 37, f. 88, 'Proposals for supplying country parishes with skilful midwives' (n.d.).

13. See Nina Gelbart, 'Midwife to a nation: Mme du Coudray serves France' in Marland, *The Art of Midwifery*.

14. NHSA: GRHB 1/1/3, 'West wing: plans for lying-in ward'.

15. NHSA: *Minutes of the AGM*, 1758.

16. NHSA: GRHB 1/1/4, *Minutes*, 1759, 'Description of the ward'.

17. NHSA: GRHB 1/1/4.

18. NHSA: GRHB 1/1/5, *Minutes*, 1768.

19. NHSA: GRHB 1/1/5, *Minutes*, 1768, 'Agreement with General Righton'.

20. Skene's advertisement appeared in the *Aberdeen Journal*, 29 September 1760, and 13 October 1760. He gave notice that 'any lying in Women, by applying to him will be carefully attended gratis in their own houses by sufficiently skilful midwives and such as are poor will be not only attended but maintained in Bed and Board at his expense [un]til their recovery.'

21. Dugald Baird, 'The Aberdeen Maternity Hospital', in D. Rorie (ed.), *The Book of Aberdeen* (compiled for the 107th Annual meeting of the British Medical Association, Aberdeen, 1939), p. 61. Hereafter cited as BMA 1939.

22. Scottish Record Office (SRO), Edinburgh: Sinclair of Freswick papers, GD136. This is the only early list of patients to the dispensary known to survive.

23. A copy of the treatise is in the AULSC.

24. Semmelweis was given the credit for the discovery. Gordon's contribution has been a well-kept secret outside Aberdeen.

25. See G. P. Milne, 'The history of midwifery in Aberdeen' in *A Bicentennial History of the Medico-Chirurgical Society, 1789–1989* (Aberdeen, 1989), p. 230.

26. See C. Pennington, *The Modernisation of Medical Teaching at Aberdeen in the Nineteenth Century* (Aberdeen, 1994); *Aberdeen University Review*, vol. 38 (1959–60), pp. 434–37.

27. This area is just off Broad Street, where Provost Skene's House and Marks and Spencer's store are now situated.

28. AULSC and Aberdeen Central Libraries' Local Studies Department: Aberdeen Dispensary, Vaccine and Lying in Institution, *Annual Reports* (hereafter cited as *ADAR*).

29. Andrew Inglis was the second professor of Midwifery, and held the chair for only six years, from 1869 to 1875. His predecessor from 1860 to 1869 was Robert Dyce.

30. *ADAR* 1886.

31. To set these numbers in context, the population of Aberdeen in 1887 was 115,000. By 1890 one in every twelve of the population had had medical help from the dispensary. This figure was much lower in the field of maternity care.

32. *ADAR* 1893.

33. William Stephenson was professor of Midwifery from 1875 to 1912. He was considered to be one of the best teachers of obstetrics in the country: his lectures were reputed to be both practical and entertaining. See Ian Porter's biographical notes in *Aberdeen University Review*, vol. 38 (1959-60), p. 434-35.

34. British Medical Association, *Aberdeen 1914: Handbook and Guide* (London, 1914), p. 59. Hereafter referred to as BMA 1914. The chapter on midwifery services is by Stephenson, the professor emeritus.

35. BMA 1914, p. 59.

36. BMA 1914, p. 59.

37. *Aberdeen Maternity Hospital, Annual Report*, 1912. These reports are cited hereafter as *AMHAR*.

38. *AMHAR* 1912.

39. *AMHAR* 1912.

40. BMA 1914, p. 60.

41. *AMHAR* 1919.

42. I am grateful, for this table and for all her help with this chapter, to Fiona Watson, archivist at NHSA. The figures for the table come from the *Annual Reports* of the Aberdeen Dispensary and the Aberdeen Maternity Hospital.

43. BMA 1939, p. 63.

44. NHSA: GRHB 1/1/42, Minutes 1938.

45. BMA 1939, p 63.

46. These smaller and more informal maternity hospitals have all been closed in recent years in the name of rationalisation. Their part in the history of maternity care is commemorated in ward names at Aberdeen Maternity Hospital.

47. 'Obituary' of Baird, *Aberdeen University Review*, vol. 52 (1987-88), p. 82.

48. Baird obituary, p. 82.

49. NHSA: report in the *Aberdeen Press and Journal* by Ruby Tuberville.

50. City of Aberdeen, *Report by the Medical Officer of Health for the Year 1972* (Aberdeen, 1973). Hereafter cited as *MOH* 1972.

51. For further information on the growth of family planning services in Aberdeen, see a Birth Control Campaign publication, *The Benefits of Birth Control: Aberdeen's Experience, 1946-1970* (Aberdeen, 1973).

52. *MOH* 1972.

53. BMA 1939, p. 62.

54. These figures were taken from the *Annual Report of Aberdeen Maternity Hospital*, and were provided by the Information Services Team, Grampian Health Board, Summerfield House, Aberdeen.

55. In the 'Domino' birth experience the expectant mother is attended throughout the pregnancy by the same midwife who will be with her at the birth. If everything progresses normally, the midwife delivers the baby in hospital. Mother and baby will then return home very quickly after the birth (often only six hours later). It is a safe compromise for mothers who would like to have their babies at home but want the security of hospital care.

8

Healing for the Body as Well as the Soul: Treatment in the Aberdeen Royal Lunatic Asylum during the Nineteenth Century [1]

Seumas Lobban

The Broadsea fishwife, Christian Watt, described what happened in the Aberdeen Royal Asylum (ARA) as 'healing for the body' – by which she meant the physical aspects of the mind. The treatment provided in the asylum complemented the care for the soul offered by the church.[2] The author of the well-known *Christian Watt Papers* spent over forty years in the ARA during the late nineteenth and early twentieth centuries. Her memoirs paint a very positive picture of the asylum. They are not used as evidence in this chapter (their complete authenticity is itself the subject of historiographical debate), but are quoted as a way of introducing a critical, historical analysis of the view that the ARA was a benign and curative establishment. The chapter looks first, in both a local and a national context, at why the ARA was established. The asylum's transformation from a moral reformatory into a thoroughly medical institution is then examined, along with the evolution of treatment. Finally the outcome of residence within the ARA is discussed, on the basis of a statistical study of admissions and discharges.

Scholars studying the history of asylumdom, have come up with several radically different explanations for the appearance of this new

type of institution. All agree that the rush of asylum foundations which took place in the late eighteenth and the early nineteenth century was in some way related to the great social changes brought about by commercialisation, industrialisation and urbanisation. But there is dispute about the nature of the relationship. An older generation of authors believed that a new urbanised society allowed the construction of institutions that were able to tackle the age-old problem of insanity.[3] But, more recently, others such as Edward Hare have suggested that this huge social change made people more vulnerable to insanity, implying that the opening of asylums was not so much a response to an old problem but was, rather, part of the changing nature of the problem itself.[4] Of this latter group of scholars there are those, such as Andrew Scull, who believe that the asylum was the product of a society grown less tolerant of what he calls deviant behaviour. Scull writes:

> While claims to provide cures as well as care were periodically used as a means of drumming up custom the fundamental orientation of the system [of asylum provision] was towards restraint in an economical fashion of those posing a direct threat to the social order.[5]

Michel Foucault, in his seminal account of the nature of insanity in seventeenth- and eighteenth-century France,[6] identifies the origins of the nineteenth-century lunatic asylum in the 'Great Confinement' of indigent paupers. Foucault correctly identifies institutions like the workhouse and the hospital as precursors of the lunatic asylum. However, the evidence of England in the eighteenth century suggests that instead of a 'Great Confinement' of paupers in workhouses, 'the great majority of the disturbed remained within society, kept at home or boarded out.'[7] In Aberdeen, after 1739, provision was made for the poor in the form of a workhouse; but this was abandoned as a residential building in 1768 and acted instead as the distribution centre for a monthly outdoor allowance, and we can assume that many of the indigent insane were therefore maintained on outdoor relief.[8] Eighteenth-century England did witness an expansion in the number of people confined in private madhouses. Roy Porter has described this development as entrepreneurial, comparable with developments in the professions of journalism, the general practice of medicine and estate management.[9] The rationale for confinement of the insane during the seventeenth and eighteenth centuries was that they

presented a danger to themselves and to others. With the acceptance of insanity as a secular medical diagnosis, families and physicians began to justify confinement on the basis of treatment and possible cure.[10] The lunatic asylum as a separate institution was born.

THE FOUNDATION OF THE ABERDEEN ROYAL ASYLUM

The ARA was established in 1800 by the existing management of the Aberdeen Royal Infirmary, itself established in 1739.[11] The board had originally included representatives chosen by the town council, the local kirk sessions, the guild court and the lord provost himself. By 1839 it included over sixty individuals drawn from the wealthier residents of Aberdeen, the majority of whom were members by virtue of having paid a subscription.[12] The infirmary, from its inception, had been designed to accommodate a number of the local lunatics as well as the sick and deserving poor.[13] Management minutes reveal that the cells reserved for these 'Bedlamites' were considered to be unfit for lunatic accommodation, so it was decided to build an asylum for them.[14] However, the management also explained the removal of lunatics from the infirmary as a response to the disruption they caused in a general hospital. They stated that:

> Finding from experience that it is attended with very great inconvenience and prejudice to sick patients to have those who are under mental derangement lodged within the same house.[15]

Notably absent from the initial reasons given for the establishment of the ARA was any claim to be providing a more curative and therapeutic environment: this appears to become part of the agenda only once the asylum project was under way. Indeed, in Aberdeen at the turn of the nineteenth century, with the transfer of lunatics from the infirmary to an institution with no resident physician and a lay superintendent, it appeared that madness was becoming estranged from the medical profession.

The asylum building, which was constructed in 1800, was designed to accommodate fifty patients.[16] The building itself was rectangular, with the roof sloping in towards an open courtyard, divided up with palisades. The accommodation included sixteen single cells and an unstated number of rooms for convalescents, a kitchen, accommodation for managers' meetings and for the keeper and servants.[17] It occupied

about an acre of ground and was situated on the present site of the Royal Cornhill Hospital, then a mile from Aberdeen. It was at an easy distance from the infirmary, facilitating daily visits by the latter's physicians, whose services were given without charge.

THE ABERDEEN ROYAL ASYLUM IN ITS LOCAL CONTEXT

The Aberdeen Royal Infirmary and the ARA, as Lesley Diack has made clear in the previous chapter, were part of Aberdeen's Poor Law provision, funded by voluntary contributions and administered on a strictly local basis. Aberdeen was in fact thick with charitable institutions in the first half of the nineteenth century. They were all supported by donations and subscriptions and therefore reflected the concerns of wealthier Aberdeen residents. Indeed certain individuals often appeared as members of the managements of several institutions, suggesting an inner group of active managers, motived by philanthropy and civic pride. Some of these institutions, such as the Asylum for the Blind and the General Institution of the Deaf and Dumb were educational establishments,[18] others sought the confinement of the indigent in a self-supporting manner.

A workhouse, or the Poor's Hospital, was established in Aberdeen, at the same time as the infirmary, designed in accordance with part of the central rationale of the Scottish Poor Law, which was to remove the problem of vagrants from the streets.[19] As we have seen, this was a short-lived institution,[20] but in 1836 a similar foundation, the House of Refuge for the Destitute,[21] came into being. Its purpose was succinctly stated in its rules and regulations:

> To afford on a strictly economical plan, temporary shelter, food, religious instruction and employment to the numerous classes of destitute persons who wander throughout the city and suburbs in a demoralised condition, until they can be forwarded to their parish.[22]

The Aberdeen Bridewell, established in 1809, was also designed to remove vagrants from the streets. This was an avowedly punitive institution, which later became the West Prison,[23] where people could be and were confined for begging. Inmates were imprisoned in total seclusion within cells, not unlike those existing contemporaneously in the ARA.[24] Then, in 1840 a Female Orphan Asylum was established, which trained girls for domestic service.[25] In 1841 the Aberdeen

Female Penitentiary was set up to try to keep prostitutes, victims of destitution, off the streets – the idea being to reclaim them for respectable society through the discipline of hard work and religion.[26]

This far from comprehensive list of institutions which were all products of the voluntary tradition of the Scottish Poor Law had other features in common too. All were closed institutions, confining their inmates and restricting the access of friends and relatives.[27] All relied on the reformatory power of honest toil and the religious service. Work, religion and discipline made up a 'moral treatment' that was regarded as just as appropriate for the able-bodied poor as for the insane.[28]

There were, of course, many differences between the ARA and these institutions. Mechanical restraints, like the strait waistcoat, were not considered necessary except in the ARA; while in the asylum, the role played by religion was increasingly supplemented by medical treatment. Moreover, work was not compulsory in the lunatic asylum where, if labour was expected at all, four hours were generally considered sufficient; whereas in the House of Refuge an eleven-hour working day was demanded.[29] But all these institutions deprived their patients, or inmates, of freedom, confining them in similar conditions. They satisfy Erving Goffman's criterion for a 'total institution':

> A place of residence and work where a large number of like situated individuals cut off from wider society for an appreciable period of time together lead an enclosed formally administered life.[30]

Given this institutional context, it is clear that the lunatics resident in the ARA were seen by the wealthy and influential members of Aberdeen society as a social problem comparable to pauperism, prostitution and crime. An institutional response to these social problems proved so popular not only because it offered a custodial solution through the segregation of deviants from society, but also because it promised their moral regeneration. The ARA was not simply a receptacle for the unwanted of Aberdeenshire society, but neither was it, at its inception and during its early years, a truly medical institution. It looked back to the eighteenth-century tradition of confining the mad because they presented a danger to other people and themselves, as well as forward to the medical aspiration to identify madness as a disease and cure it.[31]

[134]

EARLY TREATMENT

The ARA provided the only lunatic asylum accommodation in Aberdeen, serving both town and county, for almost the whole of the nineteenth century. It accepted both pauper and private patients. As the century unfolded the ARA, in common with all asylums, grew in response to the perennial increase in the number certified insane. Medicine in the ARA came to play a dominant role, personified by the physician superintendent, who exercised almost absolute authority over the asylum's staff and patients. The ARA's official annual reports place an increasing emphasis on the importance of therapy, and in particular the separate philosophies underlying medical and moral treatment. Moral treatment was made famous after its development and implementation at the Retreat near York, a private asylum for Quakers. It paralleled the moral training, based on religion, work and discipline, described in Aberdeen's varied institutions, in that it concentrated on the 'rational and emotional rather than the organic causes of insanity'.[32] Patients in the Retreat were to be encouraged and cajoled back to reason free from the most coercive forms of mechanical restraint, in a supportive – almost a family – atmosphere, and with the aid of productive occupations. Genuine attempts were made to introduce moral treatment into the ARA.[33]

In 1814 the keepers, Mr Anderson and his wife, visited the Retreat near York in order to learn the ways of moral treatment.[34] There is evidence that, following these moves, attempts were made to interest the patients in productive labour in the asylum fields, and claims were made in the *Annual Medical Reports*, that mechanical restraint was used less frequently.[35] The *Annual Medical Reports*, written for public consumption, were, of course, designed to show the asylum in a favourable light. They describe a range of occupations and amusements provided: patients played chess, bagatelle, draughts and were even allowed to keep pets. Books, papers and periodicals were provided for the more settled patients and some were encouraged to write articles which appeared in the in-house magazines of other Scottish asylums, such as the *New Moon Magazine* produced at the Crichton Royal Asylum in Dumfries, or the *Morningside Mirror* from the Royal Edinburgh Asylum.[36] While Europe and Britain reeled from the revolutions and unrest of 1848, lunatics in the ARA were encouraged to debate the issues of the day: 'It is amusing but at the same time gratifying to hear the topics of the day discussed in our little political circles, and to

observe that almost universally their members take part with the lovers of order and good government.'[37]

However, despite these colourful descriptions, the reception of moral treatment at the ARA was never more than piecemeal. Regular complaints were made by the visiting physician and the inspecting sheriff that there was not enough employment available for the patients, that living conditions were poor[38] and that far from drastically reducing mechanical restraint, methods of restraint like the muff and strait waistcoat remained in regular use.[39] Fifteen years after the introduction of the first resident physician at the ARA, the Royal Commission of 1855, appointed to examine the state of lunatic asylums in Scotland, concluded that the level of mechanical restraint in the ARA was excessive:

> The principal defects of management are the employment of trough-beds with drains, the use of strong dresses for male and female refractory patients, too frequent seclusion in cells and 'seclusion yards', and a great deficiency of means of occupation and amusement, and of extended exercise.[40]

Mechanical restraint as a means of controlling troublesome patients fell into disrepute after Dr John Connolly successfully removed it from the country's largest asylum at Hanwell in 1839.[41] The amount of mechanical restraint employed at the ARA in the first half of the nineteenth century suggests that the creation of a family atmosphere achieved for a time at the Retreat was not a realistic proposition in Aberdeen. This was hardly surprising for an institution that was constantly overcrowded, underfunded, and not well endowed compared with, for example, the Crichton Royal in Dumfries. The ARA in fact regularly ran at a deficit of up to 20 per cent in its first thirty years of operation.[42] Indeed, apart from the *Annual Medical Reports*, designed for public consumption, the asylum's records do not show much concern with the philosophy of moral treatment. While the management minutes record the mundane details of the administration of the institution, the case records invariably concentrate on the prescription of medicinal treatment.

MEDICALISATION

The lay superintendence, to which the ARA was initially intrusted, proved to be an unmitigated disaster, with the dismissal of three

keepers in the first thirty years – for offences ranging from drunkenness through to embezzlement and the abuse of patients.[43] The medical men alone combined the requisite professional respectability with at least some claim to expertise in the treatment of insanity. Dr MacRobin was appointed as the first resident physician in 1830.

When the ARA had been established, it appeared as if the physicians of the Aberdeen Royal Infirmary had been physically distancing themselves from the insane. In fact, the ARA, in common with all lunatic asylums, by bringing together those considered by society to be insane, facilitated the development of psychiatric medicine. This tendency has often been seen as medical aggrandisement. Michel Foucault commented:

> It is not as a scientist that *homo medicus* has authority in the asylum, but as a wise man. If the medical profession is required it is as a juridical and moral guarantee not in the name of science.[44]

This argument has been taken to its logical conclusion with the suggestion that medicine merely legitimised the confinement of the troublesome and inconvenient.[45] But before a further assessment of the treatment provided in the ARA can be made, it is necessary to investigate the argument that asylum patients were not suffering from any mental aberration or derangement.

Even a cursory glance at the medical case notes of the ARA physicians reveals a record rich in aberrant behaviour. For the historian, it is a record which cannot be easily explained away simply as social deviancy. To take one case more or less at random, John Henderson, a journeyman tailor from Aberdeen, was admitted to the ARA on 17 November 1842. The initial entry is as follows:

> Has for some time been travelling about seeking work in various places and his insanity is thought to be the consequence of poverty, anxiety, hardship and fatigue, acting on a delicate frame of a body. He returned home from Edinburgh on foot, about three weeks ago, emaciated, in rags, and in his present state of derangement. He has gradually grown worse saying that the French are bent on taking his life, has a dread of poison, and has been violent towards his mother who he blames for bringing him into the world and says he wishes she would cut his head off.[46]

Always assuming that the symptoms observed are not pure invention on the part of the physicians involved, we are forced to conclude that this patient was certified for something other than being an unwanted member of society. It remains possible, of course, that many symptoms were the product of institutionalisation itself: what Erving Goffman has described as the self-defence mechanisms of people confined within a total institution.[47] However, the fact that these symptoms appear to be unique to the patients of the ARA and other lunatic asylums, and were not exhibited by the residents of other institutions where similar conditions prevailed, suggests that they were correctly regarded as being physiologically distinct. Moreover, if the certification papers of patients drawn up before their admission are compared with subsequent observations in their case notes, the same symptoms can be found, suggesting that they were not the product of institutionalisation.[48] Of course if patients were suffering from what may loosely be termed 'mental derangement', it remains possible that the real reason for their certification was the unacceptable behaviour their conditions produced. Indeed, as we shall see, attitudes to the insane were coloured by preconceptions that had little to do with the nascent science of psychiatry.

The domination of the medical profession did not eliminate the asylums' custodial aspect. On the contrary, as the ARA grew in response to ever increasing numbers of certifications, it became necessary, in the second half of the century, to regulate and regularise the asylum regime. The reports of the Scottish Lunacy Commission, established after the Royal Commission of 1855, leave little doubt that living conditions improved considerably in the ARA. The asylum was no longer criticised for failing to provide basics such as warmth and clothing:[49] instead the emphasis of the commissioners was on overcrowding and a lack of occupation.[50]

The Lunacy Commission also described how, as the asylum grew into an institution for hundreds of patients, the superintendent, Dr Robert Jamieson, developed a rigid patient management policy to allow his overworked staff of attendants to control and treat their troublesome charges. Gone are the references to exotic pets, political debates between patient and doctor, and picnics in the Aberdeenshire countryside. Such frivolities receded into the background to be replaced by the reality of an asylum day. This began, for all patients, at six in the morning and ended at nine at night, with patients moved around the asylum in a body and given set eating, working and rest periods.[51]

It may have been warmer and more comfortable, and the evidence suggests that patients were less likely to be abused,[52] but it was a far from stimulating environment.

DR ROBERT JAMIESON

Dr Robert Jamieson was physician superintendent of the ARA from 1852 to 1884. Born in 1808 in Aberdeen, the son of a jeweller, educated at Marischal College in Aberdeen and then at Edinburgh University, he spent most of his working life in the ARA. Even after his retirement in 1884, he continued to live in the asylum grounds, where he died, predeceased by his wife and without son or heir. Not a major figure in the psychiatric profession, on the model of W. A. F. Browne or David Skae, he nevertheless became, in 1845, the first-ever lecturer in mental diseases at Marischal College,[53] and the following year he began lecturing in medical jurisprudence at King's College, then still a separate university.[54] He has also bequeathed to us a small body of writing on the nature and treatment of insanity and this, in conjunction with the medical records from the ARA, allows a comparison to be made between the theory of asylum treatment and the reality.

For Jamieson, as for all writers on the subject of insanity in the nineteenth century, aetiology was a major concern. The possible causes of insanity were divided into predisposing and exciting, and normally it was assumed that a person who developed insanity had suffered from both a predisposing and an exciting cause.[55] There were, however, several causes which, revealingly, were considered sufficient to bring about insanity in isolation. These were intemperance, domestic unhappiness, joy or grief, head injury and religious excitement.[56] It is no coincidence that what were considered to be especially virulent causes of insanity parallel the social concerns of the time. For example, domestic unhappiness was of constant concern because of the strain it put on the family unit, at a time of frightening social change. Connected with this in the middle-class mind was the problem of vice in general and intemperance in particular, considering the devastating effect heavy drinking could have on an individual's physical constitution, family and socio-economic position. Religion, always a powerful force in Scotland, was also an area which aroused passions. During the religious revival which flourished around 1860 in the north-east,[57] the incidence of patients diagnosed as suffering from devotional excitement noticeably increased. Devotional excitement was normally rarely

given as the cause of insanity, in one case each year at the most, but in 1859 and again in 1860 devotional excitement was the ascribed cause in four cases, and the number rose to five in 1861.[58] It would appear that, as was also true in northern Ireland, a number of people suffering from religious excitement, or fits, were considered to have been driven into this insane condition by the revivalist fervour. [59]

Jamieson's comments and observations on the insane are, in their overwhelming majority, not condemnatory in tone. However, in the last pamphlet he wrote, published in 1875, disillusionment with the continuing increase in the numbers of certified insane had clearly set in, and he explained the increase solely in terms of degeneracy:

> It seems to me the natural power of the nervous centre in resisting malignant influences is in these days impaired by mistakes of education and training, unsuitable marriages, defective nutrition of the nerve tissue through poverty, over-indulgence in stimulants – tobacco and narcotics – over-reading, moping and unhealthy habits, unseasonable hours, defective and disordered religious impressions. [60]

Insanity had become for him the scourge of civilisation and he vented his spleen against it. He wrote:

> The disease increases in the population, growing like a malignant fungus living on the decaying vitality of the trunk from which it has parasitically sprung. [61]

It would, however, be grossly unfair to let these quotes stand as an illustration of Jamieson's overall attitude to his charges throughout a long and dedicated career, but combined with occasional comments in which he equated insanity with criminality,[62] the mad with the bad, they illustrate the fear and resentment insanity generated. It is little wonder that scholars have seen the whole asylum enterprise as an exercise in confining the socially unacceptable, and argued that nineteenth-century insanity was a social construct.

There was nothing unusual in Jamieson's attitude towards the insane. More surprising perhaps was the lack of originality in the diagnostic system he used. Despite the presence of the medical school (or schools) in Aberdeen, and the prestigious Royal Asylum, Jamieson showed no evidence of innovation in diagnostic or treatment techniques. The classification used included four major types of insanity: mania, monomania, melancholia and dementia. Mania and melan-

cholia were considered curable, while monomania and dementia were deemed chronic. There were also the far less common diagnoses of epilepsy, general paralysis and puerperal insanity.[63] Dr Jamieson produced a series of lectures which outlined the symptomatology of each type of insanity and the medical treatment that was to be provided for those who were considered curable. For example, mania, which was said to be characterised by convulsions, illusions and then delusions, was to be treated by being locally bled, using leeches placed on the head. Later the patient was put on a high or rich diet, given brandy, wine and opium to relieve the excitement and sleeplessness.[64] When we compare theory with the reality of diagnoses in the ARA's medical records, we can see a clear correlation between the lectures and the case notes. However, what is also clear is that the physicians were treating the symptoms rather than any actual type of insanity. For example, patients suffering from general paralysis, which was later discovered to be a tertiary form of syphilis and was a chronic condition from which no one recovered, were given treatment in response to their symptoms despite their terminal condition.[65] Medical treatment was not provided on the basis of a rigorous classificatory system; instead patients were given those treatments which appeared to alleviate their symptoms. Most telling of all is the limited number of patient case-records which show regular medical treatment, suggesting that the majority of patients resident at any one time were not receiving any.

THE RESULTS OF TREATMENT

Unfortunately it is extremely difficult, and far beyond the limits of this study, to tell what direct effect these treatments had on the patients of the ARA. It is possible, however, to analyse certain aspects of the statistical record of admissions and discharges in order to discover the influence which treatment, or indeed mere residence, in the ARA, had on patients. It should be said, however, that the results presented here are highly selective. They have been chosen because they add a statistical weight to assertions which, using conventional qualitative historical research techniques, could be no more than speculative. My calculations are based on a 17 per cent sample of patients admitted between 1821 and 1900.[66]

Firstly it is important to point out that 75 per cent of admissions to the ARA were discharged, whether designated recovered, improved or unimproved. The remaining 25 per cent died in the asylum. The dis-

charge of three quarters of admissions undermines the contention of some historians that asylums were 'dumping grounds for social misfits'.[67] The 25 per cent death rate, however, is not an insignificant figure and it remains possible that the poor living conditions and ill treatment was causing a proportion of these deaths. If this was the case, we can assume that the pauper patients would suffer most, since they received poorer quality food and lived in more cramped conditions (see appendix: graphs 1–6.)

Pauper patients, however, were only marginally more likely to die in the asylum than private patients (appendix: graphs 1–2, which cover the period after the 1857 Lunacy Act only), suggesting that the poorer food and living conditions endured by the pauper lunatics did not seriously affect their mortality. Looking at the whole period under study, and breaking the social class of patients into four groups according to the social classification adopted by Anne Digby in her study of the York Retreat (appendix: graphs 3–6),[68] adds further support for the contention that poorer patients did not fare significantly worse either because of their poorer condition on admission, or because of the poorer treatment and diet they received. Indeed mortality is remarkably constant throughout the four social classes. What the four figures do show is a steady progression in the numbers discharged unimproved from the highest to the lowest classification. Perhaps this was due to the inferior treatment provided for the poorer patients, but the steady mortality rate suggests different discharge policies for different classes. Pauper patients were often transferred to the poorhouses, in the interest of Poor Law economy and in order to make space in the ARA, and this increased the numbers discharged as improved. Private patients, who could afford to stay, may well have remained in the asylum, allowing later discharge in a better condition. Moreover, when a private patient was discharged, there was a natural tendency on the part of asylum staff to emphasise the beneficial effects of asylum treatment, since it was on such a basis that the ARA justified its fees. The same pressures would not be so apparent when it was the parochial board or the parish that was paying the fees, and when the custodial, rather than the curative, aspect of the asylum was the greater concern.

In analysing the effect of social class on the outcome of treatment, there has been an underlying assumption that residence in the ARA was not simply a custodial experience, and that it actually had an effect on the well-being of patients. Strong supporting evidence for this

assumption is provided in graph 7 (see appendix). It indicates that patients who had suffered longest before admission were most likely to die in the asylum. Those, on the other hand, who have been suffering for less than three months, were far more likely to be discharged recovered. Either admission to the asylum, or removal from a particular environment, for example family or location, had a beneficial effect on patients.[69]

CONCLUSION

The ARA was established when ideas about the care and confinement of the insane were in a state of flux. When looked at from the perspective of its later development into a mental hospital, the ARA appears as a medical institution designed to cure the problem of insanity. However, when placed in a local institutional context, the ARA takes on the characteristics of a moral reformatory.

As the first half of the century unfolded, the ARA evolved into a fully medical institution. Treatment was provided by way of experimentation, as the nascent science of psychiatry tried to make sense of a bewildering range of symptoms. It is doubtful that any of the medicinal treatments provided had any significant effect on patient conditions, and yet admission to the ARA sooner rather than later in the development of a patient's condition clearly had a beneficial effect. Why this should have been the case, is not known. Perhaps the most likely explanation is the one advanced by nineteenth-century 'alienists' themselves: namely that removal from the source of mental irritation allowed the patients to recuperate and recover. If this was the case, the ARA was operating as an asylum in the original sense of the word – a place of refuge.

ABBREVIATIONS IN NOTES

AUL: SC –   Aberdeen University Library, Department of Archives and Special Collections

GRHBA –   Grampian Regional Health Board Archives (now renamed as the Northern Health Services Archive)

SRO –   Scottish Record Office

T –   pamphlets collected by Alexander Thomson of Banchory, in AUL: SC

NOTES

1. This chapter derives from material in Robert Seumas Lobban, 'Healing for the body as well as the soul: the Aberdeen Royal Asylum in the nineteenth century' (University of Aberdeen M Litt thesis, 1994).

2. David Fraser, *The Christian Watt Papers* (Ellon, 1988), p. 107.

3. Kathleen Jones, *Lunacy, Law and Conscience 1744–1845: the social history of the care of the insane* (London, 1955); Kathleen Jones, *Mental Health and Social Policy 1845–1959* (London, 1960); David Kennedy Henderson, *The Evolution of Psychiatry in Scotland* (Edinburgh, 1964).

4. John Cooper and Sartorius, 'Cultural and temporal variations in schizophrenia: a speculation on the importance of industrialisation', *British Journal of Psychiatry* (hereafter *BJP*), no. 130 (1977), pp. 50–55; Edward Hare, 'Was insanity on the increase?', *BJP*, no. 142 (1983), pp. 439–55; Edward Hare, 'Schizophrenia as a recent disease, *BJP*, no. 152 (1988), pp. 521–31.

5. Andrew Scull, *Museums of Madness* (London, 1979), p. 29.

6. Michel Foucault, *Madness and Civilisation: a History of Insanity in the Age of Reason* (London, 1987).

7. Roy Porter, *Mind-Forg'd Manacles* (London, 1987), pp. 110–11.

8. William Kennedy, *Annals of Aberdeen* (Aberdeen, 1818), vol. 2.

9. Porter, *Mind-Forg'd Manacles*, p. 164.

10. Porter, *Mind-Forg'd Manacles*, p. 155.

11. GRHBA: *Minutes of the Aberdeen Royal Asylum* (1794–1902), 2/1/1, p. 1.

12. AUL: SC, *Annual Medical Report*, 1939.

13. GRHBA, *Minutes*, 2/1/1, p. 1. Lunatics were to be found accommodated in other hospitals around Scotland, for example, Edinburgh, Inverness and Dumfries. Francis J. Rices, 'Madness and industrial society' (University of Strathclyde PhD thesis, 1981), pp. 234–35.

14. SRO: volume of miscellaneous material arising from the duties of the Aberdeen-shire sheriff concerning lunatics, 1815–1830, SC1/18/1, p. 9.

15. GRHBA, *Minutes*, 2/1/1, p. 1.

16. GRHBA, *Minutes* (1794–1902), 2/1/1, p. 1.

17. GRHBA, *Minutes* (1794–1902), 2/1/1, p. 1.

18. AUL: SC, *Report of Trustees of the Aberdeen Asylum for the Blind*, 1850, T. 96, no. 10; *Account of the General Institution for the General Instructions for the Education of the Deaf and Dumb, on the Principles of Abe Sicard*, 1837, T. 326, no. 12, p. 3.

19. Jean Lindsay, *The Scottish Poor Law: its operation in the north east, 1745–1845* (Ilfracombe, 1975), p. 81.

20. Kennedy, *Annals of Aberdeen*, vol. 2.

21. AUL: SC, *General Rules and Regulations of the Aberdeen House of Refuge for the Destitute*, 1837, T. 326, no. 12, p. 3.

22. *General Rules.*

23. Joy Cameron, *Prisons and Punishment in Scotland from the Middle Ages to the Present* (Edinburgh, 1981), chap. 5.

24. AUL: SC, *Descriptive Sketch of the Aberdeen Bridewell or the House of Correction for the City and County of Aberdeen and the System of Management*, 1827, T. 194, no. 6.

25. AUL: SC, *Abstract of the Regulations for conducting the Aberdeen Female Orphan Asylum, Albyn Place*, 1840, T. 111, no. 16.

26. AUL: SC, *Seventh Report of the Aberdeen Female Penitentiary* (Aberdeen, 1846), T. 96, no. 6.

27. In the Aberdeen asylum, for example, prospective employers were allowed regular access to the girls but friends were only allowed to visit once every three months.

28. Erving Goffman, *Asylums: the Social Situation of Mental Patients and Other Inmates* (New York, 1961), p. 13.

29. AUL: SC, *General Rules and Regulations of the Aberdeen House of Refuge for the Destitute*, 1837, T. 326, no. 12, p. 9.

30. Goffman, *Asylums*, p. 13.

31. Porter, *Mind-Forg'd Manacles*, pp. 155, 164.

32. Anne Digby, 'Moral treatment at the Retreat 1796–1846', in W. F. Bynum, Roy Porter and Michael Shepherd (eds), *The Anatomy of Madness: Institutions and Society*, vol. 2 (London 1985), pp. 50–72.

33. See also Anne Digby, *Madness and Medicine; a Study of the York Retreat 1796–1914* (Cambridge, 1985).

34. AUL: SC, *Annual Medical Report*, 1815, p. 4.

35. AUL: SC, *Annual Medical Report*, 1818.

36. AUL: SC, *Annual Medical Reports*, passim.

37. AUL: SC, *Annual Medical Report*, 1848.

38. SRO, volume concerning duties of the Aberdeenshire sheriff 1815–1830: SC1/18/1, p. 12.

39. GRHBA, *Inventory of the Aberdeen Royal Asylum*, completed by Thomas Boys (Superintendent), c. 1824–17, unclassified, pp. 126, 154.

40. *Report of Her Majesty's Commissioners Appointed to Enquire into the State of Lunatic Asylums in Scotland – 1857*, Irish University Press Series of British Parliamentary Papers, vol. 7, 'Mental Health' (Dublin, 1969), appendix B, no. 1, p. 44.

41. See Jones, *Lunacy, Law and Conscience*.

42. AUL: SC, *Annual Medical Reports*, passim.

43. GRHBA, *Minutes*, 2/1/2, pp. 59, 283; 2/1/3, p. 212.

44. Foucault, *Madness and Civilisation*, p. 270.

45. Scull, *Museums of Madness*, p. 29.

46. GRHBA, *Case Notes*, 2/4/7, pp. 93, 94.

47. See Goffman, *Asylums*.

48. See for example, GRHBA: Lunacy Forms (1858–1887), 2/5/1 and Case Book, (1858–1862), 2/4/11.

49. GRHBA, *Minutes*, 2/1/2, p. 236.

50. SRO, *Annual Reports of the General Board of Commissioners in Lunacy in Scotland*, 1887, MC/11/29, p. 49; 1872, MC/11/14, p. 180: 1863, MC/11/5, p. 133.

51. GRHBA, *Guide to the Attendants' Duties in the Aberdeen Asylum*, 2/10/4, 1873, p. 4.

52. The appointment of the resident physician solved the problem of abuse by the lay superintendent. However difficult working conditions and poor pay meant that the attendants charged with the day to day care of patients continued to abuse them. The level of abuse is impossible to quantify, but it was significant enough to create an embattled atmosphere in the refractory wards. See SRO: *Annual Reports of the General Board of Commissioners in Lunacy in Scotland*, 1871, MC/11/13, p. 49; 1864, MC/11/6, p. 31; GRHBA: *Register of Attendants Leaving between May 1873 and May 1881*, 2/3/75.

53. Peter John Anderson, *Kings College Officers and Graduates* (Aberdeen, 1898), vol. 2, p. 70.

54. Anderson, *Kings College Officers*, p. 856.

55. A predisposition to insanity was caused by the degeneration of a person's brain as result of their own actions, or was passed to them as a Lamarkian inheritance from their parents. In believing that the acquired characteristics of the parents were inherited by the children, Jamieson along with several subsequent generations of British alienists was heavily influenced by the French degenerationist psychiatrist, Benedict Morel (1809–73).

56. AUL: SC, MS2813: 'Lectures on lunacy' given by Dr Robert Jamieson at the Lunatic Asylum, Summer Session 1861, transcribed by John Barclay: lecture 4.

57. Andrew Drummond and James Bulloch, *The Church in Victorian Scotland 1843–1874* (Edinburgh, 1975), p. 185.

58. Statistical appendices to *Annual Medical Reports*, 1859, 1860, 1861, in AUL: SC.

59. James G. Donat, 'Medicine and religion: on the physical and mental disorders that accompanied the Ulster Revival of 1859' in W. F. Bynum et al. (eds), *The Anatomy of Madness*, vol. 3, pp. 124–50.

60. Robert Jamieson, *Recent Increase of Mental Disease: an Address to the North of Scotland Medical Association* (Aberdeen, 1875), p. 11.

61. Jamieson, *Recent Increase*, p. 9.

62. 'Insanity is not in every instance want of wisdom merely, but often want of virtue also; it may have the aspect of crime as well as that of folly': Robert Jamieson, *Lectures on the Medical Jurisprudence of Insanity* (Aberdeen, 1850), p. 53.

63. Jamieson, 'Lectures'.

64. Jamieson 'Lectures', lecture 6; GRHBA: *Admission Register 1858–1873*, 2/3/9: and case notes, 1866–69, 2/4/13, pp. 54, 80, 82, 86, 87. For a more detailed discussion of how theoretical classification corresponded to actual diagnosis and treatment see Lobban, 'Healing for the body'.

65. GRHBA, case notes, 1866–69, 2/4/13, pp. 153, 127, 148.

66. A database was constructed using Dataease version 4. Each entry included details of a single patient's admission. These factors were then used in various transformation passes in the statistical analysis package spss/pc+. The years 1821–24, 1831–34, 1841–44, 1851–54, 1861, 1864, 1871, 1884 and 1894 were selected.

67. Charlotte Mackenzie, *Psychiatry for the Rich: a History of the Ticehurst Private Asylum* (London, 1992), p. 121.

68. Anne Digby, *Madness, Morality and Medicine*, p. 183.

69. The assertion that prompt admission to the asylum was essential to allow recovery, was regularly made. For example: 'application for admission to the Asylum is deferred . . . the unfortunate patient is reduced to a state of helpless idiotism, for whose support they are unable to provide, throw him upon the charge of the parish, and when in this incurable condition, an application is made for his admission to the Asylum'. AUL: SC, *Annual Medical Report*, 1832, pp. 1–2.

APPENDIX: RECOVERY DATA

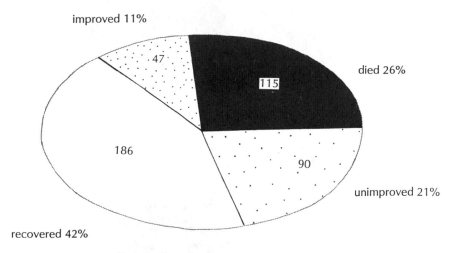

improved 11%

47

115

died 26%

186

90

unimproved 21%

recovered 42%

Graph 1. Results for pauper patients (post-1857).

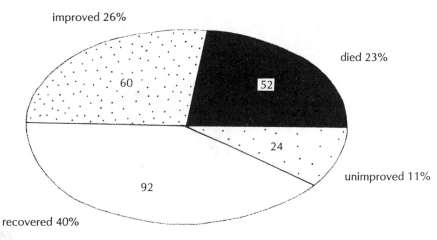

improved 26%

60

52

died 23%

24

92

unimproved 11%

recovered 40%

Graph 2. Results for private admissions (post-1857).

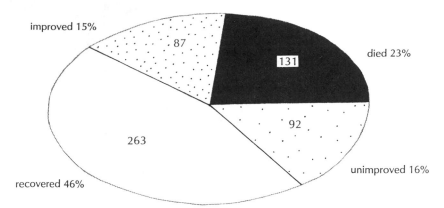

Graph 3. Results for unskilled labourers, sailors, soldiers and fishermen.

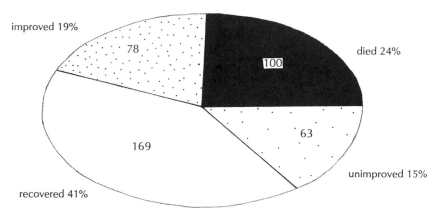

Graph 4. Results for semi-skilled workers, wright, blacksmith, pensioner, crofter, gardener.

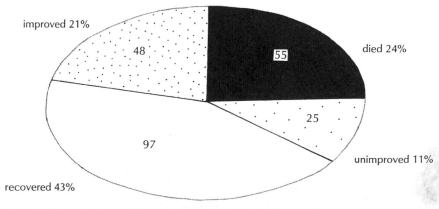

Graph 5. Results for retailers, craftsmen, teachers, clerks, students, farmers, excise officers, and inspectors of roads.

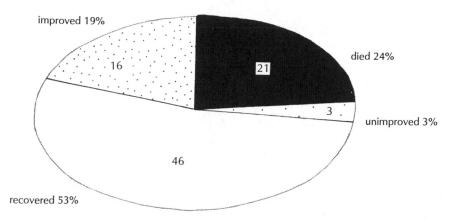

Graph 6. Results for landowners, merchants, bankers, professionals, and gentlemen.

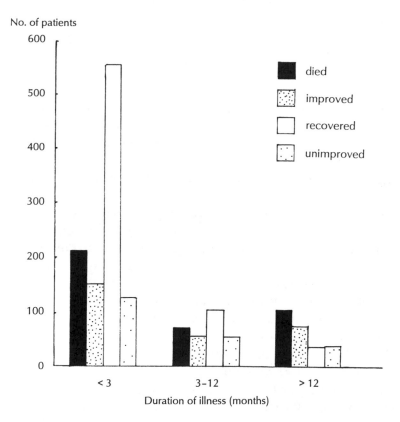

Graph 7. Duration of illness prior to admission.

9

'No mean city'?[1]
The Growth of Civic Consciousness in Aberdeen with Particular Reference to the Work of the Police Commissioners

Rosemary Tyzack

Like many Victorian cities, Aberdeen, with its increasing population and diversifying economy, faced new or exacerbated problems of poverty, public health and law and order. It sought to solve them through a mix of voluntary organisation, diverse and often overlapping municipal institutions, private enterprise and the encouragement of individual self-help – the precise emphasis changing as the nineteenth century progressed. This chapter looks at changing views of civic responsibility for the well-being of individual citizens, and of the appropriate institutions and organisation to achieve it. It does so by examining the work of the Aberdeen Police Commission from its establishment in 1795, through the 1820s when it dealt with schemes to provide water from the River Dee, and on through the period when its responsibility for public health was progressively expanded, to the early 1870s when its functions were taken over by the town council.

A study of the struggles the police commissioners had in meeting their responsibilities for provision of public health and policing – in co-operation, or often in conflict, with other municipal institutions such as the town council or the parochial boards – has broader implications. It allows us to reflect, both on the difficulties public authorities in the

localities had in coping with the new scale of social problems, and on the way in which perceptions of what the police commissioners could and should provide changed over time. With their powers over property, their ability to raise a considerable rate, and the authority they derived from being elected on a more popular franchise than most other municipal institutions, the police commissioners' activity (or inactivity) also generated strong, if intermittent, public debate. This could be about both what was the proper scope of community provision for basic services, such as water, gas, sewerage and a properly structured police force; and also about whether the community was better served by specialist boards or by a multi-purpose town council. Aberdeen's experience in coping with new urban problems had distinctive features, but consideration of the city's experience can contribute to the wider debate about the relative importance of local initiatives and central government directives, of municipal institutions and voluntary organisations, in making Victorian cities easier to live in and worthier of their citizens' pride and sense of identity.

The idea of a police commission for Aberdeen was mooted in the 1770s in what can be termed the 'paving and lighting era' of policing. But the first police commission was not established until 1795.[2] The board was to consist of thirteen commissioners, who had to be residents of property valued at £15 annual rental; and who were to be elected by inhabitants of property valued at £5. At the end of every two years the outgoing commissioners were to select five of their number for a further term of office, while eight new commissioners were to be elected. The remit of the commissioners was to see to the better paving, lighting and cleansing of the streets, to remove obstructions, to secure a better supply of water, and to open up new streets. To finance its work the commission was allowed to raise an assessment of one shilling (5p.) in the pound, to borrow money to a limit of £5000, and, possibly, to receive help from the common good fund of the town council. Initiated by the dean of guild together with the town council, the Aberdeen Police Commission was intended to meet the needs of a growing population for water and for space; and particularly to deal with overcrowded streets. It was also to relieve the town council of responsibility for the wells, and still more for the well debt, financing its operations through a new rate rather than the town's Common Fund. Originally it was intended that the town council and convener of the Incorporated Trades should keep a firm control over the commission, which would have had *ex officio* members and a relatively restrictive

property qualification both for membership and for the franchise. But this intention was thwarted by the supporters of burgh reform, led by John Ewen, who wanted local government to be more popular and accountable.[3] On the other hand, the original plan had been to permit women who met the property qualification to vote as well as men, whereas in the event women were excluded.[4]

We can already see in these arrangements some of the hazards the Police Commission would face throughout its existence. It had limited finances and strictly regulated financial powers, coupled with airy promises of funding from the town council. And there were inevitable tussles with the council, which was self-selecting prior to the 1833 Burgh Reform Act, and thereafter elected on a narrower franchise than the commission: the more popular basis of the latter meant that it could become a focus for radicalism.

Such hazards became early apparent in the 1790s, in the struggle over plans to enlarge the Police Commission's powers, and in the way it was bypassed when, as discussed in chapter two, the New Street Commission was established. The Police Commission began its work with commendable zeal, passing regulations against nuisances, organising the wells under Commissioner Anderson, removing safety hazards such as outside staircases and sharp granite corners to buildings and paving. Despite phasing in improvements, however, it ran out of funds.[5] The town council having refused help from the Common Good Fund, the police commissioners resolved to put the financial position to their electors; and to ask either for permission to increase the rates from one shilling to one-and-sixpence (7½p.) for a limited period of five or seven years, or for a new act making the commission permanent and giving it enlarged borrowing powers.[6] The town council in collaboration with the Incorporated Trades seized the opportunity to curb the commission by ensuring the failure of the proposal for a new act, and by establishing a New Street Trust – from which the police commissioners were excluded – to open up the South and North Roads, and to bring water from the Hazlehead spring to sell to private households. This plan was sold to the General Meeting of Electors of the Police, and to the inhabitants more generally, on the grounds that it would be self-financing at the very least – the dues on feus paying for opening up the streets, and the sale of water paying for its supply. Ultimately, it was argued, the scheme would even provide a surplus for the use of the community.[7]

While King Street and Union Street were to be of inestimable benefit

in the long run to Aberdeen, and were probably more adventurous projects than anything the commissioners could have afforded, they did nothing to contribute to the more mundane improvements Aberdeen badly needed or to deal with the growing problem of law and order. And the disputes tended to mean that the Police Commission lost much of its momentum. Commissioners became lax in attending meetings (people even spoke disparagingly of 'Mr Ewen's Commission'); and, having failed to get a new bill introduced in 1799, they were reluctant to try again. Not until 1815 and 1816 did they take the initiative, through public advertisement, and this evinced no popular response. Only when the crime-wave after the Napoleonic war hit Aberdeen, and the subsequent attempt to establish voluntary support for a watch failed, were the police commissioners to get their new bill, which became the Police Act of 1818.[8] The changed mood was, no doubt, in part also a reflection of a conservative reaction after the French Revolutionary and Napoleonic wars.

The Police Acts of 1818 and of 1829[9] strengthened the powers of the commission but perpetuated its rivalry with the town council. In 1818 the police commissioners were given enlarged powers of enforcement in established areas such as drainage, paving and lighting, and the control of nuisances. Their remit was enlarged to include a new night watch. Their resources were increased through the imposition of a higher rate of one-and-sixpence, and a separate police rate; and their borrowing powers were enlarged.[10] But the act also brought a permanent town council presence on to the Police Commission.[11] At a time when Scottish burgh reform was again on the national agenda, and the Conservative government was trying to fend off demands to change the self-selection procedure for town councils with promises to open up the council accounts, the provost of Aberdeen, in the teeth of the opposition of the police commissioners and the General Meeting of the Inhabitants, was able, with government support, to secure *ex officio* seats on the Police Commission for himself, the dean of guild, and the convener of the Incorporated Trades.[12] The town council also retained responsibility for daytime policing through its town sergeants, meaning that there was dual control over the policing of crime, which was only partly remedied when the police commissioners gained powers to raise their own day police force in 1829.[13] Similarly the Police Commission's ambition to take responsibility for, and enlarged powers over, Aberdeen's water supply – in particular the Hazlehead springs – was thwarted, until the pressing need for water both for

[153]

domestic and for manufacturing consumption led to its being empowered to take water from the Dee in 1829.

The 1829 Police Act, indeed, marked an important stage in the transition of the Police Commission from an essentially paving and lighting authority towards being a public health authority. The Dee water scheme made Aberdeen a pioneer in the provision of water through a large-scale capital project run by a municipal board. The records of the police commissioners and town council, and the columns of contemporary newspapers, show that many Aberdonians had doubts about the gamble involved in the enterprise. There was a hunt for alternative sources such as the Culter Burn, the Loirston Loch, the Loch of Skene or the Aberdeen canal; but experts were called in to show the water was undrinkable. It was optimistically hoped that a private water company might come to the rescue;[14] and, indeed, Aberdeen may have got its municipal water in part because private investors were not interested. Furthermore, the restrictions on the capital sum to be raised, £36,000, and on the rates to be levied, reflected Aberdonian suspicions of municipal debts, following the city bankruptcy in 1817.[15] This worry seems to have been shared by some of the newly elected police commissioners, who were afraid they might personally be held liable for Police Commission debts.[16]

For the Police Board the municipal water scheme meant negotiation with local landowners, especially Menzies of Pitfodels, over access, and with salmon fishers over river levels;[17] hiring an Edinburgh-based civil engineer, Mr Jardine, who directed operations through flying visits and long-distance correspondence; wrestling with suppliers of substandard pipes, who might be all too well known to board members;[18] and then persuading Aberdonians that river water was fit to drink. For many people the odd colour and the 'foreign bodies' in the river water were off-putting, whereas at that time nothing was known of the germs in wells near the graveyards.

The police commissioners also looked on the provision of water as a business – the more people who could be persuaded to have water piped into their own houses and pay private water-rents the more financially viable the scheme became.[19] Press advertisements for houses show two differing trends in Aberdonian responses. More and more houses were put up for sale with bathrooms and piped water supply, while others were advertised as outwith the Police Authority area, with good wells and no water rates. Water was provided initially for domestic consumption through public wells or private pipes but

the police commissioners had also to confront the demand for water from business – notably the big textile firms, the gasworks and the slaughterhouses. Whether their motive was financial or to please the local industrial bigwigs, or the need to promote the city's economy, the police commissioners increasingly began to supply water to business. Their shifts of strategy between individual negotiations with firms and the charging of fixed tariffs[20] raised dark suspicions of favouritism among rival concerns, and among private citizens who were not sure whether business should get public water at all.

The commissioners had also to work out a compromise with 'the suburbs' which had initially stoutly maintained that they could provide their own policing and cleansing, and which had their own wells. They were brought within the powers of the act for policing and cleansing, but were able to remain outside the water scheme until inhabitants paying over half the assessed rental petitioned through a general meeting to be included.[21] The commissioners had to balance the financial advantages of bringing them within the act against the potential supply of water. They had also to raise the capital for the water schemes, largely through local bonds.[22]

Provision of water was, of course, taking on new dimensions nationally with the growth of the public health movement in the 1830s and 1840s. The very fast growth of the large industrial cities like Manchester, Leeds and Glasgow, with attendant occupational and environmental health hazards, and the outbreak of cholera in the years from 1830 to 1832, with its unknown causes but cross-class impact (it was no respecter of upper and middle class areas), gave point to the earlier work on public health of doctors and academics, such as Robert Graham, Robert Cowan and James Cleland. Surveys of local health conditions by local statistical societies – in Manchester for example – were strengthened by parliamentary investigations such as Chadwick's in 1842, and the Health of Towns Commission in 1844. These pointed to the importance of personal cleanliness, sewerage, and piped water; of adequate ventilation within houses and lodgings; of the layout of streets; of the need to tackle problems such as overfull graveyards; and of appointing professionals, whether they were doctors to check on work conditions and public places or engineers to oversee the new drainage systems.[23]

The growing national concern for wider public health reform impinged on Aberdonians. The report submitted to the Chadwick Commission by Dr Kilgour and Dr John Galen on behalf of the town

[155]

council amply demonstrates both Aberdeen's problems and the potential solutions.[24] Aberdeen suffered three epidemics of fever in 1817–19, 1831–32 and 1838–40. The city's sewerage system was virtually non-existent.[25] Many areas were without common sewers, there being only twenty-eight in existence, mainly in the recently built streets. Many of these were very small (nine inches to one-and-a-half feet); and some were open, some closed. Similarly such cesspools as existed were confined to the new streets. Aberdeen dealt with its night soil through daily collection, the dustcart announcing its arrival by bell; but not all families were assiduous in putting out their filth. Nor did the Police Commission encourage them by providing proper facilities. Ash pits in many areas were few and far between, as also were privies. The report noted, for instance, that the Gallowgate with its 44 courts had only 17 ash pits and 10 privies, North Street, similarly densely packed, had 12 receptacles for filth and no privy.[26] Nor did private enterprise really help. Very few stablers provided privies. And if lack of sewers and drains was one problem, what to do with the filth was another. Many sewers and drains emptied into the Denburn and it, along with other burns, handily emptied into the harbour, the surface of which bubbled with fetid, noxious gas at low water, giving forth a most intolerable stink perceptible in the town at a considerable distance,[27] although the prevailing winds kept it away from the west end.

Overcrowding of the poor was also commonplace. They lived in cramped streets, three-storey buildings and courts, with one- or two-room homes for families. Such of the ventilation as there was came about by accident rather than by design, through the failure of the landlord to repair the windows in the common-stairs.[28] The Kilgour-Galen report took a poor view of certain landlords in particular, the new rack-renters who had replaced the old custom of twice-yearly rent collection with four-weekly payment, and were careless to whom they let property, or of keeping it in good repair, whitewashed and painted.[29] While deploring the failure of the poor to help themselves by opening windows and by taking out their filth, the doctors also recognised the need to encourage effort by providing facilities and a cleaner environment.

The report however was concerned not only to paint a rather unsavoury picture of Aberdeen's environment, but also to suggest the remedy. Kilgour and Galen advocated:

(1) The extension of police powers, on the lines of suggestions made by Dr Arnott and Dr Kay for London; planning to ensure widths of

streets; proper sewerage charged to the owners of new property; the connecting of all habitations with the main sewer; effective drainage of land and collection of rubbish; inspection of lodging houses and powers to enforce whitewashing of houses by the owners.[30] The suggestion was not that police commissioners were not using their powers, but that they did not have the right powers.

(2) The establishment of a committee of the police commissioners, or of the town council, or of both, to be elected annually as a Board of Health. This was a proposal which subsequently emerged in the 1848 Public Health Act for England and Wales.[31]

With such a damning indictment of public health conditions in Aberdeen, and with proposed solutions, why did Aberdeen not get its new Public Health Act until 1862? Not that it was alone in this: Edinburgh and Glasgow also hastened slowly. J. H. F. Brotherston, in his *Observations on the Early Public Health Movement in Scotland*, suggested that Scottish towns moved slowly because medical opinion was divided over the causes of fever. Chadwick and his supporters stressed 'miasma', the stench from rotting vegetation and waste; whereas Scottish medical opinion often stressed contagion and poverty. Another factor was indifference among the better-off toward the conditions of the poor. This, along with vested interests, could operate against acceptance of public responsibility for health.[32] A further cause of the slow progress arose from the technical problems of improving drainage and sewage-disposal. The Aberdeen doctors (Kilgour and Galen) concentrated in their report on epidemic fever, and tended to gloss over endemic fevers. They pushed for improved sanitation but they also saw contagion as a cause of disease, stressing the problems of overcrowding and poverty, which they related particularly to old age, single-parent-hood, and the loss of work through sickness. In proposing remedies, they reported divisions of opinion amongst those they had consulted: for Mr Leslie, Mr Frazer and Kilgour himself, better allowances from the poor's fund were needed; for Dr Keith and Mr Wood extending the means of religious instruction and training as a corrective to the physical and moral degeneration of the poorer classes were equally important, if not more so.[33]

The preoccupations and priorities of the doctors reporting to the Chadwick Commission were only partly reflected in the wider views of Aberdonians in the 1840s. Aberdeen had its Health of Towns Association, and the press continued to take an interest in public health issues. But, with some notable exceptions, there seems generally to have been

little sustained pressure from Aberdeen medics for public health reform, either through the universities' medical schools or through the Medico-Chirugical Society.[34] This was in apparent contrast to Edinburgh and Glasgow. Aberdonians in the 1840s and 1850s were more concerned over poor law reform, or Sheriff Watson's industrial schools, or the local soup kitchens, and saw their civic obligations in these more traditional social terms. At least some Aberdonians who had been police commissioners turned their efforts to the new Poor Law Boards.

In the 1840s and 1850s, economic boom was followed by severe depression which hit many traditional textile companies very hard. Aberdeen's accepted political and social leadership was badly affected. Quite apart from the upheavals associated with the 1843 Disruption in the Church, therefore, these were difficult times in which to launch new and expensive community projects. In the heady days of prosperity in the earlier 1840s, while some Aberdonians continued to look to municipal institutions to improve the city's well-being, others looked to private enterprise. This can be seen in the debates over the new market and gaslight company. Alexander Anderson's plans for the market would, it was hoped, not only attract business to Aberdeen, but also provide a means for slum clearance and street improvement by the removal of much insanitary property. Against this, not surprisingly, some argued that in supporting the market scheme the police commissioners were being manipulated by the slum landlords.[35] Similarly, the divisions in opinion over the proposed municipalisation of the gas supply reflected not only the debate between supporters of private enterprise and supporters of municipal provision, but also diverse approaches to the purpose of municipal trading services – whether they should promote more efficiency and lower prices in the supply of essential commodities such as gas or generate profits which might be ploughed into other municipal enterprises. Lured by promises of cheap gas supplies and by rumours that municipalisation of the old gas company was designed to benefit the pockets of the old gas company proprietors, and stricken with doubts about using gas profits for other projects, Aberdonians rejected the chance to be one of the first to municipalise its town gas.[36] Municipalisation was only undertaken in 1872. In the aftermath of the local economic crisis of the later 1840s, the city was neither in a position to seek the necessary legislation, always a costly process in itself, nor to launch expensive new municipal projects.

If times were not propitious for securing a new local act, the police

commissioners could seek to make more use of their existing powers and exploit recently enacted measures of general legislation, such as the 1847 Water Works Clauses Act, the 1847 Town Improvements Act, the Nuisances Acts of 1848 and 1856, and the 1856 Police Act. Under the Nuisances Acts, the removal of nuisances became part of the board's responsibilities. In practice, however, a division of labour was worked out between the Police Commission and the Parochial Boards, with the police commissioners looking after external nuisances, and the Parochial Boards dealing with internal nuisances.[37] A Sanitary Committee was established and a renewed assault made on nuisances such as the loch and the Denburn. These efforts were prompted or supported by the St Nicholas Poor Law Board, which, in the event of an epidemic, could, on instructions from the Board of Supervision in Edinburgh, issue directives and regulations for its control and for the provision of medicines and other medical aid, including hospitalisation.[38] The 1848 act also gave the police commissioners power to regulate lodging houses. The commissioners became more pressing in pursuit of proprietors who would not stump up for paving or drains – those of George Street and Upperkirkgate, for example – and were more willing to give a subsidy to encourage them to comply.[39] They began to make provision for public privies. Reliant still on the scavenger system for cleansing, the commissioners experimented with cleansing machines for the streets and new, more easily maintained, filth boxes. But there was increasing frustration with the limitations on the commissioners' powers. As a body they were concerned to improve the supply of water to the poor districts, but some went further and wanted to have water piped into the houses of the poor, with a differential water rate for private pipes to houses with low rentals or help for the New Model Lodging House experiment by supplying not only water but also connecting pipes free of charge. The commission, however, did not have the powers to do this.[40] The constant campaign to clean up the Denburn was also frustrated by the mill-owners' demand for water, as well as by squabbling amongst the police commissioners, the town council and the parochial board over which institution should pick up the bill for the improvements.[41]

Provision for public health was one aspect of the Police Commission's responsibilities, but it was responsible for law and order, whether through the provision of street lighting or, after 1818, of a watch or police force. In contrast to public health, where progress, however piecemeal, was often made from within the community, Aber-

deen exhibited considerable insouciance or small-town mindedness over its police forces. The major impetus for these came from outside, through the Counties and Burghs (Scotland) Act 1857 as implemented particularly by the police inspector, Colonel Kinloch. At a national level, attitudes to law and order were changing as Britain moved from a deterrent criminal code, with its use of the death penalty for many minor offences such as theft, to reliance on a regular police force to prevent crime by its physical presence,[42] and on improved detection leading to the punishment and rehabilitation of criminals in prisons and reformatories. This change was seen in the Counties and Burghs Police (Scotland) Act of 1857, with its provision for the national inspection of forces and its sweetener of financial support for local police reforms. Aberdeen was perhaps lucky in that it had a relatively homogeneous population, migrants who often came from the country-side close by, and small-scale industries with, relatively speaking, greater face to face contact – all factors likely to act as restraints on crime. But, with a rising population, it still had its share of thefts, drunken brawls, juvenile delinquency and vagrancy, as well as much-publicised murders and periodic riots. However, the police commissioners, the town council and the Harbour Board – which shared responsibility for polic-ing until 1862 – and Aberdonians in general, remained relatively con-tent to have police forces thin on the ground, poorly paid, largely un-trained and subject to divided control.

Town serjeants under the magistracy provided the first day patrol, but no provision for a night watch was made until a force was organ-ised by voluntary subscription in 1817 largely on the initiative of local advocates. The police commissioners gained the powers to organise a night watch in the 1818 Police Act[43] and a day patrol in the 1829 Police Act.[44] A police court was established in 1829, and gas lighting introduced for part of the town in 1827.[45] Aberdonians were clearly looking for the physical presence of the police, rather than for their in-telligent anticipation of crime or detective abilities, to deter criminals. Under pressure from police superintendents whom they recruited from Bow Street London, Glasgow and Dundee, the police commis-sioners introduced codes of discipline, uniforms, and gratuities for the number of criminals caught, but they clearly did not envisage policing becoming an attractive career. Salaries were low, and numbers were cut back in hard times. There were few officers and scant chances of promotion or pay rises; and there was an invidious distinction main-tained between the day patrol and the despised night watch – the

former being deemed to have the harder task and to merit more pay and better uniforms.[46] Divided responsibility between the town council and the police commissioners led to jealousies between the different police forces. The intermittent refusal of the town council to make a proper contribution from the rogue money to assist the police commissioners led, in the most extreme instance, to the commissioners disbanding their day patrol in 1837, leaving day-policing to just six town serjeants.

That Aberdeen was more receptive to new ideas about rehabilitating criminals can be seen from such philanthropic endeavours as the house of refuge, the industrial schools and juvenile reformatory school. But the state of its prison, especially for those on remand, left a great deal to be desired. While the Aberdeen Police Commission was willing to use extra powers – such as those conferred by the Public House Regulation Act of 1854 to control rowdiness and drinking – Aberdeen only began its move to a more effective and organised police force after the compulsory inspection made, in 1859, by Colonel Kinloch in his capacity as inspector general of police in Scotland.

Kinloch's report was damning about the city's outdated and inadequate approach to policing.[47] Aberdeen, with an 80,000 population, had eighty in its police force, but only three were officers. The report recommended at least ten officers at a rate of pay which would attract good men; a properly graded and paid constable service to retain those who so often left for the higher-paid county force; the ending of the distinction between night and day policing; the establishment of proper police headquarters; and the improving of the prisons. The police commissioners stoutly opposed the initial investigation as being dangerously centralising[48] and defended local pay bargaining and other practices.[49] Aberdeen, it was argued, was a cheap and pleasant place to live and work in, so salaries could be modest. The night patrol's greatcoats and staves were suitable for the climate, and for the men's dual role as members of the watch and as lamp-extinguishers. With the lure of a national subsidy of just over £5000, however, those police commissioners in favour of improvement were able to persuade their colleagues to upgrade their force, to provide police housing, and a new police headquarters – but not superannuation. [50]

The frustrations of the 1840s and 1850s over public health and policing were to be partly overcome by the 1862 Police Act.[51] This gave the police commissioners the powers to supply water from the Cairnton works on the Dee and to provide a sewerage system; increased their

authority to deal with nuisances; gave them greater planning controls and in particular the right to insist that owners of houses provide sinks, water closets, and privies; made them responsible for the fire service; enabled them to maintain the new police force; and assigned to them the function of dealing effectively with vagrants, prostitutes, unruly hackney cab drivers, and – a sign perhaps of a developing tourist industry – bathers on the beach, who also required the provision of bathing machines. Significantly the commissioners might, with the agreement of a specially convened ratepayers' meeting, purchase and run the gasworks, though any profits were to go to lowering the cost of gas. Again with the ratepayers' approval, they could provide municipal slaughterhouses, public parks and public baths, particularly for the working classes.[52]

The act, passed in a period of economic revival, shows clearly how expectations about public health and policing had changed since 1818 and 1829 – both in the range of powers given, and the options open, to the commissioners; and in the investment to be made in public health. The Police Commission was now able to press ahead with the Cairnton works, for which scheme alone £166,000 was to be raised. It also proceeded with the sewage system, and the extension of its services to people living outside the police boundary. The Police Act did not, however, tackle the question of rivalry between different municipal authorities, which had been at the centre of the storm between 1868 and 1871.

In 1871, the Police Commission was merged with the town council. In the rather dirty fight over the merger, the provision of gas and water did concern some of the combatants. But the central issues had more to do with changing attitudes to community and to political participation than with the effective provision of public health and policing as such. The extension, in 1867 and 1868, of the parliamentary and the burgh franchise to incorporate the urban working-class voter, taken together with growing pressure in the Liberal Party for social reform, and with the comparative prosperity of the later 1860s and early 1870s, accounts for the emergence in Aberdeen of a new political grouping loosely labelled the 'Party of Progress'. It aimed to bolster city development through, for instance, harbour improvements and the expansion of the city into Torry. It sought to make the town council the power centre of Aberdeen by taking over the commissioners' duties and by its increased influence on the Harbour Board. It campaigned to revamp the composition of the council itself, by eliminating the seats of old

vested interests, such as the convener of the Associated Trades and the dean of guild; and by giving it greater financial strength through taking over the collection of the police rates. Some progressives also argued that the Guildry funds were monopolised by the few at the expense of the many,[53] and should be transferred to the council.

As the Party of Progress supporters put it in their very strenuous campaign in the 1870 elections, and in the town council committee report on the merger, amalgamation and centralisation were the way of the future, as, they alleged, could be seen in other large Scottish towns. There would be economies in management charges, allowing a saving of a shilling in the pound rate – enough to open a 'People's Park'. There would be more efficiency savings in the collection of rates. The more efficient of the police commissioners, if they were not already on the town council, could be elected to serve there; and as the town council franchise was now wider than that of the Police Commission, it would allow the new voters to have a say in police matters on which the comfort of citizens depended. Besides, one exciting election a year was quite enough for the candidates, their friends, and supporters.[54]

The Party of Progress, now in the majority on the town council, had to speak the language of economy for the ratepayers; and of civic amenities for progressive Liberals and, especially, for the working-class voters. It tried to avoid awkward questions such as those about the rocketing costs of town council projects like the building of the County and Municipal Buildings; about the price of land in Torry; and about what it intended to do with the Guildry funds. The progressives' proposals met with a barrage of opposition from those who deplored the new popular politics; from the Incorporated Trades, the Guild Brethren and the vested interests they represented; and from those doubtful of the competence of the new town councillors who were thought to be running up debts, to have ridden roughshod over apparent statutory requirements in some of their financial dealings, or to be involved in shady contracts and land deals.

From the Police Commission's point of view, or at least that of the majority of the commissioners, the proposed changes were not necessary, advantageous or desirable. The commission provided an opportunity for more people to serve the community, took on a considerable burden of work, and collected their rates more efficiently than the town council. It already had the requisite powers to expand services like gas and slaughterhouses, and to extend its boundaries.[55] At a polit-

ical level, while some commissioners and their supporters argued that the Police Commission was comparable to a joint stock company, providing services, to be judged by results rather than representation, others took a more democratic approach and wanted the franchise qualification lowered to bring it into line with that for elections to the town council and parliament. These commissioners were above all opposed to the concentration of powers in the hands of one municipal institution. They wanted to ensure wider popular participation through retaining a number of municipal boards, as was still the case in other Scottish cities, and in this they no doubt had the support of their colleagues on the school board and parochial board. [56]

It would be easy to see this conflict in terms of democrats against non-democrats, or nascent municipal socialists against obscurantist ratepayers. But this would seem to simplify the dividing lines. There were improvers both on the council and amongst the police commissioners. The improvements they envisaged were still in many ways in the tradition of land improvement, harbour improvement and civic building, and of the provision of basic amenities, rather than of extensive social services such as school meals and council-housing. There were, moreover, supporters of more popular politics in both camps. The argument revolved around questions such as what was the best way for the community to reach decisions about the scope of its collective responsibilities and how community spirit could be most effectively maintained in the new political climate of the 1860s.

The arena in which these conflicts were resolved, as had been the case with the dispute generated by the 1818 Police Act, was a parliamentary committee – this time the one set up to consider the Aberdeen Municipal Extension Bill – a pro-amalgamation measure. The town council with its access to Common Good funds had the edge over the police commissioners in putting its case. The latter were not allowed to use money from the police rates and had to finance their case out of their own pockets.[57] The largely Liberal parliamentary committee was, in any case, likely to be sympathetic to the idea of reinforcing the powers of town councils, on grounds of general principle alone.

How, in conclusion, should Aberdeen's experience be judged in the wider Scottish, or British, context? Traditional accounts of the progress of public health and policing painted a picture of central government and parliamentary committees pushing reluctant local boards – mindful of their ratepayers and their landlords – into making improvements. More recent investigations have stressed the pioneering work of

many local authorities. It has been argued that the worry about the rates was reasonable when all the necessary money was still raised locally, and when there were many calls on the community purse – whether for public projects, philanthropic endeavours, or investments in industry which provided employment. And it has been suggested that divisions among the experts – whether medics or sanitary engineers – about what needed to be done justified caution in tackling public health provision. Such accounts have noted the good as well as the bad performance of private water companies or gas companies; and have pointed to the reluctance of ordinary folk to have people meddling in their lives – especially if those people were middle-class do-gooders who did not seem to appreciate that opening windows let out expensive heat.

What happened in Aberdeen shows that there was a considerable increase in municipal enterprise between, say, 1818 and the 1870s. The range of the police commissioners' powers grew substantially – with or without town council support – and there was increasing popular acceptance of these powers. Aberdeen took the initiative over municipal provision of Dee water. The police commissioners, together with the parochial boards, utilised the Nuisance Acts to attack health hazards – sometimes, it is true, under pressure from the Board of Supervision in Edinburgh. And the city was kicked or bribed into good policing by the outside intervention of Colonel Kinloch. Aberdonians were pragmatic in their approach to whether services should be provided by private companies or by municipal boards, as was seen in the saga of the gas company. While most citizens took the need to keep rates low for granted, the community poured increasing investment into municipal enterprises such as the new sewerage and gasworks. And to maintain its sense of being a close-knit community, it was prepared to see a hike in the police rate to support an ever-widening range of philanthropic endeavours. There were, of course, landlords who resisted bills for drains or inside improvements, ratepayers who wanted to keep rates down, and entrepreneurs who sought to manipulate the police commissioners or the town councillors. Rivalry between municipal institutions could hold up the provision of public health or policing. As a result of much trial and error, local initiatives and outside pressure, however, Aberdonians increasingly recognised the need to provide basic services in public health. And they came to accept policing as a community responsibility, which involved much of the time and effort of their police commissioners, their town council-

lors, and the members of their parochial boards; and which required controls over the activities of individual citizens. If this was accepted, it was at least in part because they – like the citizens of other expanding Victorian municipalities – wanted to be able to say that they lived in 'no mean city'.

NOTES

1. The earliest use of this term is, apparently, to be found in the 1611 translation of the Bible: *Acts*, xxi, 39.
2. 35 George III s. xxxvii.
3. City of Aberdeen Archives. Minutes of the Police Commissioners (hereafter MPC), vol. 1, pp. 1–7, 6 June, 3 and 7 July 1795.
4. 35 George III c.
5. MPC, vol. 1, p. 160, 5 November 1798.
6. MPC, vol. 1, p. 164, 4 February 1799.
7. MPC, vol. 1, pp. 171–72, 4 March 1799.
8. 58 George III c. lix.
9. 10 George IV c. xli.
10. 58 George III c. lix, s. lxxvi.
11. 58 George III c. lix, s. vi.
12. MPC, vol. 2, pp. 164–67, 28 April 1818.
13. 58 George III c. lix, s. lxxi.
14. MPC, vol. 13, p. 371, 14 September 1826, pp. 372–73, 20 September 1826.
15. MPC, vol. 3, pp. 517–18, 20 October 1828.
16. 10 George IV c. xli, s. cix.
17. MPC, vol. 3, pp. 576–78, 7 November 1828, vol. 4, pp. 17–18, 25 March 1829.
18. MPC, vol. 4, p. 175, 26 April 1830.
19. MPC, vol. 4, 9 December 1829.
20. MPC, vol. 4, pp. 353–54, 21 March 1831, pp. 395–97, 6 June 1831.
21. MPC, vol. 3, pp. 530–32, 10 November 1828, pp. 540–41, 24 November 1828.
22. 10 George IV c. xli, s. cx; MPC, vol. 4, p. 209, 19 June 1830.
23. See A. S. Wohl, *Endangered Lives: Public Health in Victorian Britain* (London, 1983); J. H. F. Brotherston, *Observations on the Early Public Health Movement in Scotland* (Edinburgh, 1952).
24. *Sanitary Conditions of the Labouring Population: Local Reports for Scotland* (1842), vol. 28, pp. 286–302.
25. Ibid., p. 292.
26. Ibid., p. 294.
27. Ibid., p. 295.
28. Ibid., p. 296.
29. Ibid., p. 297.
30. Ibid., p. 299.
31. Ibid.
32. J. H. F. Brotherston, *Observations*, p. 83.

33. *Sanitary Conditions of the Labouring Population*, p. 298.

34. See Minutes of Medico-Chirugical Society, passim.

35. MPC, vol. 7, pp. 428–29, 11 December 1843, pp. 430–34, 18 December 1843, pp. 427–40, 15 February 1844, p. 446, 27 February 1844.

36. *Aberdeen Journal*, 1844, passim.

37. MPC, vol. 8, pp. 557–59, 26 September 1853.

38. For a general view of the work of the Board of Supervision in poor relief, medical relief and public health, see S. Blackden, 'The Board of Supervision and the Scottish parochial medical service', *Medical History*, vol. 30 (1986).

39. E.g. MPC, vol. 8, pp. 430–31, 8 December 1851, p. 543, 18 July 1853.

40. E.g. MPC, vol. 8, p. 121, 25 May 1846, p. 214, 28 February 1848.

41. MPC, vol. 9, pp. 248–49, 11 December 1848, pp. 484–85, 16 August 1852.

42. See, for a general view, V. A. C. Gattrell, B. Lenman, G. Parker (eds), *Crime and the Law: a Social History of Crime in Western Europe* (London, 1980).

43. 58 George III c. lix, s. lxxi.

44. 10 George IV c. xli, s. clxviii.

45. 10 George IV c. xli, s. clxxxix; *Form of Procedure for the Police Court of Aberdeen* (Aberdeen, 1829).

46. See H. Irvine, *The Diced Cap: the Story of Aberdeen City Police* (1972), for a general account of Aberdeen City Police.

47. MPC, vol. 9, pp. 370–72, 13 June 1859.

48. MPC, vol. 9, pp. 387–91, 10 October 1859.

49. Ibid.

50. MPC, vol. 9, pp. 428–39, 15 May 1860.

51. 25 and 26 *Victoria* c. cciii.

52. Ibid., s. 434–56.

53. *Aberdeen Journal*, esp. 20 July 1870, 26 October 1870.

54. *Aberdeen Journal*, 8 February 1871, 15 February 1871.

55. MPC, vol. 14, p. 161, 9 May 1870.

56. MPC, vol. 14, pp. 350–51, 30 January 1871, pp. 369–75, 20 February 1871.

57. See House of Commons, *Select Committee on Private Bills Group B* (1891), Aberdeen Municipality Extension Bill.

10

Aberdeen into Parliament: Elections and Representatives, 1832–1865[1]

Michael Dyer

Between 1707 and 1832, Aberdeen shared a member of parliament with Inverbervie, Montrose, Brechin and Forfar. He was nominated and chosen by an electoral college consisting of five electors – each close burgh corporation appointing a single elector. Similar arrangements applied to all the other royal burghs, with the exception of Edinburgh. Consequently, as the radical Committee of the Friends of the People observed in the early 1790s, 'the burgesses and inhabitants at large were disfranchised,' and an 'evil felt by the great commercial towns, [was] being classed with insignificant and obscure burghs.'[2] The principles behind the Scottish reform legislation of 1832 sympathised with the frustrations of the disfranchised urban middle class, the act seeking to remedy the problem by creating a burgh franchise based on a qualification requiring residence, as true owner or occupier, of property valued at £10 annual rental and by restoring separate representation to the big cities. A main beneficiary of the changes was Aberdeen, whose new Parliamentary Burgh, extending beyond the royalty, not only re-established the separate representation it had enjoyed in the pre-1707 Scottish parliament, but created a constituency of independent electors beyond the reach of local powerbrokers and ministerial

manipulation. Dod, in his *Electoral Facts*, noted that in Aberdeen – as in Edinburgh and Glasgow – 'no personal influence prevails'.[3] The major theme of this chapter, then, is the lack of deference shown by voters to both old and new elites. In the light of the tendency amongst political historians to stress the continuing force of tradition in the way in which the reformed parliamentary system in Britain operated, this may seem surprising.

The autonomy enjoyed by individual electors was reinforced by the factional character of political conflict, because each contest restructured electoral choice, requiring an elector to consider his vote anew. Party organisations were virtually non-existent. Campaigns centred on the activities of leading families, groups of citizens and candidates, who formed ad hoc election committees, serviced by a variety of law firms, to advance their respective causes. In order to demonstrate the popularity of their candidates, contending factions published lists of their election committees in the press, which, in 1841, included almost half those who eventually voted. A vigorous political debate was sustained by public meetings, pamphleteering, and local newspapers, including the Tory *Aberdeen Journal*, the Whig *Aberdeen Herald*, the Non-Intrusionist *Aberdeen Banner*, and latterly the Liberal *Aberdeen Free Press*.

Apart from free trade, the issues confronting the electorate – even when, as for example with municipal and ecclesiastical reform, they were national in character – had a distinctly local focus. That was particularly the case after the Conservatives ceased to contest the seat following the general election of 1841. Some matters, particularly the question of civic improvement, were purely local, and cut across conventional partisan and religious divisions. There were also geographical differences of interest within the constituency, dividing those living in the old royalty, from those in the new suburbs and from others outwith the municipality altogether; these were reflected in the shaping of electoral choice. Thus, the interpretation of elections involving competing Liberals cannot be reduced to a one-dimensional explanation, based on religion or a conflict of Whig versus Radical – even to the extent that those terms had any precise meaning. The selection of candidates deliberately to obfuscate the boundaries between competing social categories, and thus to maximise support, only adds to the historian's problem. Indeed, as we shall see, the outcome was so confused in 1857 that the local press itself was at a loss to explain it.[4]

BACKGROUND TO VOTING DATA

In 1832, 2,024 £10 residents became the arbiters of representation in the new Parliamentary Burgh of Aberdeen. By 1852, their number had risen to 4,547, but following the Burgh Registration Act of 1856 this fell away, in 1857, to 2,346 and only rose to 3,996 in 1865.

The electors were distributed amongst five wards, four of them within the royal burgh (see appendix: table 1). Wards 1 to 3, accounting for three fifths of the electorate, constituted what had been until the early nineteenth century the whole of the urban part of the royalty, confined on the east by the North Sea and to the west by the Denburn valley. Ward 1, centred on the harbour, was characterised by shipbuilding, commercial and trading interests, and latterly included the railway station. Ward 2 incorporated the Town House, the Sheriff Court and the North of Scotland Bank (virtually a single complex in the heart of the city), Marischal College, the younger of the two universities, and the 'Mither' Kirk of St Nicholas to which the council paraded each Sunday. Ward 3 was dominated by manufacturing and retail interests, though not significantly more so than its neighbours.

Ward 4 was a new residential suburb immediately to the west of Wards 1, 2 and 3, whose development had been made possible in the early years of the nineteenth century by the construction of Union Street and the bridge across the Denburn. The separation of this new quarter from the old city was more than geographical, because it became the focus of the new middle-class revolt against the traditional urban leadership, and was an important location for the new Free churches following the Disruption.[5] Ward 5 was outwith the municipal boundaries. It included Old Aberdeen, a burgh of barony with sixty-four inhabitants huddled around King's College, the older university, and St Machar's Cathedral.[6] It also incorporated Woodside, an industrial village which later became a small burgh, an agricultural hinterland, and textile mills along the River Don, including that owned by the Haddens, the arbiters of Aberdeen politics in the years prior to reform.

Differences of character between the wards were predictably reflected in the occupational composition of their electorates (see appendix: table 2). In 1857, for example, against an overall 47.6 per cent of the electorate engaged in manufacturing and retail, those so employed accounted for around three fifths of the voters in Wards 1 and 3, and more than half in Ward 2, but less than a third in Wards 4

and 5. The drink interest (mostly grocers) and food retailers comprised more than a fifth of the voters in Wards 1, 2 and 3. In Ward 4 a quarter of the electors were associated with the professions; three in ten voters in ward 5 were engaged in agriculture. These occupational differences in some measure help to explain differences in voting behaviour between the various parts of the constituency.

The electoral history of Aberdeen between 1832 and 1865 falls under three headings: the Whig-Liberal ascendancy of 1832 to 1841, characterised by competition between Liberal and Conservative candidates; the Free Church and new middle class revolt, 1847–1852, which saw a rejection of traditional elites; and the waning of old alignments, 1857–1865, when earlier alliances became confused.

THE WHIG-LIBERAL ASCENDANCY, 1832–41

The first phase was dominated by a conflict between two local families, the Haddens (Tory) and the Blaikies (Whig), and their respective allies. The Haddens had been the incumbent power in the city for at least thirty years prior to reform. James Hadden of Persley, textile manufacturer and father of the modern city, was lord provost from 1801 to 1803, from 1809 to 1811, and again from 1832 to 1833. And his brother, Gavin, held the office from 1820 to 1822, from 1824 to 1826, and then from 1830 to 1832. Their power rested on the control they exercised over the close corporation and the patronage they exerted with respect to municipal improvements, harbour and kirk works, and the appointment of ministers and the professors of Mathematics and Divinity at Marischal College.[7] They were largely responsible for the bridging of the Denburn, which had laid the foundations for Aberdeen's expansion and increased prosperity. The Haddens were also landowners, and had close connections with agricultural proprietors. They opposed burgh, parliamentary, and ecclesiastical reform, and supported protection. The *Journal*, whose editor, David Chalmers, was a member of the unreformed corporation, gave the Haddens its support.

As part of an interconnected commercial aristocracy, the Blaikie Whigs had more in common with their opponents than with the new £10 voters. Like the Haddens, they were involved in textile manufacturing and the law. They also had interests in iron founding and shipbuilding. If there was a distinction between the Whigs and Tories it was that the former were more exclusively tied to the commercial activ-

ities of the burgh than their opponents.[8] The main conflict between them was a political struggle for the control of municipal affairs. The Blaikies were particularly concerned about the mismanagement of harbour improvements arising 'from the vast preponderance of self-selected magistrates'[9] on the board of trustees. Following burgh reform, the Blaikies assumed municipal leadership, the lord provostship being held by James Blaikie from 1833 to 1836, and by Thomas Blaikie from 1839 to 1847, and again from 1853 to 1855.

Close allies of the Blaikies were the Bannermans. Alexander Bannerman, a wine importer, who became the Liberal candidate in 1832, had previously been appointed to the council by James Hadden, but in 1812 had been forced to leave over a dispute about the appointment of a minister. The mouthpiece of the Whigs was the *Herald*, whose editor, James Adam, an anti-clerical in the European mode, disliked the enthusiasm of the Non-Intrusionist Evangelicals even more than the outlook of the Moderates in the Church of Scotland. [10]

Exclusion from political patronage led the Whigs to identify with the movement for reform. Bannerman blamed the bankruptcy of the council in 1818 on the incompetence of the Haddens, and suggested that the improvements they had effected had been done for private rather than public gain. In 1830, he organised a reform petition signed by 121 members of the Seven Incorporated Trades and Burgesses of Guild, which was rejected by James Hadden. The strength of support for political change and free trade amongst even this conservative section of the trading and manufacturing community underlined the wide base of Bannerman's coalition. He also identified with Non-Intrusionist sentiment within the kirk, although the political significance of this issue was less central in 1832 than it was to become later in the decade. Given the antipathy towards the Tories for having opposed reform, it was not surprising that James Hadden withdrew his intention to contest the seat in 1832.

The wisdom of Hadden's retreat was soon confirmed, when the Whig-Liberals carried every seat on the reconstituted burgh council in 1833. Although six candidates were returned in each of three wards,[11] all former members of the corporation who stood were defeated. In Ward 3, James Blaikie topped the poll, with James Hadden 92 votes behind the candidate returned in sixth place. In a separate election for the dean of guild, Thomas Bannerman defeated David Chalmers, editor of the *Journal*, by 283 to 145, underlining the extent of business support for Whiggery. It was not until 1837 that the first Tory was re-

turned to the reformed council. [12]

The Whig apotheosis came with the general election of 1835, when Bannerman received 71.6 per cent of the votes against a Tory, Admiral Sir Arthur Farquhar, a landowner with a town house in Aberdeen (see appendix: table 3). Although the committee lists are too limited to make a comprehensive analysis of party support, it is instructive to note that, while no fewer than forty-nine of the signatories to the 1830 petition requesting burgh reform were members of Bannerman's election committee, only two declared themselves for Sir Arthur. It is noteworthy, too, that in the industrial and commercial wards (1, 2 and 3), the sitting member received more than three-quarters of the vote. Even in the fastnesses of Ward 5, the admiral failed to win forty per cent of the poll. The lesser support for Bannerman in Wards 4 and 5, nevertheless, indicated a weakening of Whig influence away from the commercial and manufacturing heart of the royal burgh.

Given the outcome in 1835, it was no surprise there was an unopposed election again in 1837, but by 1841, as part of a general trend in Scotland towards the Conservatives, there was a significant diminution in Bannerman's popularity (see appendix: table 4). To a certain extent that reflected a weakening of gratitude towards the Liberals for the Reform Act, but more specifically it indicated strains within the Whig-Liberal coalition precipitated by the crisis in the Kirk.

In many respects the reform alliance between the Whig elite and the new middle class had been one of convenience, for while the former had been prepared to ride the tiger of reform to replace the Tories as the arbiters of social control, they did not share the desires of the latter for a fundamental transformation of the political, social and ecclesiastical establishment. As long as the Kirk remained unified, the Whigs could temporise with Non-Intrusionist sentiment, but as it became more insistent and drifted towards schism, the alliance could not be sustained. Furthermore, whereas in 1832 the Non-Intrusionists had been politically unorganised, by the end of the decade they had established a network of connection outwith the traditional urban leadership, and had founded their own newspaper, the *Banner*, to press their case.

In response, the *Herald*, formerly a bitter opponent of the Haddens, voicing the opinions of the Whig leadership, advocated a rapprochement between the Whigs and Tories to resist those who were to become the Free Churchmen. By 1839, local government elections were being contested by Whig-Tory Moderates (i.e. Intrusionists),

thereby effecting a political alliance between the Haddens and the Blaikies, against Non-Intrusionist opponents. The new local government alignment was particularly problematical for Bannerman because it opened a rift between his major backers and the majority of his voters, whose evangelical cause he could not ignore.

Bannerman was fortunate that he faced a Conservative (Innes of Raemoir, a Kincardineshire landowner), rather than a fellow Liberal, at the general election of 1841, because it revived the reform coalition which had broken down at local government level. Although his election address made no mention of the crisis in the Kirk, he could not ignore the 'very delicate' religious question. As a non-presbyterian dissenter he attempted to distance himself from the issue, and waffled his way between support for 'any new measure to give the people a substantial choice in the choice of their ministers', and opposition to proposals 'intended to give the clergy more power'.[13] Thus, he sought to satisfy the demand of the Non-Intrusionists for greater control by congregations over their own affairs; while, at the same time – and in order to placate the Voluntaries – distancing himself from evangelicals who sought a significant secular role for the Kirk in a spiritually re-formed Establishment. The fudge proved acceptable to the *Banner* and the *Herald*, but risked alienating traditional Kirkmen.

Although Bannerman won comfortably, a drop in overall support of 12.9 per cent on 1835 indicated a weakened alignment. While the parameters of support remained essentially the same as before, with the inner city wards most supportive, Bannerman's decline in Wards 1, 2 and 3 of 15.9 per cent was almost twice as much as in Wards 4 and 5 (where the drop was 8.5 per cent). The greater movement of traditional Aberdeen towards the Conservatives suggested a firmer affection for the Auld Kirk than was the case in the suburbs. As the *Banner* noted on 10 July 1841, 'A number of Whig-Moderates refused to vote, notwithstanding the editor of the *Herald*'s "satisfaction" with Mr. Bannerman.'

In occupational terms, electors engaged in manufacturing and retail were strongly behind Bannerman (see appendix: table 4). Collectively, they constituted 59 per cent of his election committee and 71.3 per cent of all manufacturers and retailers who declared their affiliation. Food retailers (72.3 per cent) and the drink trade (75.0 per cent) were particularly supportive. It was, however, a reflection of the Hadden influence that those connected with textiles were hardly more Liberal than the constituency as a whole. By contrast, Innes had the over-

whelming backing of those associated with banking and insurance (66.7 per cent) and the professions (59.8 per cent). He enjoyed a clear lead among those engaged in agriculture (53.4 per cent), and had an almost equal share (48.7 per cent) of the residenter vote. Consequently, in terms of occupational background and economic interest, there was a clear distinction between the profiles of Liberal and Conservative support. Whereas three-fifths of all Liberals were associated with manufacturing and retail, as against 49.2 per cent of all voters, only 36 per cent of Conservatives were so engaged, and although only 37.8 per cent of those declaring their voting intentions were classified as residenters, or were connected with the professions, banking, insurance, and agriculture, they accounted for 52.8 per cent of all Conservatives as against 26.6 per cent of Liberals.

THE FREE CHURCH AND THE NEW MIDDLE CLASS REVOLT, 1847-52

Whig-Tory co-operation in local politics reflected a mutual commitment to civic improvement and commercial development, in which the principals drew little distinction between their own private ambitions and the public interest. (The Blaikies, for example, made sewage pipes for some of the projects Rosemary Tyzack has discussed.) These efforts were stimulated by the North of Scotland Bank, the creation of a Tory, Anderson, but the directors of which, including Lord Provost Blaikie, were predominantly Whig. The bank, appealing to local patriotism, attracted investors from the new middle class and advanced cheap loans to its friends, notably Thomas Bannerman & Co., Hadden & Sons, and Masson & Co. It also advanced a substantial loan to Adam & Anderson to assist the promotion of a railway bill.[14] There was additionally a Masonic link, Alexander Hadden and Thomas Blaikie being quondam master and deputy master of the Provincial Grand Lodge. The apotheosis of the Whig-Tory alliance came with the formation of the Aberdeen Marketing Company in 1839 under the chairmanship of James Hadden, with James Blaikie as a co-director. It was a measure of their accord that at the opening of the covered market in 1842, a project which included the building of new streets, Blaikie said of Hadden that, 'No man has ever done so much for the improvement of the city.'[15]

The Hadden-Blaikie accord, which sustained the lord provostship of Thomas Blaikie from 1840 to 1847, was based on a dynamic civic leadership, which established a coalition that extended across the

religious spectrum from Tory Episcopalians to Liberal Voluntaries, leaving the Evangelicals isolated. In 1840, for example, the Non-Intrusionists attributed their poor performance in the local elections to 'worldly-minded Churchmen, Episcopalians, and revilers of scriptural principles'.[16] And it was said of the first post-Disruption municipal election in 1843 that 'not a single candidate of Moderate views in Church matters [took] the field but his starting is forthwith traced to the intrigues of the Market Company';[17] and that 'of the three candidates started by the Non-Intrusionists . . . not one [was] returned'.[18]

In the latter half of the 1840s, however, an economic recession weakened confidence in the traditional leadership, and in 1847 the initiatives of the Haddens and Blaikies were brought to an end when a meeting of citizens rejected an improvement plan that involved, inter alia, the municipalisation of the gas company, a matter also discussed in the previous chapter. This event was the first in a chain of crises which was to undermine the foundations on which the old civic leadership had been secured.

A leading opponent of improvement had been Alexander Dingwall Fordyce of Brucklay, a landowner and former naval captain, living in Ward 4, who between 1842 and 1844 had been a town councillor. He was also an ordained elder of the Free Kirk.[19] From 1845, he had begun to canvass support as a Liberal opposed to Bannerman, and had secured not only Liberal support but also that of Conservatives opposed to improvement, including David Chalmers of the *Journal*, who disagreed with the Haddens in this matter. With his electoral coalition divided, the Blaikies having lost the confidence of their municipal supporters, and with Fordyce strategically placed to win the Free Church vote (the largest tranche of the electorate), Bannerman, on the eve of the dissolution, decided to retire from parliament rather than face a contest. As a riposte to Fordyce, the Blaikies and Haddens (with the backing of the *Herald*) jointly put forward an Anglican Englishman, Colonel Sykes, a director of the East India Company, as a Liberal. As a candidate removed from a direct involvement in the complexities of Scottish presbyterian factionalism, his selection was designed to appeal to the commercial instincts of the electorate and to minimise the importance of the religious question. His selection also reconciled local and national political alliances, which had been at odds in 1841.

The strengths of Fordyce's candidature were that he not only identified with the Free Churchmen, but that, as a landowner, he could appeal to Tories of a similar social (though not religious) background

in the countryside, and that as an anti-improver he could attract lower-middle-class Conservative electors who had lost confidence in the Haddens. On his committee the *Herald* identified 'Roman Catholics and Unitarians, ultra-Moderates and Ultra Frees, Puseyites, Presbyterians, Dissenters, Congregationalists and Baptists, Free Episcopalians, and Episcopalians free and easy'.[20] Consequently, he attracted a level of support only marginally less than that of Bannerman in 1835 and won more votes across all wards than had his predecessor in 1841 (see appendix: table 5; and compare with table 3). It is, however, significant that Fordyce did best in Wards 4 and 5, covering the area outwith the commercial heart of the city, where Bannerman had always been weakest. Explaining the outcome, the *Herald* concluded:

> Captain Fordyce had the ultimate support of three or four distinct parties. . . . First, the Free Churchmen . . . bound to him hand and foot. . . . Then came the Dissenters, who continued to bore a hole in Captain Fordyce's endowment principle, and then shrank from their own Voluntarism. . . . After the Disestablishers came the Anti-Improvement faction – the most vicious, the most influential, but the least numerous of Captain Fordyce's supporters. . . . Lastly came the Chartists, or rather, perhaps, a few of them, with Mr. John MacPherson at their head'.[21]

In occupational terms, the voters were significantly less polarised than in 1841, so that the profile of support for each of the candidates was remarkably similar (see appendix: table 6). Reflecting his appeal to Conservatives, Fordyce performed substantially better than had Bannerman amongst residenters, landowner-farmers, and the professions, although the latter, dominated by lawyers who split 34 to 33 in favour of Sykes, were significantly less inclined to support the landowner than members of other professions.

The break-up of the 1841 alignments is well illustrated by the behaviour of individual electors between 1841 and 1847. A notable feature of the behaviour of 1841 voters in 1847 was that a third of those who had voted for Bannerman and almost two-fifths of those who had supported Innes failed to register a vote for either Sykes or Fordyce (see appendix: table 7). Of those who did, resoundingly rejecting their former Whig leaders, less than one in five of Bannerman's former coalition backed the colonel. Similarly, the Haddens were only able to influence 54.5 per cent of the former Innes voters who ex-

pressed a preference. Consequently, while Sykes had a majority of 29 amongst former Innes supporters, Fordyce led by more than three hundred amongst those who had voted for Bannerman; and more than 70 per cent of new electors expressed a preference for Fordyce (see appendix: table 8).

Assuming that the new voters had similar political orientations as the old voters, then four factions can be identified: (1) the Hadden Tories (Innes voters for Sykes), an estimated 19.0 per cent of the electorate; (2) the New Conservatives (Innes voters for Fordyce), an estimated 17.8 per cent of the electorate; (3) the Blaikie Whigs (Bannerman voters for Sykes), an estimated 12.6 per cent of the electorate; and (4) the New Liberals (Bannerman voters for Fordyce), an estimated 50.7 per cent of the electorate.

The rout of the traditional elite in 1847 over improvement, and their failure to secure the return of Sykes, was completed by the decision of Thomas Blaikie to retire from the council, and his replacement as lord provost by George Thomson junior, a Free Church shipowner and anti-improver, who had nominated Fordyce in the general election. The defeat of the old order was underlined a month later when the voluntaryist majority on the council reduced the status of the Auld Kirk, resolving by 13 to 4 'that it is the opinion of the Council that the procession of the Magistrates attending church be dispensed with in future.'[22] More traumatic for the commercial and manufacturing establishment was the collapse of the textile industry in 1848, with default on unsecured loans (especially those of Leys, Masson, and Hadden & Sons), almost bringing down the North of Scotland Bank.[23] Although the reconstituted board included most of the former directors, including Lord Provost Thomson and Thomas Blaikie, greater concern for the interests of investors in its practices completed a shift in power towards the new middle class that had already taken place in the Kirk and politics. The new social synthesis was typified by Lord Provost Thomson, who combined his close commercial contacts with the Whig-Tory establishment with a cautious approach to municipal expenditure and strong commitment to the Free Kirk.

When Fordyce announced his intention to retire from parliament in February 1852, a meeting of his election committee, consisting of around fifty people, met to discuss the matter. After expressing their regret at the M.P.'s decision, several members proposed that ex-Provost Thomson be adopted in his stead. Thomson initially declined, but agreed to reconsider. Councillor Torrie (a Churchman), however,

who was in correspondence with Colonel Sykes, demurred:

> Why, if a candidate was to be fixed upon, not call all the
> electors. . . . Captain Fordyce's election committee had been
> composed of all parties – Whigs, Tories, Conservatives,
> Liberals, Radicals and Chartists – why not allow all these
> parties a voice. . . . It was an easy way of making Liberals
> assume, as several gentlemen had done, that this was a Liberal
> committee. He [Torrie] used to be called a Conservative, and
> there were other Conservatives present. . . . He had been
> present at many meetings and words failed him to characterise
> the manoeuvre attempted to be palmed upon the independent
> electors of Aberdeen.[24]

Others expressed the view that the supporters of Hay (a Liberal
already in the field) should also be given an opportunity to participate.
Consequently, although the Fordyce committee was to form the core
of Thomson's committee, after he had agreed to stand, it had to be reconstituted on a somewhat narrower base. A major gain for Thomson,
however, was the endorsement of the *Herald* (which had deserted the
Blaikies in this matter) because of 'steadfastness in the cause of Free
Trade'.[25] Although not approving of his sabbatarianism, the paper
noted his backing for voluntaryism and a national system of education,
and 'forgave him his leanings towards the Pharisees, and the Puritan-
ical nomenclature of his ships.'[26]

Thomson's opponent, Sir Andrew Leith Hay, a soldier and landowner, who had been governor of Bermuda from 1838 to 1841 and
was a former member for the Elgin Burghs, had only supported free
trade with qualifications. He was backed by the Blaikies, but the
Haddens took no interest in the contest – none of them even bothered
to vote. A meeting of Conservative electors failed to take a collective
decision on which candidate they preferred, although of the sixty-five
present twenty-nine eventually voted for Hay and only five for Thomson.[27] Given the hostility of the press, the indifference of the Haddens,
and the reduced influence of the Blaikies, it is somewhat remarkable
that Hay polled 56 more votes than had Sykes in 1847, whilst Thomson
ran 236 votes behind Fordyce (see appendix: table 5).

As in 1847, a notable feature of electoral behaviour was the substantial turnover of electors. Of the 1847 participants, 49 per cent
failed to register a preference in 1852; 35.6 per cent of those who did
vote were first-timers. Of those who had supported Fordyce, 40.8 per

[179]

cent went to Thomson and 12.6 per cent to Hay, whereas only 11.1 per cent of former Sykes voters backed the ex-provost, and 34.4 per cent moved to Sir Andrew (see appendix: table 9). Of the Conservative electors who had backed Innes in 1841, and who voted in 1852 (64.4 per cent did not), 55.4 per cent voted for Hay – virtually the same proportion as had declared for Sykes in 1847. On the other hand, while the 45.5 per cent of remaining 1841 Bannerman voters favoured Thomson with 68.6 per cent of their preferences, it was significantly less than the 80.3 per cent that had endorsed Fordyce. New voters broke 55.6 per cent in favour of Thomson. Thus, while the basic parameters of the Fordyce coalition had been sustained, it was not without amendment.

Thomson was clearly less popular than Fordyce in all wards. Only in Ward 4, dominated by the Free Church, did he almost match his predecessor (see appendix: table 5). Hay, by contrast, had a more variable performance. Despite improving overall on Sykes' vote, Hay ran behind the colonel in Wards 1 and 2, which covered the harbour and administrative centre of Aberdeen, but he significantly out-polled his opponent in Wards 3 and 5. He even polled better than Sykes had done in Ward 4, despite Thomson's strength there. In relative terms, Thomson performed much better in Wards 1 (66.3 per cent) and 4 (65.1 per cent) than in 5 (54.9 per cent), 3 (54.2 per cent) and 2 (50.0 per cent).

The significantly greater strength of Thomson in Wards 1 and 4 reflected his shipping interests and religious convictions. Thomson's success in the harbour ward, however, was somewhat ambiguous, for although he retained the bulk of continuing Fordyce voters and attracted 43.6 per cent of continuing Sykes electors (as against less than a quarter of former Sykes voters across the constituency), under half the 1847 electorate participated in the 1852 contest (see appendix: table 9). Significantly, Ward 1 contributed a smaller share of the total vote than in any election of the period (see appendix: table 1). It would appear, therefore, that while Thomson commanded the favours of harbour-based electors because of his shipping interests, his Free Churchmanship was a liability. Rather than vote for him or his opponent, a significant number of electors abstained. Elsewhere in the Old City (Wards 2 and 3), however, antipathy towards the Free Church candidate remained as pronounced as in 1847.

Thomson's clearest strength came from the Free Churchmen. Fully eighteen per cent of all his votes came from Free Kirk elders and

deacons, who split 135 to 15 in his favour. Significantly, Ward 4, which contributed its highest proportion of the electorate in any election of the period, included three in ten of all Thomson voters. It was a reflection of the importance of the Free Churchman in this suburb, that a higher proportion of former Fordyce voters turned out for Thomson that in any other ward (see appendix: table 9). Conversely, a smaller proportion of ex-Sykes voters in Ward 4 switched to the ex-lord provost than in other wards, suggesting that in this ward religious polarities, established in 1847, were particularly important.

The contrast with 1847, therefore, reflected differences in the social characteristics of the candidates representing the two coalitions, and the ending of the improvement issue that had enabled Fordyce to establish a broad-based coalition that cut across the religio-political divide. Unable to combine the radicalism of the new urban middle class with a traditional rural interest, as his predecessor had done, Thomson's 'great victory over a combination of city and county magnates,'[28] was heavily dependent on his Free Churchmanship.

WANING OF OLD ALIGNMENTS, 1857-65

Thomson had been a reluctant candidate in 1852 and announced his retirement on the eve of the 1857 general election. This led to the most confused election of the period, mainly due to a split in the Free Church vote.

The two candidates in 1857 were John Farley Leith and Colonel Sykes, making a second attempt to capture the constituency. Leith was the son of a military officer and son-in-law of an Aberdeen doctor. Five years after graduating from Marischal College and University in 1825, he was called to the bar at the Middle Temple, and lived on an estate in Essex. Colonel Sykes had maintained his connections with Aberdeen after 1847, becoming university rector in 1854, and by 1857 was chairman of the East India Company. Thus, for the first time since 1832 there was no local candidate.

Thomson claimed that he left parliament due in part to his opposition (expressed in the lobbies) to the Opium War, described by the voice of progressive mid-century Liberalism in the region as 'one of the darkest chapters in our national history'.[29] Leith was the most obvious successor to the former lord provost in that he too opposed the opium trade. He also identified with growing disestablishment sentiment amongst both the Free Church and presbyterian dissenters, and

[181]

approved of Thomson's parliamentary votes against the state subsidy
of religion in Ireland – which involved not only a grant to the Roman
Catholic college at Maynooth but also financial assistance to Irish presbyterians, and particularly the Episcopal Church of Ireland. Sykes, by
contrast, was deeply implicated in the Indian poppy industry, and as a
member of the Church of England supported the claims of the Church
of Ireland.

Leith, however, failed to command the support of Thomson and his
allies, ostensibly because he had been canvassing before the ex-lord
provost had indicated his decision to retire. Consequently, having
nominated Fordyce in 1847, Thomson declared for the colonel. At
the same time, Sykes rejected his former, profitless alliance with the
Blaikies and Haddens, and created a base amongst Free Churchmen
through his commercial contacts, who incidentally included Thomson.
Both his proposer and seconder, then, were Free Churchmen who had
previously voted for Fordyce and Thomson.

As a result of these manoeuvrings, Leith found himself representing
a motley coalition that included the conflicting leaderships of the previous three decades. His principled stand on the main issues of the day
attracted the support of Free Church ministers, and of John MacPherson, a leading Chartist; whilst Sykes' desertion of his 1847 backers
brought Leith the endorsement of the spurned Blaikies and Haddens.
Sykes, however, had secured the Free Church secular leadership
through Thomson, and commanded the favours of the Conservative
Journal. He also enjoyed the support of the *Free Press*, which ignored its
own opposition to the opium trade and the Maynooth grant, and in-
sinuated (without evidence) that Leith was a government nominee,
claiming that in contrast Sykes was free from sectional interest.[30] The
new alignment of forces brought the comment that:

> Not only do the ties of political party seem fairly dissolved, but
> even the stronger bands of ecclesiastical connection and
> sympathy. It is not now the old antagonism of Tory and Whig,
> or the more recent conflict between Conservative and Liberal –
> it is not even that of Churchman and Dissenter, of Voluntary
> and Anti-Voluntary, no, not even that of Old Church and Free.
> All the recognised, inveterate ambitions are at an end in Aber-
> deen, and out of the clouds two new ones are extemporised.
> For on the one side you see at the foot of Market Street, all
> those elements in happy (if but temporary) harmony, and

coalescence, yet bristling all over with antagonisms to a like strange conglomerate at the top![31]

The result of the election, in which Sykes won 54.9 per cent of the votes, was the closest of the period, and attracted the most voters, 1,884 – eighty one per cent of the recently purged register. Almost three-fifths of those participating (1,126) had not voted in 1852, and 45.9 per cent (865) voted in an Aberdeen parliamentary election for the first time. The overall geographical pattern of the result was less reminiscent of the outcome in the two previous contests than of those in 1835 and 1841, in which the victor, basing his appeal on business interests, ran best in the Old City and was at his weakest outwith the royalty (see appendix: table 10).

Despite a smaller overall share of the poll than Thomson, Sykes won a larger proportion of the poll than the ex-provost in Wards 1, 2 and 3, running best in Ward 1 (63.2 per cent) and Ward 2 (59.2 per cent), where non-1852 voters broke particularly strongly in his favour. By contrast, Sykes was at his weakest in Ward 5 (41.9 per cent), where his vote made him the first winning candidate not to carry all the wards. It was notable that whereas 55.7 per cent of continuing Thomson voters across all wards backed the colonel, in Ward 5 only 35.4 per cent did so, (see appendix: table 12).

Sykes proved especially popular with those engaged in commerce and trade. The shipbuilding and harbour interest gave him 85.1 per cent of their votes (see appendix: table 11), and he carried the support of 70.0 per cent of those engaged in food retailing, and 62.9 per cent of the drink vote, which formed the basis of his success in Wards 1 and 2. Amongst most other categories, however, Sykes ran below the overall distribution of the vote.

Leith's association with the Blaikies and Haddens helps to explain his strength amongst manufacturers, particularly foundrymen (57.4 per cent), and those engaged in the construction industry (58.3 per cent) – which was reflected in the outcome in Ward 3. The growing rivalry between the new railway companies and established shipping lines brought Leith the backing of 58.6 per cent of those employed in non-maritime transport. And agriculturalists, almost a third of the voters in Ward 5, favoured him with 64.2 per cent of their registrations.

A critical dimension to the election was the behaviour of the Free Church vote. Leith, with his principled stand on foreign policy, opposition to Maynooth and leanings towards voluntaryism (increasingly

popular with urban Free Churchmen), was the Free Church choice in religious terms. Indeed, all eleven Free Church ministers along with almost all dissenting ministers – the Wesleyan Methodist being the exception – voted for Leith. By contrast, as would be expected, ministers of the Auld Kirk and Episcopalians supported Sykes. Elders and deacons of the Free Church, however, split only 83 to 70 in Leith's favour. It would seem reasonable to assume that ordinary members of the Free Church congregations with the vote were more likely to reflect the divisions among their elders than the unanimity of their ministers. Indeed, with Thomson's continuing voters giving Sykes 55.7 per cent of their vote, there is strong *prima facie* evidence to support this proposition (see appendix: table 12).

The probable behaviour of the Free Church vote is well illustrated by the outcome in Ward 4, the most religiously polarised ward in its voting behaviour. In 1852, Thomson had inherited 82.7 per cent of the continuing Fordyce vote, and Hay had carried 91.9 per cent of the continuing Sykes vote – from 1847 (see appendix: table 9). In 1857, however, although Leith shaded Sykes amongst former Hay electors, with 52.9 per cent of their continuing vote in Ward 4, he carried only 41.9 per cent of the continuing Thomson electorate (see appendix: table 12). It is, therefore, quite probable that ordinary members of the Free Kirk on balance preferred Sykes. Had Leith won the same share of the poll in Ward 4 as had Thomson, and the results in the other wards remained as they were, Leith would have come within six votes of Sykes (939 to 945). One is tempted to conclude that many Free Churchmen preferred – as we know Thomson did – their commercial and economic interests (represented by Sykes) to their religious scruples (represented by Leith).

The most instructive feature of this election was the way in which it underlined the rapidity with which the political influence of elites and their alliance changed in the quarter of a century after 1832. Leith's supporters included the Haddens, who had controlled politics in pre-reform days; the Blaikies, who had defeated them in the 1830s; and the Free Church ministers who had led their flocks against both Tories and Whigs. All of them together now lacked the ability to see their preferred candidate home, even with the help of John MacPherson, the leading local Chartist. On the other hand, the combined efforts of the *Journal* and *Free Press* and some leading laymen in the Free Church helped to produce only the narrowest of victories.

The fluidity of electoral alliances between 1841 and 1857 is well

illustrated in table 13 (see appendix), where it is found that the alignments of 1857 bore little relationship to those of previous elections. Even those who had supported Sykes in 1847 were no more disposed to back him in 1857 than were those who had supported his former opponent, Fordyce. Of those who had voted together in earlier elections, the most distinctive in 1857 were the previous supporters of the Conservative, Innes: on balance they preferred Leith (53.7 per cent) and were 8.6 per cent less favourable to Sykes than the electorate as a whole. Sykes' best performance was amongst the Bannerman coalition of 1841, where he ran 3.2 per cent ahead of the general distribution – but that is hardly a significant figure.

In the final analysis, the selection of Sykes rather than Leith was not of great importance, because it indicated the waning of old conflicts rather than the emergence of any significant new political demarcation lines. The *Free Press*, for example, chose to explain the outcome more in terms of Leith's tactical failure than as the triumph of any particular political principle:

> Should he [Leith] seriously regard the history of Colonel Sykes' relations to the electors of Aberdeen as affording a 'precedent' applicable to his own case, he may find, that he has failed to bring some elements into the probationary contests, which, in the gallant Colonel's case, have contributed not a little to his ultimate victory.[32]

Despite the narrowness of his victory in 1857, Sykes was returned unopposed until his death in 1872, the doubling of the electorate in 1868 notwithstanding. Having seemingly taken the advice of the *Free Press*, Leith returned to take the seat at the consequent by-election against Liberal and Conservative opposition.[33]

CONCLUSION

To a large extent the ambitions of the reformers of 1832 to create independent constituencies were realised in Aberdeen. The city had a strong locally based economic elite which had the skills and financial resources sufficient to provide political leadership within the framework of local government, which, as Rosemary Tyzack has shown, was so important at this time. It was also able to arrange for national representation in line with constituency values and interests. At the same time, the local establishment, whose composition was ever-changing as

the city expanded, was often divided on the definition of those values and interests, and was forced to seek adjudication from an electorate capable of making up its own mind. If necessary, the voters were prepared to reject long-standing social leaders in favour of new ones whose aims were more compatible with their own needs and wishes. Political debate was sustained by a lively, informative, and diverse press, though, with such a small electorate, its influence was perhaps subordinate to less formal conversations conducted in board rooms and between leading members of the various religious congregations. Although in its particulars the politics of Aberdeen was *sui generis*, it was that very quality which characterised the politics of all the independent Scottish burghs in the period between the first and second Reform Acts.

NOTES

1. This chapter is based on material used in M. Dyer, *Men of Property and Intelligence* (Aberdeen, 1996), and is printed with the permission of the Scottish Cultural Press.

2. As reported in T. H. B. Oldfield, *Representative History of Great Britain and Ireland* (4 vols, London, 1816), vol. 4, pt. 2, pp. 130, 131–32.

3. C. H. Dod, *Electoral Facts Impartially Stated* (London, 1852), p. 105.

4. This examination of voting behaviour in Aberdeen is based principally on the membership listing of the Conservative and Liberal Election Committees of 1841 (the equivalent of 45 per cent of the actual vote received by the candidates in both cases; occupations of committee members were included); the Poll Book, 1847, held at Aberdeen Central Library; the Poll Book, 1852, which does not include the occupations of electors, and the Poll Book, 1857, both held in Aberdeen University Library: Special Collections. For details of religious affiliation a major source was the *Post Office Directories*. Interpretation of the data is greatly assisted by A. A. MacLaren, *Religion and Social Class: the Disruption Years in Aberdeen* (London, 1974). Other relevant secondary material includes Alexander Keith, *The History of the North of Scotland Bank, 1836–1936* (Aberdeen, 1936), and J. A. Ross, *Record of Municipal Affairs in Aberdeen Since the Passing of the Burgh Reform Act in 1833* (Aberdeen, 1889). Relevant government publications are: *Report upon the Boundaries of the Several Cities, Burghs, and Towns in Scotland in Respect to the Election of Members to Serve in Parliament*, Parliamentary Papers (hereafter PP) 1831–32, vol. 42; and *Municipal Corporations (Scotland), Local Reports of Commissioners*, part I, *from Aberbrothwick to Fortrose*, PP 1835, vol. 29.

5. MacLaren, *Religion and Social Class*, pp. 4–5, 61–62.

6. PP 1835, vol. 39, p. 49.

7. PP 1835, vol. 39, p. 20.

8. MacLaren, *Religion and Social Class*, pp. 19–22.

9. 'Statement as to the Harbour of Aberdeen transmitted to the Commission by James Blaikie, esq., provost of the city' in MacLaren, *Religion and Social Class*, p. 43, in which he also pointed out that until 1829 all the trustees had been magistrates. At the passing of the act in 1810, Telford, the engineer, had informed the committee that the work would be completed within five years. See PP, 1835, vol. 39, p. 46.

10. MacLaren, *Religion and Social Class*, pp. 56–57.

11. The municipal wards were not the same as the parliamentary wards.

12. Local elections, however, were not fought under national party labels.

13. *Banner*, 3 July 1841.

14. Keith, *North of Scotland Bank*, pp. 49–51.

15. *Herald*, 30 April 1842.

16. *Banner*, 7 July 1840.

17. *Herald*, 21 July 1843.

18. *Herald*, 11 November 1843.

19. MacLaren, *Religion and Social Class*, p. 233.

20. *Herald*, 17 July 1847.

21. *Herald*, 7 August 1847.

22. Ross, *Record of Municipal Affairs*, p. 101.

23. Keith, *North of Scotland Bank*, pp. 48–60.

24. *Herald*, 21 February 1852.

25. *Herald*, 3 April 1852.

26. *Herald*, 28 February 1852.

27. Though the preferences of this faction were not representative of former Innes voters as a whole, who split more evenly.

28. *Herald*, 10 July 1852.

29. *Free Press*, 6 March 1857.

30. *Free Press*, 20 March 1857.

31. *Free Press*, 27 March 1857.

32. *Free Press*, 3 April 1857.

33. The electorate, however, had been much changed by the Second Reform Act. The result was J. F. Leith (Lib), 4,392; J. W. Barclay (Lib), 2,615: J. Shaw (Con) 704.

APPENDIX: TABULATED VOTING PATTERNS

Table 1. Proportion (%) of voters in contested elections, 1835–1857, by ward.

	1835	1841	1847	1852	1857
Ward 1	20.7	18.6	21.4	17.9	21.6
Ward 2	17.1	16.9	17.5	15.5	14.7
Ward 3	22.1	22.4	21.0	22.6	21.1
(Wards 1-3)	(59.9)	(57.9)	(59.9)	(56.0)	(57.4)
Ward 4	20.8	23.7	23.5	27.2	26.2
Ward 5	19.3	18.3	16.6	16.8	16.3
All	100.0	99.9	100.0	100.0	99.9

Table 2. Aberdeen voters in 1857 in percentages by occupational categories and ward.

	Ward 1	Ward 2	Ward 3	Ward 4	Ward 5	All
drink	16.5	14.8	15.8	8.1	10.7	13.0
food retail	6.6	5.4	5.5	2.4	1.3	4.2
textiles	10.1	8.7	12.6	6.5	6.5	8.9
leather	5.2	4.3	4.8	4.0	3.6	4.4
engineering & allied trades	5.7	5.8	6.0	3.6	3.6	4.9
foundry & forge	2.7	2.9	5.5	1.6	1.6	2.9
other manufacturers	4.2	4.7	3.5	3.2	1.6	3.5
miscellaneous sales	7.6	7.2	7.8	3.2	3.6	5.8
(manufacturers & retail)	(58.6)	(53.8)	(61.5)	(32.6)	(32.5)	(47.6)
service	3.2	3.2	2.5	2.0	2.3	2.6
construction	4.4	3.6	4.5	7.9	5.8	5.5
shipping/harbour	9.3	3.6	1.3	3.4	1.3	3.9
non-maritime transport	3.2	4.3	2.0	3.8	1.9	3.1
banking/insurance	4.7	6.1	2.5	4.5	0.3	3.7
the professions	7.9	13.0	13.3	25.3	12.3	15.1
residenters	4.7	3.2	3.0	6.5	10.1	5.5
agriculture & fishing	3.9	8.3	8.8	12.8	30.8	12.3
other	0.2	0.7	0.5	1.0	2.6	1.0
Total	100.1	99.8	99.9	99.9	99.9	100.3

Table 3. The results of the Aberdeen elections 1837 and 1841 by ward.

	1835			1841*		
	Bannerman no.	Farquhar no.	Bannerman %	Bannerman no.	Innes no.	Bannerman %
Ward 1	200	70	74.1	150	91	60.2
Ward 2	170	53	76.2	137	81	61.2
Ward 3	228	61	78.9	181	109	60.5
Ward 4	184	87	67.9	183	124	59.2
Ward 5	156	96	61.9	129	108	53.3
All	938	367	71.9	780	513	59.0

* In 1841, a Chartist won 30 votes or 2.3 per cent of the poll (8 votes in Ward 1; 6 votes in Ward 2; 9 votes in Ward 3; 2 votes in Ward 4; and 5 votes in Ward 5).

Table 4. *Profiles of Liberal and Conservative support at the General Election of 1841 in percentages by occupation based on the composition of the election committees.*

	Bannerman share of poll	above/below overall share	profile of Bannerman support	profile of Innes support
drink	75.0	+14.8	12.7	6.4
food retail	72.7	+12.5	4.5	2.6
textiles	62.2	+2.0	13.6	9.9
leather	76.0	+15.8	5.4	2.6
engineering & allied trades	68.6	+8.4	6.8	4.7
foundry & forge	69.2	+9.0	2.5	1.7
	75.0	+14.8	4.2	2.1
miscellaneous sales	70.2	+10.0	9.3	6.0
(manufactures & retail)	(71.3)	(+10.1)	(59.0)	(36.0)
service	66.7	+6.5	0.6	0.4
construction	70.6	+10.4	6.8	4.3
shipping/harbour	65.2	+5.0	4.2	3.4
non-maritime transport	50.0	−10.2	0.6	0.9
banking/insurance	33.3	−26.9	1.1	3.4
the professions	39.8	−20.4	12.2	27.9
residenters.	51.3	−8.9	5.7	8.2
agriculture & fishing	46.6	−13.6	7.6	13.3
other	58.3	−1.9	2.0	2.1
(non manufacturers and retail)	(49.4)	(−10.8)		
All	60.2		99.8	99.9

Table 5. *The results of the Aberdeen elections 1847 and 1852 by ward.*

	Fordyce no.	1847 Sykes no.	Fordyce %	Thomson no.	1852 Hay no.	Thomson %
Ward 1	200	87	69.7	138	70	66.3
Ward 2	139	95	59.4	90	90	50.0
Ward 3	193	89	68.4	142	120	54.2
Ward 4	222	93	70.5	205	110	65.1
Ward 5	164	58	73.9	107	88	54.9
All	918	422	68.5	682	478	58.8

Table 6. Profiles of support for Fordyce and Sykes at the General Election of 1847 in percentages by occupation based on the Poll Book.

| | Fordyce's above/below | | profile of Fordyce's support | profile of Sykes's support |
	share of poll	overall share		
drink	70.0	+1.5	12.2	11.6
food retail	75.4	+6.9	4.7	3.3
textiles	68.5	0.0	10.2	10.2
leather	65.1–3.4	4.5	5.2	
engineering & allied trades	75.3	+6.8	7.0	5.0
foundry & forge	63.4	–5.1	2.8	3.6
other manufacturers	75.0	+6.5	5.9	4.3
miscellaneous sales	75.9	+7.4	7.2	5.0
(manufactures & retail)	(71.1)	(+2.6)	(54.5)	(48.2)
service	26.7	–41.8	0.4	2.6
construction	70.1	+1.6	6.0	5.5
shipping/harbour	66.7	–1.8	3.9	4.3
non–maritime transport	89.5	+21.0	1.9	0.5
banking/insurance	68.1	–0.4	3.5	3.6
the professions	58.2	–10.3	12.4	19.4
residenters.	70.6	+2.1	3.9	3.6
agriculture & fishing	67.9	–0.6	11.5	11.8
other	85.7	+17.2	2.0	0.7
(non manufacturers and retail)	(65.6)	(–2.9)	(45.5)	(52.0)
All	68.5		100.0	100.2

Table 7. Behaviour of members of the 1841 general election committees for Bannerman and Innes in the General Election of 1847.

| | 1841 Bannerman supporters | | | 1841 Innes supporters | | |
	no.	%	% of those voting in 1847	no.	%	% of those voting in 1847
Fordyce	187	53.0	80.3	66	28.3	45.5
Sykes	46	13.0	19.7	79	33.9	54.5
no vote	120	34.0	–	88	37.8	–
Total	353	100.0	100.0	233	100.0	100.0

Table 8. Derivation of support for Fordyce and Sykes in the General Election of 1847.

| | Fordyce | | Sykes | | Fordyce | majority |
	no.	%	no.	%	%	Fordyce
Bannerman*	413	45.0	102	24.2	80.2	+311
Innes*	145	15.8	174	41.2	45.5	-29
New	360	39.2	146	34.6	71.1	+214
All	918	100.0	422	100.0	68.5	+496

* Figures adjusted from Election Committee numbers.

Table 9. Behaviour of 1847 voters at the General Election of 1852 in percentages.

	Fordyce to Thomson	Fordyce to Hay	Fordyce* to Thomson	Sykes to Thomson	Sykes to Hay	Sykes* to Thomson
Ward 1	37.5	9.5	79.8	19.5	25.3	43.6
Ward 2	42.4	10.8	79.7	9.5	34.7	21.4
Ward 3	40.4	13.5	75.0	9.0	38.2	19.0
Ward 4	47.3	9.9	82.7	3.2	36.6	8.1
Ward 5	35.4	20.7	63.0	17.2	37.9	31.3
All	40.8	12.6	76.4	11.1	34.4	24.5

*Excluding abstainers in 1852 from the calculation.

Table 10. Result of the General Election of 1857 by ward comparing voters in 1852 with other voters.

	% of all voters	Sykes no.	Leith no.	Sykes %
Ward 1				
1852 Voters	40.8	98	68	59.0
Others	59.2	161	80	66.8
All	100.0	259	148	63.6
Ward 2				
1852 Voters	54.0	64	58	52.5
Others	56.0	100	55	64.5
All	100.0	164	113	59.2
Ward 3				
1852 Voters	40.0	89	70	56.0
Others	60.0	131	108	54.8
All	100.0	220	178	55.3
Ward 4				
1852 Voters	39.3	105	89	54.1
Others	60.7	158	142	52.7
All	100.0	263	231	53.2
Ward 5				
1852 Voters	38.0	48	69	41.0
Others	62.0	81	110	42.4
All	100.0	129	179	41.9
All voters				
1852 Voters	40.2	404	354	53.3
Others	59.8	631	495	56.0
All	100.0	1035	849	54.9

Table 11. Profiles of support for Fordyce and Sykes at the General Election of 1847 in percentages by occupation based on the Poll Book.

	Sykes share of poll	above/below overall share	profile of Sykes support	profile of Leith support
drink	63.9	+9.0	15.1	10.4
food retail	70.0	+15.1	5.4	2.8
textiles	54.9	0.0	11.3	5.9
leather	47.0	−7.9	3.8	5.2
engineering & allied trades	48.9	−6.0	4.3	5.5
foundry & forge	42.6	−12.3	2.2	3.7
other manufacturers	58.5	+3.6	3.7	3.2
miscellaneous sales	57.8	+2.9	6.1	5.4
(manufactures & retail)	(60.1)	(+5.2)	(51.9)	(42.1)
service	53.1	−1.8	2.5	2.7
construction	41.7	−13.2	4.2	7.1
shipping/harbour	85.1	+30.2	6.1	1.3
non−maritime transport	41.4	−13.5	2.3	4.0
banking/insurance	52.2	−2.7	3.5	3.9
the professions	54.6	−0.3	15.0	15.2
residenters.	56.3	+1.4	5.6	5.3
agriculture & fishing	35.8	−19.1	8.0	17.6
other	55.6	+0.7	1.0	0.9
(non manufacturers and retail)	(52.5)	(−2.0)	(48.2)	(58.0)
All	54.9		100.1	100.1

Table 12. Behaviour of 1852 voters at the General Election of 1857.

	Thomson to Sykes	Thomson to Leith	Thomson to Sykes*	Hay to Sykes	Hay to Leith	Hay to Sykes*
Ward 1	47.1	31.2	60.2	47.1	35.7	56.9
Ward 2	41.1	30.0	57.8	30.0	34.4	46.6
Ward 3	38.0	25.4	60.0	29.2	28.3	50.7
Ward 4	35.1	25.4	58.1	30.0	33.6	47.1
Ward 5	21.5	39.3	35.4	28.4	30.7	48.1
All	36.8	29.3	55.7	32.0	32.2	49.8

* Excluding non-voters.

Table 13. Behaviour of earlier alignments and new voters at the General Election of 1857.

alignment		Sykes votes no.	votes %	Leith votes no.	votes %	% voting in 1857
Bannerman	(1841)	165	58.1	119	41.9	36.5
Innes	(1841)	68	46.3	79	53.7	28.8
Fordyce	(1847)	215	53.6	186	46.4	43.7
Sykes	(1847)	105	55.6	84	44.4	44.8
Thomson	(1852)	251	55.7	200	44.3	66.1
Hay	(1852)	153	49.8	154	50.2	64.2
New Voters	(1857)	496	57.3	370	42.7	100.0

Aberdeen and Holland: John Forbes White and the Scottish Fascination with Dutch Art, 1860–80

John Morrison

The twenty years covered in this chapter constitute a significant period in the history of Scottish painting. The period begins with the emergence of the Robert Scott Lauder pupils, trained in Edinburgh at the Trustees' Academy, covers their pre-eminence, and stretches to the beginnings of their eclipse as the avant-garde by the 'Glasgow Boys'. [1]

A consideration of Aberdeen from 1860 to 1880, and the developments in painting and patronage in the city, is also reasonable. During that period Aberdeen was the centre, or at least – along with Dundee – one of two centres of innovation in the Scottish art world. Edinburgh held artistic hegemony in Scotland in the nineteenth century. It was the home of the Royal Scottish Academy (RSA), and success in painting terms at that time meant success at the RSA. As late as 1888 the RSA, a national body, had only one member or associate member who did not live in Edinburgh or had not been living in Edinburgh at the time of his election. This absolute power, it seems clear, led to the stifling of innovation and the promotion of a narrow, insular and self-satisfied view of the art world outside Scotland. Tales of Edinburgh parochialism are legion. In the 1880s, at an after-dinner address, the president of the RSA said of west coast painters' complaints that their works were always badly hung at RSA exhibitions, 'What do they want

here at all? If they are badly hung in Edinburgh I am sorry for it but we must look after ourselves.'[2] This, remember, was the president of a *national* institution.

By 1889, when these remarks were made, Glasgow, in the persons of the eponymous 'Boys', had become the centre for innovation in Scottish painting. They had not burst fully formed upon a wholly moribund scene however. The upper echelons of the RSA may have been a stultifying influence but for at least the previous twenty years Scotland had possessed a group of younger artists and patrons, of necessity working within the RSA system, who were in very close contact with more progressive developments in Europe. This group, led by the Aberdeen mill owner John Forbes White, pioneered a more realist British approach to landscape and figure painting, and was amongst the first in Britain to appreciate contemporary French and Dutch painting and to adopt and adapt continental techniques. Uniquely, its members studied in Holland with the premier masters of the Hague School and fostered strong ties with the Dutch. This resulted both in radical changes in Scottish painting and in the creation of early and large collections of contemporary Dutch art in Scotland.

Before considering the activities of White, his Aberdeen associates and their links to Holland, it is necessary briefly to explain why the Scots in the early 1860s should be so well disposed towards the Dutch. By the beginning of the nineteenth century Scotland had had strong economic and intellectual links with Holland for very nearly 400 years. Since 1407 Scots merchant burgesses had traded through the 'staple' port, sometimes Bruges, sometimes Middleburg, but from the early sixteenth century, Campvere.[3] This meant that whichever of these towns of the Low Countries held the staple had a large Scottish community. All Scottish exports of raw materials (hides, wool, coal, salt and salmon) went through the Netherlands. Campvere granted Scots customs and docking privileges and there was a Scottish court and a Scottish kirk. The Dutch brought much to Scotland as well. Physically the trading ports on the east of Scotland were built on Dutch lines, sometimes even of Dutch materials brought over as shipping ballast. Settlers arrived in Scotland from Holland. New weaving techniques which spread through the country came from the Netherlands.

Scotland of course had strong links with France. In the sixteenth and early seventeenth centuries large numbers of Scots lived in French Calvinist towns (held under the edict of Nantes) and studied law. There were so many in fact that in 1617 the Erskine family, who were

living in Bourges, left because they 'could not have lernit the Frence' there.[4] There were so many of their countrymen in Bourges that they had no opportunity to speak anything but 'Scotis'. From the middle of the seventeenth century the study of law also moved to Holland, specifically to the University of Leyden. In the first half of the eighteenth century there were some 658 Scottish students studying at Leyden, 302 of them law students.[5]

Apart from a very strong historical link, there were other factors which encouraged Scots to look to Holland. These elements are less a matter of historical fact than of practical observation. The sober, presbyterian background of nineteenth-century Scotland had its affinities with the moral and religious values of seventeenth-century Holland. In short, Dutch society naturally appealed to the Scots. There was also an inherited tradition in artistic terms of looking to Holland. From David Wilkie the Scots had inherited a view and an appreciation of the Dutch seventeenth-century 'old masters', albeit a view with a distinctly Scottish slant. As the pre-eminent Scottish painter of the first half of the nineteenth century, Wilkie was the model for many later nineteenth-century Scottish artists. Elected an associate of the Royal Academy in November 1809 and a full member eighteen months later at the age of only twenty-five, his work was admired and studied by younger painters. Painters who exerted an influence on Wilkie then would also have an influence, at second hand, on later Scottish artists. These influences were predominantly Dutch. It is this tradition which Wilkie handed down to later Scottish painters – a tradition of looking to Holland and abstracting from Dutch painting while producing works characteristically Scottish in outlook.

In looking to Holland, Scottish patrons and artists found paintings congenial to their tastes. The mid-nineteenth-century Dutch painters had something important in common with Wilkie – they were rediscovering Dutch painting of the 'Golden Age'. As a contemporary writer observed,

> In the sixties, the Dutch after a long dull interregnum and affectation were reawakening to the artistic possibilities of a national intimate and emotional art. Above all Josef Israels had a few years before shaken off the trammels of historical convention, and in the work of Rembrandt, and in Dutch cottages found the material and the method which yielded such a rich harvest.[6]

Both Wilkie and The Hague School, (the informal group in which Josef Israels was a leading figure) were looking back to the seventeenth-century Dutch masters for guidance. Given the later and strong Scottish historical links to the Netherlands, their inherited inclination towards a subject matter similar to the Dutch, and the basic similarities in outlook between themselves and Wilkie and the Hague School, the idea that the Scots looked towards and learned from Holland seems only natural.

These conditions of course prevailed across the whole of the country, not just in Aberdeen. The insularity of Edinburgh, where in the 1870s it was stated by a senior member of the RSA that there were sufficient painters in Scotland to fill the walls of the Academy and therefore there was no need to have any foreigners exhibiting, meant that any inclination to look outwards from Scotland was stifled. It was left to the provinces to take the lead and in the form of John Forbes White they did.

White was an extraordinary man. Originally intended for the medical profession, he entered Marischal College in 1844 as first bursar. He was the most distinguished graduate of his year in 1848 but his subsequent medical studies were interrupted when his father died. His elder brother Adam became a missionary and so John Forbes White took over the running of the family milling business at the age of twenty-one. Nevertheless, he was a classical scholar of very considerable attainments and continued to study Latin and Greek throughout his life. He both spoke and wrote Latin fluently, contributing to a edition of celebrated translations from Hadrian.[7] He became vice-consul for Sweden and Norway and was also consular agent for France. After invitation he contributed a number of articles to the *Encyclopedia Britannica*. He was a fellow of the Society of Antiquaries of Scotland, an early member of the Aberdeen Philosophical Society, and a founder member of the Aberdeen Hellenic Society. He was chosen as assessor for the General Council of Aberdeen University to the University Court and was later awarded an honorary degree by the university.

White was a central figure in a distinguished intellectual, cultural and social circle in Aberdeen in the years after 1860. This group included William Robertson Smith, the internationally renowned theologian and biblical scholar, Sir David Gill, later the astronomer royal, Sir William Geddes, the professor of Greek at Aberdeen University, Dr John Kerr, the educational reformer and Sir George Reid, later a liberal president of the RSA. It was no inferior rustic grouping. It was a diverse and

Painting 1. John Forbes White, by G. Reid (reproduced with permission of City of Aberdeen Art Gallery & Museums Collections).

highly cultured assembly. At the very least its members were respected figures in their own fields and frequently they were polymaths of note. It is against these personal circumstances and this cultural background that White's activities as a patron and a collector have to be set. Given these conditions it is not surprising that White's activities were both original and influential.

In 1867 *The Scotsman* published an obituary of the thirty-four years old Dutch painter, Alexander Mollinger. It said: 'His works have acquired a large amount of popularity, and generally formed one of the chief attractions of the landscape department of the (RSA) Exhibition'.[8] Five years before, the artist's work had been unknown in Scotland yet by his death his reputation was considerable. Mollinger's popularity marked the beginning of the Scottish passion for contemporary Dutch art and the first Mollinger to arrive in Scotland came as the property of John Forbes White. Mollinger's 'Drenthe' was purchased for £45 by White at the London International Exhibition of 1862. It was a large landscape, now lost, probably more than 48" wide. As was to be typical of White, he was not satisfied with simply owning the work. He wished to know its history and to find out all he could about its creator. He wrote, therefore, to Mollinger in Utrecht and discovered that the painter was a young man, not yet thirty, and that he was one of a number of younger artists in Holland who were beginning to work in the manner exemplified by 'Drenthe'. White must have delighted Mollinger by immediately commissioning another large landscape and by making arrangements to visit him in Utrecht. That visit took place in 1863 and during his stay White was introduced to the painter Josef Israels from whom he also commissioned a painting. This was 'The Departure', the first Israels to come to Scotland.

It would be possible to document the growth of the White collection of Dutch painting, detailing what was purchased and when, but if White is to be promoted as a major formative influence on Scottish taste and Scottish painting then there are more important matters to consider. White's new interest and concern for contemporary Dutch painting are significant, but if all that had happened when he purchased the paintings was that they were hung in his Aberdeen homes at 269 Union Street and at Seaton Cottage, then little would have come of his innovations. In fact, White actively promoted this new fashion. One of the ways in which he encouraged the spread of Hague School ideas among Scottish painters was by financing one of the foremost of the younger generation of painters, George Reid, to

Painting 2. 'Meerkirk, clearing up after rain' by Alexander Mollinger, 1866 (reproduced with permission of City of Aberdeen Art Gallery & Museums Collections).

study for two months in Holland. It was White who made the initial approach to Mollinger to inquire if he would accept Reid as a pupil, and White who both provided Reid with the money to live in Holland, and, by buying some of the work Reid produced there, enabled the artist to get established when he returned home.

By the mid-1860s White was becoming a major figure for the rising generation of Scottish artists. His biographer notes that, 'J. F.'s house was becoming a Mecca for young Scottish painters. His hospitality and geniality were unbounded, and with increasing links with well-known Dutch, French and English artists, his influence was much extended to help rising painters in Scotland.'[9] The painters who visited him were invariably introduced to White's growing collection. Thus artists such as George Paul Chalmers and Hugh Cameron encountered the works of Mollinger, of Israels and of other members of the Hague School.

The path to acceptance for the new approach was not a smooth one. When he returned from his studies in Utrecht, Reid was called before Sir George Harvey, the president of the RSA, and pilloried for studying in Holland. He was recommended to return to his former methods and subjects and to work in the manner of more traditional Scottish painting. When that failed to have any effect an influential collector

Painting 3. 'Montrose' by George Reid, 1889 (reproduced with permission of City of Aberdeen Art Gallery & Museums Collections).

was organised to invite Reid to his home, show him his collection and then attempt to dissuade him from his new Dutch-influenced method.

Reid's new technical methods – that is using thicker, drier paint – and his new subject matter – concentrating on more intimate, human subjects instead of Romantic evocations of castles and mountains – were not simply imports into Scotland from Holland. The Scott Lauder generation was working along similar lines; the contribution of White's activities was to point out the similarity of approach of the Scots and the Dutch, and also similarities to the French Barbizon and Realist painters, thus re-establishing Scottish painting within the mainstream of European developments. It was White who, in 1870, arranged for Josef Israels to visit Scotland and stay with him in Aberdeen. The Scottish painters, Chalmers and Cameron, who had been introduced to Israels' work by White, now met the artist himself and went with him on a painting trip around Scotland. George Reid, who by this time had already spent six weeks working under Israels in the Hague, also met the artist again. All four artists painted a commemorative portrait of

Painting 4. 'The Errand' by Josef Israels, c. 1865 (reproduced with permission of City of Aberdeen Art Gallery & Museums Collections).

Israels to mark the occasion of his visit (Painting 5). They inscribed it 'A notre ami White', and presented it to the collector. The fact that such a collaboration was possible is significant: it could only happen because the methods and ideas of all four artists were compatible. These commonly held techniques and convictions about painting became highly successful in Scotland, not because the Scots learnt a brand new approach from Israels and the Hague School, but precisely because the new approach was not a foreign import. It gave expression to a set of ideas and beliefs which were identifiably Scottish. White's role was to give Reid and the others the chance to develop that expressive language, and to establish that it was a language which Scottish painters shared with many of the more progressive painters of Europe. This sense of a common perception with Europe certainly contributed to the success of the new generation, and it was White's dedicated support which encouraged European painters to consider Scotland as a worthwhile place to exhibit.

Apart from promoting the new method among Scottish painters, White also spread the taste for Dutch painting among fellow collectors. He did this not only indirectly by lending out his paintings at every opportunity to exhibitions all over Scotland, but also by taking an

Painting 5. 'Josef Israels' by George Paul Chalmers, George Reid, Hugh Cameron and Joseph Israels, 1870 (reproduced with permission of City of Aberdeen Art Gallery & Museums Collections).

active part in the mounting of loan exhibitions. He was the central figure in the genesis and organisation of the Aberdeen Art Exhibition of 1873. White served on both the Finance and Arrangements Committee and on the Art Committee.[10] The exhibition was staged, according to an anonymous reporter from the *Aberdeen Journal*, 'not only to delight the senses, but to improve the human character, to improve the

human mind and to develop in the highest manner those qualities whose cultivation tend to benefit mankind, to spread civilisation and to benefit the world at large.'[11] White certainly shared this view of the moral, educational role of art. He later delivered a paper on precisely that topic.[12] The exhibition had other more practical purposes as well. It both celebrated the opening of the new County and Municipal Buildings and it raised money, from the admission charges and through the sale of catalogues, for the Association for the Poor. It can be supposed that for White the exhibition served another purpose. It allowed him to lend out some of his paintings and to promote further Hague School painting and Scottish artists who worked along related lines. White loaned no fewer than forty-four paintings to the exhibition. Of these, twenty-three were by modern Dutch painters and eleven by related contemporary Scottish painters. There were five paintings by Reid and Chalmers and the four-handed collaborative portrait of Israels was also shown. The message could not have been more clear. For White this was the way ahead for Scottish painting.

Although White was the leading figure who first brought Hague School painting to Scotland, he was certainly not the only significant collector in Aberdeen. White was particularly friendly with Alexander Macdonald of Kepplestone, the owner of a granite works, and another major collector of contemporary Scottish painting. Macdonald, like White, was a patron of George Reid and, also like White, was keen to acquire some of the work which Reid produced during his periods of study in Holland. Indeed the two collectors appear to have had a disagreement about who should be allowed to buy 'Broadsea', the most important painting that Reid brought back from his 1869 studies with Josef Israels. Given Macdonald's disposition and enthusiasm, White obviously did not have to work hard to persuade him to buy Hague School paintings, and he soon owned a number by Mollinger, Israels and others. That Macdonald had very strong connections with both Scottish and English artists of the period is shown by his collection of ninety-four cabinet portraits of artists with whom he was friendly. At his death in 1884 he owned large and important paintings by Mollinger, Israels and David Artz, and also by William Roelofs, Mollinger's master. His collection is now in Aberdeen Art Gallery.

In addition to the collections of contemporary Dutch paintings by these major figures, Aberdeen was home to numerous smaller ones, many of which were the direct or indirect result of the activities of John Forbes White. Alexander Walker, for example, had a small collec-

Painting 6. 'Le Bonheur d'une Mère' by David Artz, c. 1870 (reproduced with permission of City of Aberdeen Art Gallery & Museums Collections).

tion of paintings which was almost a White collection in miniature. A city wine merchant, Walker was a close friend of George Reid from an early date. Like White he owned paintings by Chalmers, Cameron and Reid, and was directly influenced by White's support of Dutch painting. While George Reid was studying in Holland he wrote to Walker

and persuaded him to buy paintings by Mollinger.

So successful did Mollinger become in Scotland, indeed, that he referred to it as the 'land of my success' and viewed it as one of the most likely places to sell his paintings. Very quickly after the arrival of the first modern Dutch work in 1862, there emerged in Scotland a powerful fashion for Holland. Initially it was concentrated more on the east coast, but by the late 1870s Glasgow too became a major centre for the buying of contemporary Dutch painting. Alexander Reid, the most successful picture dealer in Glasgow in the late nineteenth century, is primarily associated with the promotion of contemporary French painting, and his influence on the Burrell collection has been used to illustrate this. But the mainstay of his business was his dealing in Hague School pictures. Even to William Burrell he sold far more Dutch paintings than he did French.

Something of the flavour of the Scottish passion for Dutch art can be seen in the circumstances surrounding John Charles Bell's purchase of his first Mollinger in 1866. Bell wrote to Mollinger in June 1865, commissioning a painting for £20. The popularity of Dutch painting had grown so swiftly that Bell was quite prepared to take whatever Mollinger painted for him without seeing it. Furthermore the matter was urgent because Bell wished to lend the painting to an exhibition as soon as he had it. Keen to keep his popularity in Scotland growing, and to make the sale, Mollinger wanted to be able to agree, but he was on the Mediterranean coast at the time and not able to work. He wrote from Menton to his friend and patron VerLoren van Themaat in Utrecht:

> You may know that Mr J. Charles Bell [of Dundee] has asked me for a painting for £20 or a little more to be ready by January 1866. What to do? I should like to earn that £20 but I have no painting. It strikes me that the paintings from Dublin should be coming home any day and if Mr Bell has not visited the Dublin exhibition I should be able to send him the tall painting entitled 'The White House Under the Oaks' and for the time being write to him that I'll do my best to finish the painting by mid-January. If you feel able to agree to this plan would you be so kind as to write to him in English. [13]

By 1866 Mollinger was obviously under considerable pressure to produce paintings for Scotland. The Scottish press also began to comment very favourably on his work. In another letter to VerLoren

van Themaat, Mollinger included cuttings from *The Scotsman* and from *The Daily Review*, which praised him highly. Mollinger had gone south for his health; he had tuberculosis and the damp winters in Utrecht were bad for him. White had arranged for his brother-in-law, a Dr. Drummond, to treat the painter but in spite of this Mollinger died in Utrecht in the autumn of 1867. He had become so successful in Scotland, and so many of his paintings were there, that his reputation abroad was considerably higher than it was at home; his paintings fetched higher prices in Scotland. When Mollinger died John Forbes White was in Paris. He had intended to meet Mollinger and George Reid there and for the three of them to visit the International Exhibition together but Mollinger had withdrawn because of his ill-health. White went directly to Utrecht from Paris and arranged to take the entire contents of Mollinger's studio back with him to Scotland. He sold the paintings and drawings in Scotland on behalf of Mollinger's family, knowing that more money would be raised there than in Holland. This was a genuinely philanthropic act for White made no money from the sales. While the fashion for Holland initiated by White means that all of Scotland's galleries have large holdings of Hague School paintings, the collector's particular ties to Aberdeen mean that that city now has the single biggest collection of Mollinger works in existence. There are five oil paintings and two pencil drawings in Aberdeen Art Gallery.

The Hague School also became popular in England, but the fashion started far earlier, with more lasting impact, and produced more interesting home-grown variants in Scotland. So powerful was the force which White unleashed that when Scotland came to stage the first of its two great International Exhibitions of the 1880s, in Edinburgh in 1886, the painting collection was dominated by Hague School and related French Barbizon painting. In his preface to the catalogue, the organiser of the collection rather despairingly described the fact that 'this collection was to a large extent confined to the French and Dutch painters' as 'more of an accident than the result of any preference on my part for these schools'.[14] There were 106 French paintings and 192 Dutch paintings on display. This is a far cry indeed from the situation sixteen years earlier when George Reid struggled to have his new approach to painting accepted and White was attempting to promote Dutch painting in Scotland. In that climate the issue arose of the RSA exhibiting a painting by Josef Israels. In a letter to White, Reid described the course of an RSA council meeting:

There was some talk in the council about Macdonald's (the Aberdeen collector) Israels – They had never heard of him before and did not know that there was any celebrated Dutch artist living at present, Rembrandt being the last they had heard of. Fortunately Cameron was there and spoke . . . and so the council was appeased. They seem to inherit the Barbarians' traditional mistrust of foreigners. [15]

Beleaguered in 1870, White had effected a revolution in taste which was complete by 1886. Its consequences continued, however, well into the 1890s and ultimately it significantly affected the course of not one but two generations of Scottish painting and collecting.

NOTES

1. For further information on the Scott Lauder pupils and Glasgow Boys see Lindsay Errington, *Master Class. Robert Scott Lauder and His Pupils*, National Galleries of Scotland (Edinburgh, 1983) and Roger Billcliffe, *The Glasgow Boys* (London 1985).

2. William Fettes Douglas: reported in *The Scotsman*, 2 March 1889, p. 6.

3. The 'staple port' was that European port which had the Scottish trading monopoly. Individual cities competed by offering differing commercial and social privileges in an attempt to secure the right to be the sole point of entry of Scottish goods to Europe. In the early sixteenth century there was considerable rivalry for this monopoly between Antwerp, Campvere and Middleburg. Campvere, in Zealand, was eventually chosen as the staple port in 1541 and remained so for nearly 250 years.

4. Rosalind Mitchison, *A History of Scotland*, (London 1970), p. 164.

5. Robert Feenstra, 'Scottish – Dutch legal relations in the 17th and 18th centuries', in T. C. Smout (ed.), *Scotland and Europe 1200–1850* (Edinburgh, 1986), p. 130.

6. James Caw, *Scottish Painting Past and Present 1620–1908* (Edinburgh, 1908), p. 286.

7. David Johnston (ed.), *Translations Literal and Free of the Dying Hadrians Address to His Soul* (Bath, 1876).

8. *Scotsman*, 24th September 1867.

9. C. S. Minto and Dorothea Fyfe, *John Forbes White. 1831–1904* (Edinburgh Libraries and Museums Committee, 1970), p. 12.

10. Speeches at the opening of the exhibition make it clear that White was the driving force behind it.

11. *Aberdeen Journal*, 6 August 1873, p. 5.

12. John Forbes White, 'How can art be best introduced into the houses of persons of limited income?', a paper read before the National Association for the Promotion of Social Science at Aberdeen on 24 September 1877. Printed for private circulation (Aberdeen, 1877).

13. Correspondence of G. A. Mollinger to P. VerLoren van Themaat, 4 December 1865. Held in Gemeentearchief, The Hague.

14. *Memorial Catalogue of the French and Dutch Loan Collection. Edinburgh International Exhibition 1886* (Edinburgh, 1888), p. xxxvii.

15. Correspondence of George Reid to J. F. White, 4 February 1870. Held by Aberdeen Art Gallery.

PART III:

CAPITAL AND LABOUR

Aberdeen 1800–2000 AD:
the Evolution of the Urban Economy

Clive Lee

The *economic growth* of Aberdeen and its region in the past two centuries was part of the economic transformation of the western world which created a level of economic activity and widespread prosperity far in excess of the achievements of earlier generations. This process was essentially driven by market forces and was international in character. Thus it was able to draw sustenance from its own growth through the increase in personal affluence which created a demand for an ever-increasing range of goods and services which, in turn, expanded markets, stimulated the supply of new and better commodities, and extended the tentacles of trade through most of the world. Western Europe, and particularly the United Kingdom, played a prominent part in that process and many of its manifestations are found in the economic history of Aberdeen.

A crude indicator of the dimensions of this growth is provided by the population of the city. In 1801 Aberdeen numbered about 27,000 people and was therefore already substantially larger than the 8,000 estimated as the seventeenth-century population of the burgh, and had probably doubled in the previous half century.[1] After 1801 expansion was even more impressive, reaching 70,000 by 1851 and 153,000 by the beginning of the twentieth century. During the past hundred years the population has doubled again, although the area of the city has also increased as the rural fringes have been converted into suburban

housing areas. This chapter explores the economic forces that have brought about this expansion.

THE ESSENTIALS OF GROWTH

It is a truism, but nevertheless a vitally important one, that the early growth of Aberdeen was shaped by its location and the natural resources which provided its comparative advantage in both Scottish markets and those further afield. In some respects the location was not particularly favourable, being distant from the major English and European markets, while its position on the eastern seaboard effectively precluded involvement in the North American markets which had such a dramatic impact on the trade of west coast ports like Liverpool and Glasgow. But the exploitation of local resources underpinned the economic growth which had been achieved already by 1800 in the development of agriculture and the textile industry. The nineteenth-century industrialisation of Aberdeen was largely determined by the exploitation of natural resources, such as fishing and granite, and by the secondary effects of such activity. Thus the growth of fishing stimulated shipbuilding, ship repairing and marine engineering. The fact that the growth of agriculture, fishing, textiles and quarrying relied on the supply of markets far from Aberdeen meant that there was an obvious and substantial impact on transport, leading to the improvement of the harbour, the function of which was supplemented in the middle of the nineteenth century by the advent of the railway. More than a century later, the expansion of the oil industry and its ancillary activities in Aberdeen contributed enormously to the improvement of road links with the south. Further, the emergence of all these new activities necessitated the development of a commercial infrastructure in distribution, banking, insurance and a wide range of professional services.

As geographical constraints have been so important to Aberdeen, so transport considerations have played a major role in the development of the city. Prior to 1800 the sea was the main route to markets beyond the region. This remained the case until the advent of the railway in 1850 which increased both the speed and convenience of access to southern markets. These included the London meat market, access to which allowed and encouraged cattle farming on a much larger scale than hitherto. When the railway was extended to the north of the city in the 1850s, local farmers increasingly adjusted their activity to fat

stock production, and, while wishing to keep the railway off their own land, were anxious to have it pass fairly close by.[2] The new and highly effective competition offered by the railway caused problems for the coastal shipping companies. Prices were lower by rail, the journey was quicker, and no cattle were lost overboard during a storm. The Aberdeen Steam Navigation Company sought to protect some of its market by entering an agreement with the Scottish North East Railway Company, by which they shared the trade, and the shippers paid compensation to the railway in respect of 'lost' trade allocated to the shipping company under the collusive agreement.[3]

Despite competition, the growth of shipping traffic meant that the harbour was frequently expanded. Since the navigation channel was subject to silting, most of these improvement schemes were needed to deepen or keep open the entrance to the harbour. This frequently involved changing the course of the Dee, and the accidental outcome of one such scheme created the Albert Basin which became, at the turn of the century, the centre of the United Kingdom white fishing trade. The tonnage of vessels registered at Aberdeen increased from 36,000 tons in 1818 to 135,000 tons by the end of the century, while the tonnage of vessels entering the port doubled in the second half of the nineteenth century.

In a location some distance from the main commercial centres of Scotland, and with a distinctive and somewhat self-contained economy, Aberdeen was able to develop its own commercial structure, a fact helped by its position as the business centre for a large rural hinterland. Aberdeen, therefore, developed its own banking and insurance institutions which, in turn, played a major part in financing the economic development of the region. Banking companies appeared in Aberdeen in the middle of the eighteenth century, although some of them did not survive for very long. But the appearance of the North of Scotland Bank in 1836, pledged to concentrate on providing financial services for the north-east, marked an important milestone in development. It followed shortly after the launch of the Northern Assurance Company, and was the creation of the law firm of Adam & Anderson, whose partners were also involved in establishing the New Market. They played a major part in railway finance, especially the Great North of Scotland Railway Company, although they were party to the railways linking the city to north, south and west. Sir Alexander Anderson, the more prominent partner also served as lord provost and was one of the major figures in the development of early and mid-Victorian Aberdeen.

A financial institution with more modest aspirations was the Aberdeen Savings Bank founded in 1815. This institution was designed to look after the small savings of tradesmen and labourers which might otherwise 'be squandered away, unsafely deposited, or lost altogether', and to encourage thrift amongst the less wealthy members of society.[4] A room in the Poor's Hospital opened for an hour every Saturday morning to receive deposits. By the end of the century, it had become one of the largest savings banks in the United Kingdom. It attracted deposits from all parts of the north-east. Under the leadership of Thomas Jaffrey, from the 1890s on, the bank greatly expanded its activities, opening in 1896 its imposing new head office in Union Row. In the first half of the twentieth century the bank opened a host of branches, initially in the city – at Woodside and Torry – and later as far away as Fraserburgh and Turriff. At the same time it merged with a large number of smaller savings banks such as those at Stonehaven, Inverurie, Wick and Elgin.

Many of these institutions were closely interrelated. The Aberdeen Savings Bank provided an investment service for its customers, in securities such as the East India Company but also in local enterprises such as the Harbour Board. In the 1930s it lent to local authorities at rates below market value for social purposes. One such loan – of £750,000 – was provided to Aberdeen Corporation to build houses. In adverse economic circumstances the strength of local linkages could be destabilising for the entire local economy. The heavy involvement of the North of Scotland Bank in railway promotion and in making loans to local textile firms cost the bank heavily in the depression of 1848. Indeed by the end of that year the bank's liabilities and bad debts were not fully covered by its assets, although under new management it did survive and prosper. Less successful was the Aberdeen Banking Company, in operation since 1767, which had lent heavily and over an extended period to local companies. In 1828 the capital of the bank was increased to £250,000; by 1849 it had shrunk to £7,000, together with a host of bad debts and the defunct Bannermill, which had once been a bastion of the local textile trade and was valued at some £35,000. The bank only escaped collapse by being purchased by the Union Bank of Scotland later in 1849.[5]

Part of the growth of any city comes from the multiplier effects of indigenous industrial growth, as in providing essential transport and financial services for producers. But the city also generates its own autonomous growth in providing education, health, and local govern-

ment for its citizens. Furthermore the growth of the population of the city, and of the income of its inhabitants, exerts further demand for shopping facilities and a diversity of entertainments. All these activities create new jobs and incomes, and add to the cumulative process of economic growth.

ASPECTS OF DECLINE

The process of economic change, even when dominated by growth and progress in the sense of greater wealth creation, is seldom if ever totally untroubled. Change implies the decline and disappearance of once apparently secure activities as well as the appearance of impressive new developments. The substantial transition of the Aberdeen economy over the past two centuries has, of course, included such elements of decline. In a region which has relied heavily on its endowment of natural resources, it is not surprising that some of them should have become exhausted. Granite quarrying and manufacture, as well as much of the fishing industry, have suffered this fate. Eventually, oil reserves will also become exhausted or economically unviable.

The Aberdeen granite industry had its origins in the eighteenth century in open-cast workings outside the city – at such exotic locations as the 'dancing cairns' and the 'hills of Rubislaw' – initially to supply stone for local housing, the reconstruction of the harbour and, later, the inexhaustible demands of metropolitan London. Developments in transport allowed the exploitation of reserves at a greater distance from the harbour than hitherto, most notably at Kintore and Kemnay. Deeper and larger-scale workings meant the industry had to draw on the skills of local engineers for cranes and other equipment. The perfection of the technique for polishing granite mechanically by a local stonemason, Alexander MacDonald, created a manufacturing industry with an emphasis on monumental architecture.

The industry reached its high point in the last two decades of the nineteenth century. Both the coastal trade and the urban development of Aberdeen boosted demand for granite. Local stone was used to construct the tenements of Torry and the East End and granite setts supported the electric tramway system. Both production and employment fell after the turn of the century. By then the finite resources of granite were scarcer and more expensive to excavate. High production costs made it difficult for the industry to compete in markets beyond the local region. Indeed the manufacturing side of the industry already

[215]

imported supplies of granite, especially from Sweden. This part of the trade was sustained by the housing boom of the 1890s and by the American market for tombstones. After 1900 protectionist policies in the United States, and the fading of the local housing boom, cut demand. By World War I, like many British industries, granite suffered from over-capacity, and the characteristic structure of many small firms precluded rationalisation either through take-over or by agreement. Imports of granite from Europe in the 1920s made the situation worse. Even the revival of house building in the 1930s brought only a modest respite, as the characteristic houses of the time – bungalows at Angusfield and King's Gate, and modest council-housing developments – did not require large amounts of stone. The industry had remained in local control, although when the Rubislaw Granite Company floated a share issue in 1890, a substantial majority of the shares was sold to expatriate Scots in England. Eventually, in the 1960s, a series of mergers brought the major surviving companies together, but by then many of the quarries were exhausted or reduced to producing road aggregate. The visible memorial to the industry remains in imposing monuments in many parts of the world and in the characteristic architecture of Aberdeen itself.[6]

At the beginning of the nineteenth century, the textile industries represented Aberdeen's principal manufacturing activity. The Gordon's Mill on the Don, a century old, had started production in 1703, and its hosiery was well known in Europe. By 1800, textile manufacture had been extended to include carpets, cotton, linen and wool. Their producers also introduced the new machinery, which was changing textile manufacture from a craft industry into mechanised factory production – a process which increasingly exposed the city's geographical isolation from the major centres of the industry in central Scotland, northern England and Ulster. Expansion to maintain a competitive position was expensive. Leys, Masson & Company, linen manufacturers at Grandholm spent £100,000 in the first quarter of the nineteenth century in paying for land, buildings and machinery. Local competition came from Richards & Company's Broadford Mills and Milne Cruden & Company in the Gallowgate. In 1840 these three companies employed about 7,600 people. In the woollen branch, which provided work for 2,500 people, the principal manufacturers were Alexander Hadden & Sons, making hose, worsted and carpets in the Green; and Messrs Crombie at Cothal Mills on rural Donside. The principal cotton manufacturers were Gordon Barron & Company at Woodside, Thomas

Bannerman & Company at the Bannermill and Forbes, Low & Company at Poynernook, employing together 2,000 workers.[7] (The political role of some of these business families in Victorian Aberdeen has been explored by Michael Dyer above.)

The general depression of 1840 proved devastating for the Aberdeen textile manufacturers. In 1848 two of the largest companies in the district failed – Leys, Masson & Company and Alexander Hadden & Sons. The latter reopened in 1850 and struggled on until 1904, but Leys, Masson, after a brief revival, collapsed finally in 1854. All the other major companies failed with the exception of Richards and Crombie. The tonnage of textiles shipped from Aberdeen harbour fell in the decade after 1845 from 81,000 bales to 9,000 bales, and little of this could be attributed to the effect of the new railway links. The immediate impact was very severe in loss of income and rising unemployment. It was estimated that the loss of wages in Woodside alone could diminish the income of the district to 16 per cent of its value in the previous decade. The firms which survived the depression were able to do so by finding niche markets for specific products, since they were unable to offer serious competition in main-line production to the massive firms established in Lancashire in the second half of the century. Hadden & Sons turned to the production of 'winceys', Richards & Company became one of the largest linen firms in Britain, while Crombie survived by eventually moving into the production of high quality products. Thus textiles and clothing remained an important source of work in the city throughout the nineteenth century. In 1841 the 4,233 jobs for men accounted for 16.2 per cent of the city's male work-force. By 1911 this had fallen to 3,436 jobs but, given the growth elsewhere in the local economy, this now represented only 7.6 per cent of male employment. For women, employment in textiles continued to grow from 4,489 jobs in 1841 to 6,889 by 1911; that share of female employment, although falling, remained very high at 50.5 per cent in 1841 and 30.1 per cent on the eve of World War I. Thereafter decline was rapid and substantial.[8]

As a seaport, Aberdeen has long been associated with shipbuilding, ship repairing and fishing. These industries had the initial advantage of a resource endowment which conferred a competitive advantage. They all experienced substantial growth in the past two centuries and eventual decline. The introduction of steam-powered ships in the 1820s shifted the balance of geographical advantage to estuaries with good access to coal, iron and engineering manufacture, that is to say,

to the Clyde, the Tyne and the Wear. Aberdeen shipyards were able to compete in the short run through specialisation in sailing vessels, and built some of the famous clipper ships, which were able to maintain an advantage over steamships on very long voyages to China and Australia, or round South America to the west coast of the United States, until the end of the century.[9] Whereas steamers needed to devote part of their space to carry coal, sailing vessels obviously did not, and were thus able to compete on long voyages until coaling-stations and improved technology eroded that advantage. With the decline of the clippers, Aberdeen ceased to be a major shipbuilding centre, although Hall Russell, the result of the combination in 1864 of two previous companies, managed to survive for more than a century, building trawlers and drifters, and making some of the diverse products of marine engineering.

Perhaps the greatest aid to the city as a seafaring port came with the boom in fishing in the 1880s, with the introduction of steam trawling. The value of white fish landed increased from £10,000 in 1882 to £730,000 twenty years later. This led to increased employment connected with fishing – in the new fish market opened in 1889; in fish curing; in storage and distribution; and in the repair and maintenance of vessels. It was estimated that in 1902 some 25,000 people depended on the trawling industry.[10] The volume of fish landed increased from 133,000 hundredweight in 1888 to 2,268,860 hundredweight in 1914, by which date Aberdeen had become the largest fishing port in the United Kingdom.[11] Between the wars the industry experienced rising difficulties. Higher costs and falling wholesale prices squeezed the profitability of the trawling fleet. Furthermore the exhaustion of stocks in the waters close to the coast, which had been heavily fished in the later nineteenth century, forced the industry to move further afield. The fleets of Hull and Grimsby were much quicker to adjust to the changed market conditions, and were readier to invest in new vessels, than were their Aberdeen competitors. By the end of the 1930s, the landings of white fish at Hull were three to four times those at Aberdeen. An ageing fleet of trawlers, and necessarily higher transport costs than their English competitors incurred in reaching the large southern markets, began the steady decline of Aberdeen as a fishing port.

Aberdeen is, in the jargon of economics, a small open economy in that it is exposed to shifts in international markets, and this constitutes another aspect of its economic vulnerability. The impact of such market adjustment was demonstrated very sharply in the 1980s when

oil prices fell dramatically on world markets. The oil industry has, of course, had a massive impact on Aberdeen and the entire north-east, since much of the activity has been concentrated in the region. But the collapse of the oil price from $27 to $8 per barrel within a few months in 1985–86 had a seismic effect on the industry. A severe curtailment of exploration and drilling activity brought massive redundancies at all the construction yards and many small supply companies were driven into liquidation. Employment fell by 15 per cent of the labour force. The buoyant housing market in Aberdeen was another casualty as prices collapsed. The industry readjusted through mergers, asset swapping agreements and rationalisation. As a result, three main conglomerates emerged controlling the industry, all of them American owned, as many of the small indigenous companies failed to survive until the industry revived again at the end of the decade. [12]

THE INFORMATION ECONOMY

As economies develop, their structures change, reflecting differences in the composition of production and the labour force. Employment structure is both a visible and important measure of the capability of an economy to sustain an active work-force. Over the past two centuries the labour force of Aberdeen has increased considerably, but it has also undergone a profound structural change. The earliest estimates of employment structure which can be regarded as credible in general terms are those for the 1841 census. This showed a classical early Victorian employment structure, with a far higher activity rate amongst men – in paid employment – than amongst women. There were over 16,100 men employed in the city compared to less than 8,900 women. The continued importance of textiles and clothing was reflected in the fact that over one quarter of employed men and half the women, a total of 8,700 workers, were employed in these sectors. The only other significant source of work for women was in the miscellaneous services sector – largely domestic service – which accounted for 40 per cent of all women in employment. The range of male activities was more diverse, including agriculture, food-processing and distribution, construction, engineering, and unspecified labouring, these being the major constituent activities of the work-force.

By the eve of World War I, male employment had increased to almost three times its 1841 level while women's employment had more than doubled. But men still accounted for two-thirds of the labour

force. In male employment the Victorian period witnessed substantial growth in almost all sectors, which easily compensated for the jobs lost in textiles and clothing. Particular growth occurred in transport (up by over 8,000 jobs), agriculture, fishing, and quarrying (up by 5,000), food processing and distribution (up by almost 3,000), construction (up by almost 2,000), and metal-working, engineering and shipbuilding (up by over 4,000). There was a total net increase of almost 30,000 jobs. Change in the female work-force was less complex. In 1911, employment remained highly concentrated in personal services, mainly domestic service (with 27.6 per cent of all jobs), textiles and clothing (with 30.1 per cent), food processing and distribution (12.1 per cent), and paper and printing (8.2 per cent). These sectors had all comprised a major part of growth in employment over the previous seventy years.

The structural change experienced by the labour force in the twentieth century was far greater than the changes of the Victorian era. The impact of structural change was more serious in the case of male employment. Total employment in 1971 was little more than it had been in 1921 and less than in 1951. This was due to the decline in employment in many productive sectors. There was a decline in non-service-sector employment by over 8,000 jobs between 1911 and 1971. Employment in transport also fell, by some 2,500 jobs. The replacement growth came entirely from the service sector, principally in distribution (by over 6,000 jobs), in the professions (by 4,000), in personal services (by 3,000), and public administration (by 2,000). The construction industry also grew by 2,000 jobs. The structure of the male labour force thus changed radically in the half century after World War I. Indeed the upsurge of activity in the oil industry arrested a pattern of decline which was becoming worryingly well established. The increase in employment for women has been a universal phenomenon of the twentieth century throughout the United Kingdom, and, indeed, the developed world as a whole. This has been especially true of the period since the 1950s. As in the case of male employment, growth has been confined almost totally to the service sector. Between 1911 and 1971, female employment in Aberdeen increased by 9,000 in the professions, over 7,000 in distribution, and over 1,000 in public administration, resulting in a net increase of over 11,000 jobs. The urban economy by the later decades of the twentieth century was thus heavily dependent on the provision of services. In the past two decades, however, this pattern has been readjusted by the advent of the oil industry.

One vitally important feature of local growth has been the impact of

education, especially higher education, on local spending. At the close of World War II the University of Aberdeen had 150 academic staff, a number which rose to a peak of 887 by the early 1980s, while total employment at the university in 1988 was 2,480. Total expenditure extends beyond employment. There is, for example, capital spending on buildings for teaching and student accommodation. Then there are the catering requirements of the university itself and its halls of residence; the demand for bookshops; and the contribution to local rates. Total university expenditure in 1987/88 reached £56 million, and if student expenditure is added, the total rose to £63.5 million. This may be compared to Aberdeen District Council's spending of £94.6 million.[13] Regional multipliers, which estimate the outward ripples of expenditure by such large institutions, suggest that the final impact could be at least 50 per cent more than the initial direct impact. A university also provides an important training function with effects on the local economy in the provision of lawyers, accountants, doctors and other professional workers. The total expenditure of the University of Aberdeen, at constant prices, increased from £4 million in 1945/46 to £56 million by 1987/88.[14] While the University of Aberdeen has a longer history than most other educational institutions in the area, it is by no means alone in contributing to the local economy. Robert Gordon Institute of Technology, now The Robert Gordon University, the Aberdeen campus of the Northern College of Education, and the vast array of further education colleges now gathered under the aegis of the Aberdeen College, all make significant contributions to local expenditure. Furthermore, even in the context of recent erosion of salaries in education as in the rest of the public sector, higher and further education establishments employ many staff at relatively high incomes and this too has an important effect on local spending power. Higher education comprises part of a wider research base which is essential for keeping a local economy viable in terms of the modern information economy. The struggle in the mid-1990s to retain the Torry Marine Research Laboratory, which was threatened with transfer to York, and which met with partial success, brought together all the higher educational institutions in the city in a common cause with the research institutes. The Torry laboratory, like the Macaulay Institute some years earlier, faced a threat arising typically from government centralisation, and rationalisation strategies which are often primarily designed to cut costs and pay little regard either to local impact or even to technological need. The future economy of the city is likely to rely heavily on such organisations,

[221]

and on their mutual interaction, particularly when the oil reserves are exhausted or no longer economically worth exploiting.

Aberdeen is fortunate in having other service industries which generate high levels of employment and sustain both high technology and human skills. The health complex centred on Aberdeen Royal Infirmary and medical school is an obvious example of this. The legal and commercial professions provide another. Any modern economy needs the sustaining help of high income professional employment which, in turn, generates spending throughout the community. Developing affluence becomes part of a beneficial process of self-reinforcing growth. Its converse, the vicious cycle of decline and depression, can be equally potent and difficult to break away from, as less fortunate regions of Scotland have found.

ABERDEEN 2000

There is no doubt that much of the prosperity enjoyed by Aberdeen and its region in the past two decades has been created by the sudden growth of the oil industry. In 1993 Grampian region had 65,816 oil-related jobs, approximately 85 per cent of all such employment in Scotland. The prosperity is manifest in new housing, improved road networks, the transformation of the harbour, the appearance of new office blocks at Rubislaw, Altens and Bridge of Don, and the burgeoning industrial estates. Many new jobs have been created by the industry, the great majority in the north-east, and spending power has been increased, as evidenced by the considerable improvement in shopping facilities. Statistical evidence of per capita income in the first half of the 1990s placed Grampian region, of which Aberdeen is certainly the most prosperous part, close to the very top of the regional distribution in the United Kingdom. In 1991 Scotland as a whole averaged 95.8 per cent of UK income per head while Grampian recorded a level of 134.8 per cent. Not surprisingly Grampian had a very low rate of unemployment, 4.6 per cent in 1993 compared to the Scotland-wide figure of 9.9 per cent.[15] It is sometimes easy to overlook the fact that this recent upsurge in economic activity and prosperity brought to a conclusion a long phase of slow decline. Oil, like other natural resources, is a finite commodity, and in due course this phase of the city's economic history will pass, as did the era of fishing and granite. The challenge for the future is thus to build on the good fortune of oil to create sustainable growth for the next century. The city is well

placed to do this. There seems little doubt that the key economic sectors of the future will be based on knowledge, and the new technologies of information handling. The city has a good resource base in its two universities, the variety of other educational institutions, its medical complex and its diverse commercial and professional sector. Aberdeen at the millennium can look forward to the coming economic challenges with some confidence.

NOTES

1. Hugh Mackenzie, *The City of Aberdeen* (Edinburgh, 1953), pp. 31–43.
2. J. H. Smith, 'The cattle trade of Aberdeenshire in the nineteenth century', *Agricultural History Review*, vol. 3 (1955), p. 115.
3. C. H. Lee, 'Some aspects of the coastal shipping trade: the Aberdeen Steam Navigation Company 1835–80', *Journal of Transport History*, vol. 3 (1975), p. 99.
4. T. Jaffrey et al., *Aberdeen Savings Bank* (Aberdeen, 1967 ed.).
5. Robert S. Rait, *The History of the Union Bank of Scotland* (Glasgow, 1930).
6. Tom Donnelly, *The Aberdeen Granite Industry* (Aberdeen, 1994).
7. Alexander Keith, *A Thousand Years of Aberdeen* (Aberdeen, 1972) p. 10; Mackenzie, *City of Aberdeen*, p. 46.
8. General Register Office, *Census of Scotland*, Occupation Tables (decennial).
9. C. K. Harley, 'The shift from sailing ships to steamships 1850–1890: a study in technological change and its diffusion', in D. N. McCloskey (ed.), *Essays on a Mature Economy: Britain after 1840* (London, 1971).
10. William Pyper, 'History of a great industry', *People's Journal* (1907).
11. Aberdeen Harbour Board Minutes (annual).
12. W. J. Pike, 'The oil price crisis and its impact on Scottish North Sea development 1986–1988', *Scottish Economic and Social History*, 13 (1993), pp. 63–67.
13. Alexander G. Kemp and Sandra J. Galbraith, 'Contributions to the regional economy: expenditure and employment', in John D. Hargreaves and Angela Forbes (eds), *Aberdeen University 1945–1981: Regional Roles and National Needs* (Aberdeen, 1989).
14. Kemp and Galbraith, 'Regional economy', p. 35.
15. Scottish Office, *Scottish Economic Bulletin*, 50 (Winter 1994/95).

Neither Parochial nor Soothing: Aberdeen and the Future of Labour History[1]

Terry Brotherstone

I

Aberdeen, *wrote the left-wing* novelist Lewis Grassic Gibbon in 1934, 'is the home of the . . . "Scotch" joke', based on a stereotype of meanness and mercenary ambition. Grassic Gibbon himself, who had a love-hate relationship with the city, thought 'bleakness . . . the key to the Aberdeen character'. (Union Street in winter he described as 'an Eskimo's vision of hell', a thoroughfare with 'as much warmth . . . as a dowager duchess asked to contribute to the Red International Relief'.)[2] Humour about Aberdeen, often originated by Aberdonians, has flowed also from the modern city's reputation for parochialism. It is untrue that the sinking of the Titanic was reported under the headline 'Aberdeen Man Lost at Sea'; but the government minister, Alan Clark, was not being 'economical with the *actualité*' when, in the mid-1980s, he described Aberdeen's daily, the *Press and Journal*, as 'resolute in its parochialism, and most soothing as a result'.[3] One purpose of this book has been to contend that Aberdeen's history is of interest far beyond the parish. And this last chapter will argue that its study is a challenging rather than a soothing exercise.

The City and its Worlds has selectively directed the spotlight on a

variety of the experiences made by Aberdonians over the past two hundred years or so, particularly in the nineteenth century. Physicians, planners and politicians; aesthetes and bibliophiles; graduates and emigrants; city fathers, the city's mothers; and a city hatter; all have had parts in the show. Aberdeen's history in this period was both typical and exceptional, in the mainstream of late-eighteenth-century and Victorian urban and social development and also relatively isolated from it. This contradiction may partly explain why the city's impact on the outside world has sometimes taken the form of a joke. But it also means that Aberdeen has great potential for affording historical insight.

Don Withrington began this book with an overview of Aberdeen's evolving appearance and personality, and in chapter twelve Clive Lee made what could have been the concluding statement. Lee demonstrates how Aberdeen's economic development can be seen as a tale of the progress of Western society – not without its problems, but marvellous nonetheless. After this relatively optimistic scenario, it may seem perverse to end on a note of crisis. But the growing consciousness in the 1990s of the importance of Aberdeen's history has not arisen purely by accident. It is at least in part a reflection of the fact that, in the last quarter of the twentieth century, the city became central to the working of the British economy. Offshore oil production, which in some respects transformed Aberdeen, also helped to underpin the socio-economic experiment known as Thatcherism. If it was ever justifiable to regard Aberdeen's history simply as local history, that time has passed. North-eastern Scotland retained a limited self-sufficiency while it participated in the economic success story of nineteenth-century Britain, but the region's relative resilience in the late-twentieth century was achieved at the expense of increasing interdependence with national, indeed global, trends. Labour historians, I think, have a particular responsibility to reflect on the implications of this.

II

'Agitationally, in spite of its unemployed,' wrote Grassic Gibbon in his 1934 essay, 'Aberdeen sleeps these days. . . .' He contrasted this with 'visions of the barricade' during the war, when he was a young journalist in the city, and 'when the mob broke up the peace [campaign] meeting in the Music Hall.' And he remembered

the founding of the Aberdeen Soviet when the news of the Bolshevik Revolution came through from Russia; and . . . I and a cub reporter . . . were elected to the Soviet Council, forgetting we were pressmen; and spent perspiring minutes with our chief reporters afterwards, explaining that we could not report the meeting being ourselves good sovietists. . . .

Twelve years later, however, he visited the city's police court, where a woman was being prosecuted for debt incurred in the purchase of a pair of knickers. Seeing this 'poor proletarian with her red-chapped hands . . . terrified face . . . and . . . stammering voice', he 'turned away [his] eyes and felt . . . sick.'[4]

We began this book with some celebration of Aberdeen's particularity, of its citizens' identification with their locality and its interconnected hinterland, and of the resilience of a pre-modern sense of community in the face of social change. Grassic Gibbon reminds us that epoch-making world events also had their impact on Aberdonians; and that Aberdeen, like more industrialised cities, witnessed the cruel face of class oppression. W. G. Carson, moreover, in his work in the early 1980s about the industry which has ensured the city's relative prosperity in the last quarter of the twentieth century, indicates that this is not the language of the past. His study of working conditions in the North Sea reminded him

of the [history of the] earliest efforts to impose statutory control upon the operations of the 'dark satanic mills' of the nineteenth century. In that era, as in the present, there were immutable laws of capital which rendered it 'imperative' that regulation should be minimized. Then, as now, it was constantly threatened that capital would flee if subjected to any more constraints. . . .

It was a case, he thought, of 'New Oil in Old Barrels'.[5] Some six years later, about ten o'clock on the night of 6 July 1988, explosions rocked the Piper Alpha production platform, about 110 miles north-east of Aberdeen. In the ensuing disaster, 167 men died, and many of the minority which survived were traumatised. Since 1991 a sculpture in the city's Hazlehead Park has commemorated the dead. It should perhaps be the starting point for all those setting out to explore the history of labour in and around Aberdeen.

III

Labour history, as an academic subject, arose as much from the labour movement itself as from the world of historical scholarship. Early practitioners – the Webbs (Sidney and Beatrice), the Coles (G. D. H. and Margaret) and, in Scotland, W. H. Marwick, for example – were all socialists and reformers as well as historians. When the Society for the Study of Labour History, and the Scottish Labour History Society, were born in the 1960s, there was at least an implicit assumption that, by taking a leading role in the more general renaissance of social history, labour historians could capture the ideological high ground in historical work and thereby serve the cause of socialism. A cursory reading of recent labour history periodicals will show that a decade and a half of Thatcherism in Britain, and the collapse of the Soviet Union, have thrown this perspective into disarray.[6] For some scholars, the response has been political pessimism and retreat into the intellectually self-validating isolation of the academy. But if labour history's origins lay partly in political commitment to social change, it seems reasonable to suggest that its revival must also partly depend, not of course on any specific political allegiance, but on a willingness to adopt a risk-attended approach which combines historical study with political discussion.

The idea that the events of 1989–91 in eastern Europe and the former Soviet Union meant 'the end of history',[7] that humanity's great ideological battles had all been fought and won, briefly canvassed in the early 1990s, is already widely discredited. But if anywhere in Britain was a potential centre for that illusion, it was Aberdeen. Surely the struggles of the past, and the social deprivation out of which they arose, had been soothed away with the economic emollient of oil. But simply to state such a proposition is to expose its absurdity. As the millennium draws to a close, poverty, gross inequality, and the necessity for political struggle have not been banished from Aberdeen.

A photograph on the wall of the Aberdeen Trades Council social club shows Union Street on 22 September 1982, playing host to one of the largest demonstrations ever held in the city – a protest against cuts in the National Health Service.[8] And the subsequent decade was far from being one of passive acceptance of the 'common-sense' of Thatcherism. The minutes of the Trades Council reflect some (though far from all) of the many struggles which took place and of the activities of support groups organised, notably for the miners in their 1984-

85 strike and the Dundee Timex workers in 1993. The bitter Aberdeen journalists' strike against union derecognition in 1989-90 is also recorded in pictures in a book entitled simply *Strike*.[9] And the cause of the offshore workers was one for which the Trades Council clearly felt particular responsibility. Aberdeen was also a major centre in the struggle against the 'poll tax', the success of which contributed mightily to Mrs Thatcher's humiliating downfall in 1991.

But Aberdeen's contemporary labour historians will have to do more than document continuing protest campaigns and class struggles. Their particular contribution will be essential to a rounded analysis of the 'oil boom' itself. A study in the late 1980s observed that

> the benefits . . . in Aberdeen have been distributed very unevenly . . . [And there] has been no serious attempt by central government to . . . reduce the adverse effects of oil activity upon Aberdeen's traditional industrial base.

It warned of the danger of 'the complete collapse of the Aberdeen economy once North Sea oil production declines' unless there was a change in government policy.[10] W. J. Pike, analysing the impact of the oil price recession of 1986-88, argued, with regard to Scotland more generally, that the oil industries 'had fallen further under external control . . . and it was, therefore, unlikely that [the resumption of rising prices would bring] much long-term [economic] benefit.'[11] When the story of North Sea oil began to be systematically told in the mid-1990s, the narrators, mindful of the contrast between private gain and social benefit, chose titles such as *Wasted Windfall* and *Fool's Gold*.[12] Tim Halford, personal assistant from 1976 to 1984 to Occidental Oil chairman Armand Hammer, recently remembered his boss standing on the Piper Alpha platform several years before the disaster, and saying, 'I can just feel those dollars going through underneath me!' Halford added, 'That's what it was all about'.[13]

In the early nineteenth century, the labour movement on the one hand and the ideas of socialism on the other arose separately but roughly contemporaneously and with the common goal of addressing, whether in practical or theoretical terms, fundamental social questions concerning wealth distribution and the planning of the use of resources to meet human need. In the 1970s and 1980s the exploitation of North Sea oil shielded Aberdeen from the full force of the economic buffeting that hit other parts of Scotland. But far from answering those fundamental questions, whether in Aberdeen or more gener-

ally, it only served to ask them in new ways. At the end of the 1980s, it became clear that offshore workers, despite operating in a new, high-technology industry, faced safety problems similar to, or worse than, those of older sections of the labour force. Far from being immune from the need for collective struggle, they had to rediscover the class traditions of the labour movement anew. Their fight for safety standards involved strike action, political protest and the attempt to build a new trade union, the Offshore Industry Liaison Committee (OILC). For labour historians focussing on Aberdeen this situation provides a fresh angle on their subject, relevant to how the more distant as well as the very recent past should be studied.

IV

If the struggle for offshore trade unionism had had few antecedents in north-eastern Scotland, it might not have had great significance for the locality itself. But Aberdeen has had a long and interesting labour history, stretching from the origins of trade unionism and from Chartism, through to the crisis of the unions and to the transformation of the Labour Party in the 1980s and 1990s. Aberdeen Trades Council, which in 1994 celebrated 125 years of its continuous existence, played in the 1890s a key role in the formation of the Scottish Trades Union Congress (STUC); and the city has been the starting point for significant figures in Scottish trade union history, ranging from Joe Duncan (1879–1964), the founder in 1912 of the Scottish Farm Servants Union; to James Milne (1921–86), a Communist Party member who was general secretary of the STUC from 1975 until his death. [14]

Labour historians seeking out the centres where the big battalions of the organised working class gathered strength in the nineteenth and the first two-thirds of the twentieth century, with a few honourable exceptions, ignored Aberdeen. But nineteenth-century militants and socialists did not. Visitors on the campaigning stump included the left-wing Chartist, George Julian Harney; the land reformer, Henry George; and the Marxists, William Morris and Marx's own daughter Eleanor.[15] None thought Aberdeen boring, though the inspirational Morris, in 1888, found his audience 'hard to lift'.[16] A committee to keep socialist ideas before the citizens of Aberdeen was formed following a visiting propagandist's meeting in 1837, and, according to E. P. Thompson, the revival of socialism in the city fifty years later involved 'a spectacular episode in the fight for free speech' which attracted national atten-

national attention.[17] The electoral history of labour in Aberdeen is also significant, and includes important episodes such as H. H. Champion's 1892 campaign in Aberdeen South, which Henry Pelling studied for his seminal work on the origins of the Labour Party.[18] Aberdeen North has been a Labour seat since 1918, except in 1931, often by massive majorities. 'Labour' members were elected to the town council in 1884, and the council first fell under Labour Party control in 1945, something which did not happen in Edinburgh until the early 1970s. [19]

It is also important not to neglect the Communist Party of Great Britain (CPGB), to which Grassic Gibbon briefly belonged, not so much because of its electoral interventions (though some were significant), but because of its campaigning role against unemployment and fascism at home and abroad in the 1930s and its activity in the trade union movement. A recent study, showing how trades council records can be used to illuminate the effect of the so-called Cold War on the British labour movement, highlights the post-war role of the party in Aberdeen.[20]

V

'Aberdeen's character in the inter-war years,' wrote Liz Kibblewhite and Andy Rigby in their *Aberdeen in the General Strike*, 'was essentially moderate'.[21] And in the 1930s, John Paton, an Aberdeen-raised socialist, wrote of the conservatism of the city into which he had been born in 1886, where 'the virtues of discreet reticence were well understood', and an 'outward show of reverence for the Christian God masked . . . an unquestioning obedience to the dictates of [the] real god, "respectability".' But he continued:

> already the forces that were completely to transform the life of this community were actively at work. . . . The vast economic and social changes that were to follow were still hidden in the womb of time, but the great powers of the world had already begun their disastrous drift to [the] catastrophe [of 1914].

Paton, in the early years of the twentieth century tried several trades, including selling false teeth to Lanarkshire miners' wives ('Eh, laddie, it's nae teeth we want but something to eat wi' the teeth we hae'). He settled on hairdressing, and, probably one of the few Aberdonians of his time seriously to have studied Marx's *Capital*, he himself had a capital effect of the city when he became the first practitioner there of

the permanent wave.[22] Union Street can surely never have looked quite the same again. But I digress. The point of Paton's comments on Aberdeen in the 1880s is that the surface appearance of calm and stability at a particular time or place does not absolve historians from penetrating to the underlying forces of change. [23]

The discussion about Chartism begun in chapter one by Don Withrington is germane; it is one pointer to an understanding of why Aberdeen could become an important centre in the regeneration of labour history. Referring to Robert Duncan's pioneering work, Withrington highlights his evidence that Aberdeen Chartism was primarily a moderate affair, rooted in the dominant local ethos, and concerned more with expanding opportunities for self-help than with what Friedrich Engels called 'proletarian Chartism' in contrast to 'shopkeepers' Radicalism'.[24]

We can also, however, look at Duncan's work from a complementary point of view. In *Textiles and Toil*, he begins an account of 'the emergence of the working class' by quoting an Aberdeen weaver poet on the need

> to expose the factory system [of the early nineteenth century], as it stood in our 'moral north'. Fairly to put the knife into the dead monster, lay bare its dark core, dissect it in broad day, that the world may see who had the fat and who the famine portion of that heartless trading.

On the whole, argues Duncan, the 'regime created' under early industrial capitalism in Aberdeen 'committed new levels of wholesale violence against more than one generation of working people.' His book concludes with an account of the first fully-fledged industrial strike in the city, by the female machinists at the Broadford mill who walked out on 7 February 1834.

> For five determined weeks, these women were in the front line of the working-class struggle, discovering and developing remarkable resources of collective action and solidarity with groups of male workers from the factories and also from traditional trades.

The women formed a Female Operatives Union, inspired by the example 'of their sisters in the West of Scotland'. By the end of February, class consciousness had developed to the point of declaring the

intention to form 'one general trades union, and to co-operate in procuring the re-dress of all grievances.' This, writes Duncan, was 'born of the realities of local struggles', but must also surely have been inspired 'by an awareness of the scheme, associated with Robert Owen,' of building, nationally, the Grand National Consolidated Trades Union. Equally, of course, the relatively ephemeral impact of 'general unionism' in Aberdeen must be ascribed to a combination of the victimisations after the Broadford strike and the decline of the GNCTU nationally. If we are to grasp the real course of class struggle in Aberdeen, we must look not at local factors in contradistinction to more universal ones, but at the way in which the two combined.

The Broadford women, Duncan goes on,

> withstood the barrage of hostility thrown at them by the clergy, the [Tory] Aberdeen Journal, and other bodies. . . . The same . . . clergy who had petitioned . . . against the scandal of child labour in the factories . . . [were] totally opposed to any attempt made by workers to form independent . . . trade unions and to engage in struggles which flexed the muscles of labour's power. . . .

The spirit of 'community' was, on this occasion, turned *against* the most oppressed members of the community. Although the employer was forced to concede on the wages question, the force of the law was used to victimise and effectively to blacklist those who had been active in the strike. The Aberdeen Female Operatives Union failed to survive, and the gains made were later undermined.

Notwithstanding Duncan's stress on the lack of violence and the ideological moderation associated with Aberdeen Chartism, then, it is clear that the movement emerged out of conditions of class struggle. Duncan thinks that experiences such as the Broadford strike

> proved to be necessary and valuable steps in the direction of seeking alternative initiatives in the abiding struggle for social justice. Having exhausted other means of struggle [mill workers, weavers, tailors and shoemakers] found themselves turning to political action . . . under the banner of . . . the 'People's Charter'. . . .[25]

Robert Duncan's work is important, not simply because it deals with neglected aspects of Aberdeen's story, but also because it places local

research in a wider historical context. It exemplifies how discussion of the (in some respects unique) experience of Aberdeen can be in the mainstream of historical debate.

VI

From Chartism to North Sea oil is a big, but not an impossible, leap. If there was any justification for the relative neglect of Aberdeen during the 1960s–80s heyday of academic labour history, it rested on the city's distance from the major areas of industrial trades unionism. The Chartist era occurred as industrialisation was entering its dominating phase in British economic history; the oil years have coincided with industrial decline. In these periods, I think, Aberdeen's development has a more general relevance than was the case during the decades of heavy-industrial dominance, when the manual unions led the British labour movement. In north-eastern Scotland there has been a close relationship between rural developments and urban social change. That on the one hand, and the region's proximity to the North Sea oilfields on the other, give Aberdeen a general significance in the early and late periods of industrial capitalism that it arguably lacked in the interim.

The first major study of industrial relations in the North Sea is due to appear in 1996 or early 1997,[26] and will provide a starting-point for those seeking to integrate the history of offshore unionism into the labour history of Aberdeen. All I can do here is to give a perhaps rather arbitrary taster of the possibilities for contemporary historians. Newspapers were vital to Chartism, and have remained so in working-class and socialist movements ever since, and the offshore workers' movement gave rise to a remarkable paper, of which researchers will surely make good use. *Blowout*, notably in its very earliest numbers, recaptured something of the spirit of the Chartist period, when workers' organisation and the mass discussion of socialist – or radical proto-socialist – ideas was just beginning. The paper's files show, furthermore, that, as was the case with earlier movements, the offshore workers not only organised a struggle with the employers and the state, but also faced sharp disputes in their own ranks amongst advocates of different courses of action.

Blowout began with an issue announcing that, on 13 June 1989, in Glasgow, OILC had 'issued a call to all offshore workers, to take 24 hour strike action' on 6 July, the anniversary of the Piper Alpha tragedy.

[233]

The call was made in response to an appeal by Bob Ballantyne, a Piper survivor, and a member of the Piper Alpha Support Group. He urged offshore workers to make the 6th of July a 'day of remembrance', not only for the men who died a year ago on Piper but for all those workers who have lost their lives in the industry over the past 25 years. . . .

The same issue reported the beginnings of substantial industrial action in the North Sea demanding that Health and Safety at Work legislation be fully implemented in the industry.[27]

Over the next few months the paper was remarkable for its raw directness of style and for the dialogue it built up with its readers, particularly through its letters columns. But *Blowout* also helps to document the difficulties of what was initially 'a liaison committee' for offshore workers who belonged to a number of different trade unions as it evolved into an independent union itself.

This history, adumbrated in the OILC publication *Striking Out*, is still to be fully told.[28] But my point here is this. The first half of the nineteenth century saw the origins of the modern labour movement, the beginning of a process through which trade unions developed from *ad hoc* fighting bodies into permanent, legally constituted organisations, with officials often at least as concerned to preserve the structures of their organisations as to ally themselves unequivocally with the perceived needs of their members directly involved in struggle. Thereby (as the officials saw it) they could develop a capacity to act as pressure groups on governments (particularly, since World War II, Labour governments) elected through the parliamentary system. OILC was created in the late 1980s, when the British government was seeking to counteract a decline in industrial profitability by dismantling the regulative apparatus which the labour movement had played a considerable part in establishing over more than a century of struggle. The new organisation found itself in the contradictory position of trying to fight again early struggles for decent working conditions, at a time when those labour movement structures, which had once seemed to hold the answers to workers' problems, now appeared to some at least to be themselves part of the problem.

The tensions within OILC emerged into the open in *Blowout* in February 1991. In the name of the organisation's standing committee, an editorial article which did not reflect OILC policy had been withdrawn, leaving one page blank but for a curt announcement. Another

article, by Jerry Chambers, was, it was announced, allowed to stand, but only because it was clearly one individual's 'contribution to the discussion'. It helps clarify what the dispute was about, and also gives some insight into how OILC had been built. Chambers wrote of how, like others, he had 'whole-heartedly promoted the aims and aspirations of the OILC, distributed "Blowout" and generally talked [his] head off on trains and on the rig.' It was difficult, he acknowledged, because 'in the drilling sector, apart from a generally hostile and vindictive management', the workers did 'not have "trade skills" and therefore [did] not possess . . . "trade union culture".' Such a culture was stronger in the engineering and catering sectors, where there had been a greater response. According to Chambers

> almost every offshore worker to whom I have spoken . . . has expressed varying levels of dissatisfaction with the official trade unions and asked about the formation of a single union for offshore workers. They want an organisation with which they can identify regardless of which sector they work in.

Chambers paid tribute to Ronnie McDonald, described by Christopher Harvie as OILC's 'articulate leader',[29] who, along with *Blowout*, had helped make the committee 'the focal point over the past two years' of the struggle to drag 'the industry into the 1990s'. But the rank-and-file had joined hoping that ordinary offshore workers would be involved at top level negotiations, and this had not happened.

Subsequent history was to turn the argument about forming a new, independent union into one of timing and method. Chambers' view was that, after the publicity won through its role in the strikes of 1989 and 1990, the organisation seemed 'to have made little or no progress':

> Trying to explain convincingly why the OILC is better off as unofficial body, untethered by the shackles of trade union law is an unenviable task when faced with disaffected comments such as "I'll follow the OILC to the end of the earth but I don't trust the unions an inch!" The fact has to be faced that the workforce continues to look for leadership. . . . Whether the official trade unions are effectively fulfilling that role is central to the debate.

OILC, said Chambers, should continue to act as a professional, advisory body for offshore workers, but should also make clear to the other unions, the TUC and the Scottish TUC – all suspicious of, if not

hostile to, new unions competing for members – that it was 'a special case', and that 'the cause of the offshore worker would be better served by a single Offshore Workers' Union', which (amongst other advantages) would make sure that safety was the top priority. [30]

Some months later, OILC did become an independent union, though one which, apart from the support of Aberdeen Trades Council, was not recognised by the 'official' movement. It sought and secured legal recognition, and remained at the forefront of campaigns on behalf of offshore workers. It probably stimulated other unions to increase their recruiting efforts, if only for fear of losing their existing North Sea membership. But the militancy of the post-Piper Alpha period was not easily recaptured. This created tensions, acknowledged in *Striking Out*, about the direction in which the organisation should go: tensions which replicated similar disputes within the labour movement over many generations.

VII

The telling of the story of OILC's origins will in itself be an important contribution to contemporary labour history. A small aspect of it has been adumbrated here to counter the idea that labour *history* has reason to lose its nerve because it has little relevance to what now happens in the labour *movement*. In the early history of OILC themes from the earliest period of trades unionism and labour politics were played again, though of course under very different conditions. A new agenda for labour history must pick up on such historical echoes in order to re-examine the past, in part at least for the benefit of those in the present who want to fight for a better future. [31]

This chapter, then, concludes *The City and its Worlds* with a proposal. Labour history – which should after all be that aspect of history *most* directly relevant to the greatest number of people – is in a general crisis, and Aberdeen is at a point in *its* history at which interest in its past is reviving, partly because its working population faces an uncertain future. This is of course true of working populations pretty well everywhere, but the difference is that, in Aberdeen, the uncertainty arises after a period when economic developments of national significance have masked the effects of underlying local changes which may, in the foreseeable future, have devastating consequences. These are issues which at least deserve more public debate, both in Aberdeen and amongst those elsewhere who have been educated to think of the

city's recent past as an unequivocal success story. Historians, I am suggesting, and labour historians especially, have – along with others, of course – a duty to contribute to, and to inform, such a discussion. [32]

NOTES

1. In the interests of space, I have cut endnotes to a minimum. A fuller version of this essay, outlining proposals for an Aberdeen Labour History Project, should become available during 1996 from the author at the Department of History, University of Aberdeen, AB9 2UB.

2. Lewis Grassic Gibbon, 'Aberdeen', in Grassic Gibbon and Hugh MacDiarmid, *Scottish Scene or the Intelligent Man's Guide to Albyn* (Bath, 1974; first published London, 1934), pp. 239–42.

3. Alan Clark, *Diaries* (London, 1994), p. 126. Clark admitted being 'economical with the *actualité*' when, as a defence minister, he was concerned with arms sales to Iraq. This led to the Scott Report which rocked the British government in February 1996.

4. Grassic Gibbon, 'Aberdeen', pp. 243–34.

5. W. G. Carson, *The Other Price of Britain's Oil: Safety and Control in the North Sea* (Oxford, 1982), pp. 302–03.

6. See, for example, the editorial in *Labour History Review*, vol. 60 (1) (1995), p. 2.

7. Francis Fukuyama, *The End of History and the Last Man* (London and New York, 1992) – an inflation of his provocative pièce d'occasion, 'The end of history?', *The National Interest*, vol. 16 (1989), pp. 3–18.

8. *Press and Journal*, 23 September 1982.

9. Roy Donaldson and Kate Sutherland, *Strike! a Pictorial Account of the 12-month Dispute at Aberdeen Journals by Sacked Photographers* (Aberdeen, 1990).

10. A. Harris, M. Lloyd, and D. A. Newlands, *The Impact of Oil on the Aberdeen Economy* (Aldershot, 1988), pp. 99, 5.

11. W. J. Pike, 'The oil price crisis and its impact on Scottish North Sea development, 1986-1988', *Scottish Economic and Social History*, vol. 13 (1993), p. 70.

12. Christopher Harvie, *Fool's Gold: the Story of North Sea Oil. How a £200 billion windfall divided a kingdom* (London, 1994).

13. *Wasted Windfall*, Channel Four TV programme, October 1994.

14. Angela Tuckett, *The Scottish Trades Union Congress: the First 80 Years* (Edinburgh, 1986), pp. 21–22; J. H. Smith, *Joe Duncan: the Scottish Farm Servants and British Agriculture* (Edinburgh, 1973); obituaries of Milne in leading newspapers after his death on 14 April 1986.

15. A. R. Schoyen, *The Chartist Challenge: a Portrait of George Julian Harney* (London, 1958), pp. 100–02, 162, 194, 201; E. P. Lawrence, *Henry George in the British Isles* (East Lansing, Michigan, 1957), pp. 64ff.; Bob [Robert] Duncan, *James Leatham 1865-1945: Portrait of a Socialist Pioneer* (Aberdeen, 1978), p. 16; Yvonne Kapp, *Eleanor Marx: the Crowded Years* (London, 1976), pp. 538–39; William Diack, *History of the Trades Council and the Trade Union Movement in Aberdeen* (Aberdeen, 1939), pp. 62–3.

16. Duncan, *Leatham*, p. 28.

17. William Lindsay, *Some Notes: Personal and Political* (Aberdeen, 1898), p. 85; E. P. Thompson, *William Morris: Romantic to Revolutionary* (London, 1977 edition), p. 474.

18. Henry Pelling, 'H. H. Champion: pioneer of Labour representation', *Cambridge Journal*, vol. 6 (1952–53), pp. 222–38, esp. pp. 231ff.

19. F. W. S. Craig, *British Parliamentary Election Results, 1918–1949* (Chichester, 1983), p. 573; *1950–1973* (Chichester, 1983), p. 593; *1974–1983* (Chichester, 1984), p. 291; Alexander Keith, *A Thousand Years of Aberdeen* (Aberdeen, 1972), pp. 414–17.

20. Till Geiger, 'Opposition in the shadow of emerging conflict: the Aberdeen Trades Council, government policy and voicing dissent in the Cold War, 1945–1955' *Northern Scotland*, vol. 13 (1993), pp. 103–36.

21. Liz Kibblewhite and Andy Rigby, *Aberdeen in the General Strike* (Aberdeen, 1977), p. 6.

22. John Paton, *Proletarian Pilgrimage* (London, 1935), pp. xi-xii, 149, 234–37.

23. Another example is the government's Gaskin Report, *North East Scotland: a Survey of the Development Potential* (Edinburgh, 1969), which attempted to analyse the economic basis for continuing stability in the Aberdeen area, ignorant of the oil which was so soon to change everything.

24. F. Engels, *The Condition of the Working-Class in England*, in K. Marx and F. Engels, *Collected Works*, vol. 4 (Moscow, 1975), p. 529.

25. Robert Duncan, *Textiles and Toil: the Factory System and the Working Class in Early 19th Century Aberdeen* (Aberdeen, 1984), pp. vii, 45–53.

26. Charles Woolfson and John Foster, *Paying for the Piper: Safety and Industrial Relations in Britain's North Sea Oil Industry* (forthcoming, 1996/97).

27. *Blowout*, no. 1, 6 July 1989.

28. Offshore Industry Liaison Committee, *Striking Out* (Aberdeen, 1991) – 'dedicated to the 729 sacked workers who, in August 1990, sacrificed their jobs in the struggle for safety and basic trade union rights in the offshore industry'; and see Woolfson and Foster, *Paying for the Piper*.

29. Harvie, *Fool's Gold*, p. 332.

30. *Blowout*, no. 15, February 1991.

31. A more politically engaged labour history would not of course be crudely partisan. Neither would it turn its back on the traditions of historical scholarship of the early labour historians, nor on the many insights to be had from the vast output of the past generation. The latter include, for example: the importance of studying work, unemployment, family and leisure, not only struggles, far less institutions *per se*; the need for gender-sensitive research; the understanding to be gained from linguistic and cultural analysis; and the fact that a labour history which does not deal more generally with social and political relations is deeply flawed.

ABERDEEN
(BUILDINGS, INSTITUTIONS)
Art Gallery 9, 204, 207
Associated Trades 163
Association for the Poor 204
Asylum 130, 132-43
Asylum for Blind 133
Athenaeum 29, 96
Bannermill 214, 217
Bridewell 133
Broadford Mills 216, 231-32
Central School 21
College (Technical) 221
Common Good 151-52
County & Municipal Buildings 163, 204
Dispensary 103, 119-22
Female Operative Union 231
Female Orphan Asylum 133
Female Penitentiary 134
Fonthill Nursing Home 125
General Institution for Deaf & Dumb 133
Girls' School 21
Grammar School 29
Guildry 151, 163, 172
Harbour Board 160
Health of Towns Association 157
Hellenistic Society 197
Hospital for Sick Children 121
House of Refuge 133-34
Incorporated Trades 151-53, 163, 172
Industrial Schools 158
Infirmary 9, 30, 98, 116-20, 124-25, 132-33, 137, 222
Juvenile Reformatory School 101
Labour History Project 236
Macaulay Institute for Soil Research 221
Maternity Hospital 116, 121-27
Mechanics' Institute 8, 100
Medico-Chirurgical Society 120, 158
Mother & Child Welfare Clinic 123
New Market Hall 175
New Model Lodging House 159
New Streets Trust 152
Northern College of Education 221

North of Scotland College of Agriculture 90
Offshore Industry Liaison Committee 229, 233-35
Police Commission 150-66
Poor's Hospital 116, 124, 131, 133, 214
Prison 98, 133
Provincial Grand Lodge 175
Public Library 8
Queen's Cross Nursing Home 125
Religious Tract Society 98
Robert Gordon's College 9, 21
Robert Gordon's Institute of Technology 221
Robert Gordon University 221
Royal Cornhill Hospital 133
St Nicholas Poor Law Board 159
Sanitary Committee 159
Savings Bank 214
School of Art (Gray's) 9
Schools 10, 18-21
Sheriff Court House 120, 170
Soup Kitchen 158
Soviet 226
Stamp Office 95
Summerfield Nursing Home 125
Torry Marine Research Laboratory 221
Town House 95, 116, 170
Trades Council 227-29, 236
Union Buildings 6
University 35, 37, 82-83, 86-90, 117, 120-22, 124-25, 139, 197, 221
   Forestry Department 90
   Medical School 119, 140, 222
     King's College 109, 139, 170
     Marischal College 4, 15, 29, 87, 106, 109, 139, 170-71, 197

ABERDEEN (DISTRICTS, STREETS)
Abercrombie's Jetty 9
Adelphi Court 34-35
Airyhall 11
Altens, 222
Anderson Drive 11

Angusfield 216
Argyll Place 6
Back Wynd 52
Barnett's Close 121
Belmont Street 6, 8-9, 106
Bon Accord Terrace 8
Bridge of Don 222
Broad Street 6, 43, 45, 95, 106-07
Broadhill 14
Cairnton 161-62
Canal 154
Carmelite Lane 101
Castlegate, Castle Street, 6, 8, 29, 95
Castle Terrace 121
Culter Burn 154
Cults 86
Deeside, River Dee 3-4, 8-10, 34, 55-56, 71, 150, 154, 162, 165, 213
Denburn 8, 27, 30, 34, 66, 156, 159, 170-71
Diamond Street 34
Don Street 85
Donside, River Don 170, 216
Duthie Park 9
Exchequer Row 8
Ferryhill Burn 8
Fonthill 8, 125
Footdee 15
Foresterhill 116, 125
Fountainhall Road 6
Gallowgate 6, 109, 156, 216
George Street 159
Girdleness Point 9
Grandholm 216
Green 216
Guestrow 121
Guild Street 70
Harbour 9, 34, 156, 162, 164, 170-72, 180, 183, 212-13, 215, 217, 222
Hazlehead 153, 226
Holburn 85
Justice Port 4
Kincorth 11
King's Gate 216
King's (Queen's) Links 6, 8-10, 212, 217

King Street 28-30, 152
Loch of Skene 154
Loirston Loch 154
Long Acre 102
Mannofield 9
Marischal Street 8, 34
Market Street 182
Mastrick 11
Mercat Cross 29
Nellfield 59
North Street 156
Northfield 11
Old Aberdeen 170
Pork Lane 8
Poynernook 217
Queen Street 45
Rettie's Court 6
Rosemount 6, 8
Rubislaw 222
St Nicholas Street 52, 54-55
Schoolhill 8-9
Shiprow 8
Smith's & Peacock's Close 6
Summerhill 11
Torry 8, 10, 34, 162-63, 214-15
Union Bridge 26, 29-31, 33, 36,
    38-39
Union Row 214
Union Street 3-6, 8, 22, 25-39,
    40-59, 68, 109, 123, 152,
    170, 199, 224, 231
Upperkirkgate 159
Urquhart Road 8
Vennel 4
Victoria Bridge 8
Victoria Park 6
Virginia Street 64
Water Lane 8
Woodside 170, 214, 217
Woolmanhill 9, 30, 116

ABERDEEN (PEOPLE)

Abercrombie, Charles 34
Aberdeen, Earl of 75
Aberdeen, Lady 75
Adam, James 14, 172, 174
Anderson, – 135, 152
Anderson, Alexander 87, 158,
    175, 213
Baird, Dugald 116, 125-26
Baird, Jean 118
Baird, Mary 125
Ballantyne, Bob 234
Bannerman, family of 172
Bannerman, Alexander, of Elsick
    4-5
Bannerman, Alexander 52,
    103-04, 172-78
Beattie, James 95
Benton, John 88

Blaikie, family of 171-72,
    174-76, 178-79, 182-84
Blaikie, James 172, 175
Blaikie, Thomas 172, 175-76,
    178
Booth, John 97, 104
Brazier, Prof. J. S. 89
Brodie, Alexander 55
Bruce, John 69
Carnie, William 48
Carson, W. G. 226
Carter, Ian 22
Chalmers, David 75
Chalmers, James 172, 176
Chambers, Jerry 235-36
Champion, H. H. 230
Connon, Elizabeth 73
Cook, A. S. 49
Courage, Archibald 110
Davies, Christopher, 84-85
Dey, John 88
Dingwall Fordyce, Alexander 95
Dingwall Fordyce, Alexander, of
    Bruckley 176-85
Duncan, Robert 13-14, 231-32
Duncan, Joe 229
Duthie, Robert 68
Elmslie, George 72-73, 75-77
Erskine, family of 195-96
Ewen, John 152-53
Farquhar, Sir Arthur 173
Ferdinands, George 85
Ferres, John 98
Fleming, Sir John 74
Foote, Rev. James 16
Frazer, – 157
Frost, Forbes 110
Galen, John 155-56
Galbraith, Sandra 83
Geddes, Sir William 197
Gibbon, Lewis Grassic 224-26,
    230
Gordon, Alexander 116, 119-20
Hadden, family of 170-79,
    182-84
Hadden, Alexander 75
Hadden, Gilbert 103, 171
Hadden, James 103-05, 171-72,
    174-75, 178
Halford, Tim 228
Hamilton, David 26, 28, 33, 36
Hay, Sir Andrew Leith 179-80
Henderson, John 137
Hill Burton, John 106
Inglis, Prof. Andrew 121
Innes of Raemoir 174, 177-78,
    185
Jaffray, Thomas 214
Jamieson, Andrew 88
Jamieson, Robert 138-41

Johnstone, James 97
Kemp, A. G. 83
Keith, – 157
Kibblewhite, Liz 230
Kilgour, Alexander 155-57
Koch, E. L. 85
Laurie, William 100
Leith, John Farley 53, 181-85
Leslie, – 157
Leslie, William, of Warthill 74
Lindsay, William 99-100
MacDonald, Alexander, of
    Kepplestone 204, 208, 215
MacDonald, Ronnie 235
Macgowan, J. G. 87
McKerracher, Hugh 71
Mackinlay, Duncan 98
MacLaren, Allan A. 14, 16, 18
Maclennan, John 70-71, 78
Macpherson, John 177, 182, 184
Macpherson, Sir John 86
MacRobin, Dr – 137
Martin, Samuel 40-59
Masson, Prof. David 4
Mather, John 86
Mayo, Isabella 85
Menzies of Pitfodels 154
Milne, A. F. 86
Milne, James 229
Milne, John 86
Mitchell, Alexander 87
Moir, Alexander, of Croix 86
Morris, William 229
Murdoch, Patrick 85
Murray, Rev. James 16
Ogilvie, John 106
Palmer, Alice 85
Paton, John 230-31
Pennington, Carolyn 83
Pike, William J. 228
Pratt, J. G. 106
Ramsay, Andrew 100
Ravenscroft, Edward 108
Rettie, James 5
Rigby, Andy 230
Righton, General 119
Ritchie, James 97
Robertson, Joseph 103, 106
Rose, Donaldson 68
Russel, William 109-10
Scharenguivel, J. L. 85
Simpson, Archibald 29-30
Simpson, David 88
Skene, Andrew 117
Skene, David 117-20, 123
Smith, George 86
Smith, George 'Chicago' 87, 104,
    107
Smith, John 29-30
Smith, William Robertson 197

Stephenson, Prof. William 121
Stewart, James 88
Sykes, Col. W. 176-85
Thomson, George jr 68, 178-83
Torrie, Councillor – 178-79
Tytler, Robert Boyd 74, 89
Van Geysel, J. L. 85
Vessie, James 109
Walker, Alexander 204-05
Walker, William 98
Watson, Sheriff William 158
Watt, Alexander 72-73
Watt, Christine 130
Watt, William 21-22
White, James Forbes 195, 197,
    199-200, 202, 204-05, 207-08
Williams, Robert 88
Williamson, Peter 77-78
Wood, – 157
Young, James 38
Yuill, G. S. 87-88

ABERDEEN (ECONOMY: GENERAL)

agricultural trade 175, 183
banking 212-13
bookselling 95-111
city improvements 3-12, 25-39,
    58, 151-66, 170-76
drink trade 174, 183
economic structures 211-23
educational services 10, 18-21,
    82-91, 221-23
emigration 62-80
employment structures 212-23
engineering 217
fishing 7, 212-13, 215, 218, 220
food retailing 174, 183
gas, gasworks 151, 158, 160,
    164-65, 176
general manufacturing 171-72,
    174-75
granite, granite works 66, 79,
    212, 215-17, 220
housing conditions 21, 156-57,
    162
insurance services 212-13
iron founding 171, 217
meat trades 155, 164
newspaper circulation 101
oil, North Sea oil 212, 219-20,
    222, 225-26, 228-29, 233-36
opium trade 181-82
population 5-6, 21-22, 41, 170,
    211-12
public health 6, 9-10, 150-58,
    161-62, 165
publishing 95-111
shipbuilding 183, 217-18
shipping 63-67, 77-79, 180,

183, 213
textiles 155, 158, 170, 174, 178,
    212, 214, 216-17, 220
timber trade 64, 66, 73
tobacco trade 66
transport services 65-66, 98,
    175, 183, 215
water supplies 9-10, 150-55,
    161-65
wine importing 72

ABERDEEN (BUSINESSES)

Aberdeen Banking Co. 214
Aberdeen Marketing Co. 175-76
Aberdeen Steam Navigation Co.
    213
Adam & Anderson 175, 213
Bannerman, Thomas, & Co. 175,
    185
Bell, Francis 45
Bennet, Mrs 45
Black, John 109
Booth, William 109
Brown & Burnett 96-97
Brown, Alexander, & Co. 95, 97,
    99, 106, 110
Burge, D. 45
Central Hat Co. 45
Collie, James 59
Craig & Anderson 43
Crombie's 216-17
Davidson, R. & J. 69
Esslemont & Macintosh 123
Forbes, Low, & Co. 217
Gordon, Barron & Co. 216
Hadden & Sons 175, 178
Hadden, Alexander, & Sons 216-17
Hadden, James, & Sons 170
Hall Russell 88, 218
Leys, Masson & Co. 178, 216-17
London Hat Company (Millar
    Bros) 45
MacKay Brothers 68-69
McLeod, John C. 59
Martin, Samuel 40-59
Masson & Co. 175
Middleton, George 109
Milne, Cruden, & Co. 216
Moffat, W. T. 69
Mudie's 109
Panton, Charles 107
Paton, H. W. 68-69
Rettie, John 109
Richards & Co. 216-17
Rubislaw Granite Co. 216
Smith, Lewis 99-100, 102-07, 110
Steele & Co. 43
Thomson, William 43
Wylie, David 109

ABERDEEN
(NEWSPAPERS, JOURNALS)

Aberdeen Banner 101, 107, 169,
    173-74
Aberdeen Censor 104
Aberdeen Chronicle 97, 101, 104
Aberdeen Constitutional 41, 101
Aberdeen Free Press 69, 84, 169,
    182, 184-85
Aberdeen Herald 14, 40-41, 46,
    48-52, 56-59, 101, 169, 172-
    74, 176-77, 179
Aberdeen Journal 59, 63-65, 67,
    70-71, 78, 94-95, 99-101,
    104, 111, 117, 169, 171-72,
    176, 182, 184, 203
Aberdeen Magazine 103-04, 106
Aberdeen Mirror 101
Aberdeen Observer 101
Aberdeen Patriot 101
Aberdeen Pirate 101
Aberdeen Press and Journal
    224, 228
Aberdeen Shaver 101-03
Aberdeen Universities' Magazine
    103-04, 106
Alma Mater 84, 88
Blowout 233-35
Bon-Accord 9
North of Scotland Family
    Journal 107-08
Northern Figaro 7, 9-10, 23
Northern Iris 104
Quizzing Glass 102
Scots Champion and Aberdeen
    Free Press 103
Striking Out 234

OTHER SCOTTISH
(INSTITUTIONS, PLACES)

Anderson's Institution, Glasgow 88
Ardrossan 38
Ayr 36-37
Ballater 98
Balmoral 45, 48, 50, 53, 55
Banff 63
Blackwood, 110
Board of Supervision for the Poor
    165
Brechin 168
Broadsea 130
Burrell Collection 206
Chambers, W. & R. 107, 110-11
Collins, William, & Co. 110
Crichton Royal Asylum, Dumfries
    135-36
Cromarty 64, 100
Deveron 71
Dumfries 135-36

Dundee 15, 18–19, 21, 27, 96, 100, 107, 160, 194, 206
East Kilbride 117
Edinburgh 3, 15, 17–20, 25–29, 31–39, 51, 90, 96, 98–99, 107, 109–11, 117, 135, 139, 154, 157–58, 160, 165, 168–69, 194–97, 199–200, 207
Edinburgh Religious Tract Society 98
Elgin 69, 179, 214
Ellon 87
Forfar 168
Fraserburgh 214
Glasgow 5, 9, 12, 14–15, 18–21, 26–27, 29, 36, 41, 63–65, 70, 88, 96, 98, 102, 107, 110, 125, 155, 157–58, 160, 169, 194–95, 206, 212
Glasgow Infirmary 36
Glasgow Religious Tract Society 98
Glasgow Technical College 88
Glasgow Trades House 36
Greenock 18
Hamilton 40
Inveraray 27
Inverbervie 168
Inverurie 214
Kemnay 214
Kintore 214
Lochbuy (Skye) 38
Loch Katrine 9
Longside 69
Montrose 84, 168
Mortloch 87
New Deer 87
New Lanark 27
New Pitsligo 22
North British Australasian Co. 74
Northern Assurance Co. 213
Northern Bank of Scotland 30
Northern Isles 64
Old Deer 87
Old Rayne 74
Oliver & Boyd 110
Paisley 18, 71
Perth 70
Peterhead 63, 74, 87, 89
Royal Edinburgh Asylum 135
Royal Scottish Academy 194–98, 200, 207
Sanitary Assocation of Scotland 9
Scottish Australian Co. 74
Scottish Farm Servants' Union 229
Scottish Labour History Society 227
Scottish Trades Union Congress 229, 235
Scrabster 64
Shetland 98

Society of Antiquaries of Scotland 197
Spey 71
Stonehaven 109, 214
Trustees' Academy 194
Turriff 71
Union Bank of Scotland 214
Wick 214

OTHER SCOTTISH
(PEOPLE, PUBLICATIONS)
Adam, John 32
Adam, Robert 28–29, 31–32, 34–36
Arnott, Neil 157
Barron, Tom 89
Bell, John Charles 206
Blackwood's Magazine 111
Brown, John 55
Burns, James 26
Burrell, William 206
Cameron, Charles 26
Cameron, George Paul 200, 205
Cameron, Hugh 200, 205, 208
Chambers, Robert 32
Chambers' Edinburgh Journal 99–100, 110
Cleland, James 155
Clerk, Sir James 33
Constable's Miscellany 106
Cowan, Robert 155
Edinburgh Magazine 96
Edinburgh Review 96
Edinburgh True Scotsman 110
Dundas, Henry 96
Fergusson, Adam 72
Fletcher, Thomas 26, 30, 33–34
Fraser's Magazine 111
Gill, Sir David 196
'Glasgow Boys' 194–95
Glasgow Mechanics' Magazine 110
Glasgow Post 110
Graham, Robert 155
Groome, Francis 3–4, 25
Hamilton, David 26, 28, 33, 36
Harvey, Sir George 200
Harvie, Christopher 235
Hogg, – 99, 107, 111
Hogg's Weekly Instructor 107
Keddie, William 9
Kerr, John 197
Kinloch, Col. 160–61, 165
Lauder, Robert Scott 194, 201
Lumsden, James 102
Mackenzie, Marshall 29
Maitland, William 69
Martin, William 40
Marwick, W. H. 229

Menelaws, Adam 26
Morningside Mirror 135
Mylne, Robert 26, 31
Mylne, William 33
New Moon Magazine 135
Niven, Frederick 77
People's Journal 100–11
Reid, Alexander 206
Reid, Sir George 197, 199–202, 204–05, 207
Scotsman 199, 207
Scott, Sir Walter 99, 106–07
Scottish Herald 107
Scottish Protestant 107
Sinclair, John 69
Sinclair, Sir John 3
Tait, William 99
Telford, Thomas 26, 84
Tennant, – 99
Wilkie, David 196–97

OTHER BRITISH AND IRISH
(INSTITUTIONS, PLACES)
Bath 36
Board of Trade 63
Bow St (Police), London 160
Bradbury & Evans 107
British Association for the Advancement of Science 9
British Medical Association 119, 123, 125
British Pharmaceutical Society 9
Cadell & Co. 107
Cambridge University 90
Cassell, John, and Co. 107
Central Midwives Board 125
Civil Service examinations 88
Colonial Office 63
Customs Department 63
Dublin 206
East India Co. 86, 181
England 83, 212, 216
General Medical Council 83
Grimsby 218
Halifax 110
Hanwell Asylum 136
Hull 96, 218
Ireland 83, 140, 181–82, 206
Lancashire 217
Liverpool 63, 65, 96, 216
London 4, 23–24, 29, 32–33, 50, 69, 71, 84, 90, 96, 98–99, 109–11, 117–18, 120, 157, 160, 199, 212, 216
London Religious Tract Society 98
Manchester 23, 111, 155
Medical Research Council 126
Milner & Sowerby 110
Newcastle 33

d, Ulster 140, 216
g Line 87
rsity 90
Asylum), nr York 135,
142
Routledge & Co. 110
St Bartholemew's Hospital,
London 84
Society for the Diffusion of Useful
Knowledge 100, 106
Society for Promoting Christian
Knowledge 110
Society for the Study of Labour
History 227
Stockport 41
Wales 83

**OTHER BRITISH
(PEOPLE, PUBLICATIONS)**

Anti-Jacobin Review 96
Artz, David 204-05
Berry, George 79
Betjeman, John 25
Black Dwarf 99
Bow Bells 110
British Statesman 110
Burney, – 99
Byron, Lord 99
Cain, P. J. 89-90
Chadwick, Edwin 155, 157
Clark, Alan 224
*Cobbett's Weekly Political
Register* 96, 98
Cole, G. D. H. 227
Cole, Margaret 227
Cornhill Magazine 111
Daily Review 207
Dickens, Charles 106, 111
Digby, Ann 142
Edgeworth, Maria 99
Family Herald 110-11
Family Paper 107, 110
Gentleman's Magazine 96
Gwynn, John 32
Hare, Edward 131
Harney, George Julian 229
Hopkins, A. G. 89-90
Israels, Joseph 196-97, 199-200,
204, 207
Kay (-Shuttleworth), James 157
Library of Useful Knowledge 106
London Journal 110-11
Monthly Review 96
Morris, William 229
Novel Newspaper 107, 110
Nonconformist 110
Owen, Robert 232
Paine, Tom 98
Palmerston, Lord 52

Penny Magazine 99-100, 107,
110-11
Popular Educator 107
Porter, Roy 131
Queen Victoria 45-46, 50-51,
53-55
Republican 99
Reynolds's Miscellany 110-11
Saturday Magazine 110
Scull, Andrew 131
Southey, Robert 95
Thomson, E. P. 229
Webb, Beatrice 229
Webb, Sydney 229
Weekly Magazine 110
Working Man's Friend 107, 110

**OVERSEAS
(INSTITUTIONS, PLACES)**

Antipodes 69, 71, 73-74
Australia 63, 71, 74, 87, 218
Melbourne 87
Sydney 88
Victoria 87
Baltic 64
Bavaria 83
Bermuda 179
British Empire 63-64, 68-77,
83-90, 212
Canada 63-64, 68-79
British Columbia: Okanagan
Valley 75
Manitoba: Winnipeg 77
New Brunswick 64
Ontario: Bon Accord 73,
75-76
Fergus 72
Nichol 72-73
Paisley 71
Toronto 72
Québec 68
St Lawrence 64
Canadian Immigration Dept 69,
78-79
Canadian National Railway Co. 70
Canadian Pacific Railway Co. 70
Ceylon (Sri Lanka) 73-74, 84-
85, 89
Ceylon Medical College 85
Ceylon Legislative Council 74
Ceylon Planters' Association 74
China 50, 87, 218
France 31-32, 46, 64, 118, 131,
195-96, 200-01, 206-07
Aix 31
Bourges 196
Marseilles 31
Montpellier 31
Nantes 195

Paris 4, 27, 31-32, 207
India 50, 84
Indian Civil Service 90
Indian Medical Service 86
Indian Public Works Dept 88
Indonesia 89
Italy 31
Rome 32
Malaysia 89
Mediterranean 206
Netherlands 194-208
Bruges 195
Campvere 195
Hague 195-202, 206-07
Leyden 196
Middleburg 195
Utrecht 199-200, 206-07
New Zealand 71, 86
Norway 197
Portugal 26
Lisbon 26
Prussia 85-86
Russia 227
St Petersburg 32
Sierra Leone 84
South Africa 71, 84, 86, 88
Transvaal 88
South America 64, 218
Sweden 197
Stockholm 32
Switzerland 55
Alps 55
Geneva 126
United States of America 26, 63-
68, 70-72, 74, 79, 87, 212,
216, 218-19
New England 66
New York, Syracuse 88
North Dakota 75
South Carolina 86
Vermont 66
Virginia 64, 68
West Indies 84
Antigua 64, 68, 118
Barbadoes 84
Caribbean 64, 68
Jamaica 74
Trinidad 118
World Health Organization 126

OVERSEAS (PEOPLE)

Blondel, – 32
Cezanne 82
Coudray, Mme du 118
Doctorow, E. L. 82
Engels, Friedrich 231
Foucault, Michel 131, 137
Fukeyama, F. 227
Gandi 85

George, Henry 229
Goffman, Erving 134, 138
Hammer, Armand 228
Haussmann, Baron 27
Henry, Rev. James 86
Laugier, l'Abbé 32
McCarthy, Mary 82
Marx, Eleanor 229
Marx, Karl 229
McKerracher, Hugh 71
Menzies, R. G. 87
Mollinger, Alexander 198, 200, 204, 206-08
Murdoch, Keith 86-87
Perronet, – 31-33
Rembrandt 196, 208
Rhodes, Cecil 86
Roeloefs, William 204
Scott, W. D. 69
Smith, J. Obed 71
Tolstoy 85
van Themaat, P. Verloren 206-07
Vermeer 82

PARLIAMENT, POLITICS

American Civil War 66
American Revolution 64
Arrow War, China 50
Bolshevik Revolution 226
burgh reform movement 153
class struggle 226-32
Communist Party of Great Britain 229-30
Crimean War 45, 47, 49-50, 52
elections, parliamentary 172-74, 177-84, 188-93
Franco-Prussian War 84-85
French Revolution 28
Gallipoli 87
General Strike 230
Indian Mutiny 50
legislation: Aberdeen
    Municipal Extention Bill 164
    New Streets Act 34, 152
    Nuisances Acts 159
    Police Act (1818) 153, 160
    Police Act (1829) 153-54, 160
    Police Act (1862) 161
    Public Health Act (1862) 157
legislation: general
    Burgh Reform Act 152
    Counties and Burghs (Scotland) Act 160
    Lunacy (Scotland) Act 142
    Midwives (Scotland) Act 123
    Public Health Act (1848) 157
    Public House Regulation Act 161

Public Libraries Act 100
    Reform Act (1832) 168, 173, 185
    Reform Act (1867) 186
    Town Improvements Act 159
    Universities (Scotland) Act 84
    Water Works Clauses Act 159
Marxism 229
mobs 14, 28, 225
municipalisation of services 9-10, 151-66
Nantes, edict of 195
Napoleonic Wars 40, 64, 153
Near-Eastern Crisis 88
occupational influences in voting 170-71, 174-75, 183-84, 188-90, 192
Opium War 181
parliamentary commissions
    Health of Towns 155, 157
    Lunacy 136
    Lunacy (Scotland) 138
    Sanitary Condition of the Labouring Population 155, 157
political affiliation
    Conservatives 153, 173-75, 177, 179-80, 182, 185
    Labour Party 229-30
    Liberals 8, 52, 69, 101, 103, 110, 162-64, 169, 171-76, 178-79, 182, 185
    radicals 105, 168-69, 179
    socialists 227-29
    Tories 101, 103, 169, 171, 173, 175-76, 178-79, 182-83
    Whigs 169, 171-75, 177-79, 182, 184
Poll tax 228
Sebastopol, fall of 47-49
Sedan, battle of 84-85
strikes 227-28, 231-32
Thatcherism 227
trade unions 216-36
Union of 1707 62, 168
World War I 83, 87, 123, 216, 219-20, 225
World War II 11, 22, 125, 221, 234

RELIGION

Aberdeen, churches and chapels
    Bon Accord 16
    East 15-16
    Gaelic 16
    Gilcomston 16
    Greyfriars 15
    Holburn 16

    John Kno[...]
    Mariner's [...]
    Melville 16
    North 15-16
    St Clement's 15
    St Machar's Cathedral 170
    St Nicholas 6, 15-16, 31, 52, 159, 170
    South 15-16
    Trinity 16
    Union 16
    West 15-16
Anti-voluntaries 182
Australia, Free Church in 87
Baptists 177
Church of Scotland 13-18, 101, 174, 176, 178, 182, 184
    Evangelicals 15, 107
    Moderates 13, 15, 172, 174, 176-77
    Intrusionists 173
    Non-Intrusionists 15-16, 101, 169, 172-74, 176
Congregationalists 17, 177
Disestablishment movement 177
Disruption 14-16, 31, 158, 170, 173, 176
Dissenters 179, 182
Episcopal Church in Ireland 182
Episcopalians 17, 175-76, 182, 184
Free Church of Scotland 15, 17-18, 103, 107, 173, 175-83
    Triple Kirks, Aberdeen 30
Glasgow, Tron Kirk 36
Maynooth College 182-83
patronage 15-16
Plymouth Brethren 84
Puseyites 177
religious revival 139-40
Roman Catholics 13, 17, 107, 177, 181-82
Unitarians 177
United Presbyterians 17
Voluntaries 174-75, 177-78, 182
Weslyan Methodists 183